Texts, Editors, and Readers

This book re-examines the most traditional area of classical scholarship, offering critical assessments of the current state of the field, its methods and controversies, and its prospects for the future in a digital environment. Each stage of the editorial process is examined, from gathering and evaluating manuscript evidence to constructing the text and critical apparatus, with particular attention given to areas of dispute, such as the role of conjecture. The importance of subjective factors at every point is highlighted. An Appendix offers practical guidance in reading a critical apparatus. The discussion is framed in a way that is accessible to non-specialists, with all Latin texts translated. The book will be useful both to classicists who are not textual critics and to non-classicists interested in issues of editing.

RICHARD TARRANT is Pope Professor of the Latin Language and Literature at Harvard University. He has long been interested in issues of editing classical texts, and has produced editions of two tragedies by Seneca (*Agamemnon* and *Thyestes*), and edited Ovid's *Metamorphoses* for the Oxford Classical Texts series. His most recent book, a commentary on Virgil, *Aeneid* Book XII, published in the Cambridge Greek and Latin Classics series, has received the Charles J. Goodwin Award of Merit from the Society for Classical Studies and the Premio Internazionale 'Virgilio' from the Accademia Nazionale Virgiliana, in Mantova.

T0384491

ROMAN LITERATURE
AND ITS CONTEXTS

Series editors:
Denis Feeney and Stephen Hinds

This series promotes approaches to Roman literature which are open to dialogue with current work in other areas of the classics, and in the humanities at large. The pursuit of contacts with cognate fields such as social history, anthropology, history of thought, linguistics and literary theory is in the best traditions of classical scholarship: the study of Roman literature, no less than Greek, has much to gain from engaging with these other contexts and intellectual traditions. The series offers a forum in which readers of Latin texts can sharpen their readings by placing them in broader and better-defined contexts, and in which other classicists and humanists can explore the general or particular implications of their work for readers of Latin texts. The books all constitute original and innovative research and are envisaged as suggestive essays whose aim is to stimulate debate.

Other books in the series

Joseph Farrell, *Latin language and Latin culture: from ancient to modern times*

A. M. Keith, *Engendering Rome: women in Latin epic*

William Fitzgerald, *Slavery and the Roman literary imagination*

Stephen Hinds, *Allusion and intertext: dynamics of appropriation in Roman poetry*

Denis Feeney, *Literature and religion at Rome: cultures, contexts, and beliefs*

Catherine Edwards, *Writing Rome: textual approaches to the city*

Duncan F. Kennedy, *The arts of love: five studies in the discourse of Roman love elegy*

Charles Martindale, *Redeeming the text: Latin poetry and the hermeneutics of reception*

Texts, editors, and readers

Methods and problems in Latin textual criticism

Richard Tarrant

Pope Professor of Latin
Harvard University

CAMBRIDGE
UNIVERSITY PRESS

University Printing House, Cambridge CB2 8BS, United Kingdom

Cambridge University Press is part of the University of Cambridge.

It furthers the University's mission by disseminating knowledge in the pursuit of education, learning and research at the highest international levels of excellence.

www.cambridge.org
Information on this title: www.cambridge.org/9780521158992

© Richard Tarrant 2016

This publication is in copyright. Subject to statutory exception
and to the provisions of relevant collective licensing agreements,
no reproduction of any part may take place without the written
permission of Cambridge University Press.

First published 2016

A catalogue record for this publication is available from the British Library

Library of Congress Cataloguing in Publication data
Names: Tarrant, R. J. (Richard John), 1945– author.
Title: Texts, editors, and readers : methods and problems in Latin
textual criticism / Richard Tarrant.
Description: Cambridge : Cambridge University Press, 2016. |
Series: Roman literature and its contexts |
Includes bibliographical references and index.
Identifiers: LCCN 2015042954 | ISBN 9780521766579 (hardback) |
ISBN 9780521158992 (pbk)
Subjects: LCSH: Latin literature–Criticism, Textual.
Classification: LCC PA6141.T37 2016 | DDC 870.9–dc23
LC record available at http://lccn.loc.gov/2015042954

ISBN 978-0-521-15899-2 Paperback

Robin Nisbet
In Memoriam

Contents

Preface

'Richard, isn't it curious that any damn fool who has edited a text thinks he can write a book on textual criticism?' (Roger Mynors in conversation, 1975). Roger's words struck me with particular force, partly because of their atypical vehemence and partly because at the time, fresh from editing a text and reviewing a couple of books on textual criticism, I had indeed begun to think that I might write a book on the subject. His remark made me postpone the project for nearly four decades. I must leave it to readers to decide whether I should have put it off still longer.

This set of essays is neither a handbook nor a history of classical textual criticism. Good examples of both genres are available, such as Martin West's *Textual Criticism and Editorial Technique* and Leighton Reynolds's and Nigel Wilson's *Scribes and Scholars*. My aim is instead to offer critical assessments of the current state of the field and some thoughts on the challenges and possibilities facing it in the near future. But I hope that the book may also serve as a way into textual criticism for classicists who do not specialize in the subject and for scholars in related disciplines.

Textual criticism affects all students of the classics, whether or not they are aware of its influence. That influence is mainly exerted by the editions that we all depend on, and so one of my goals is to provide guidance for users of critical editions, at a general level by examining the rationales that underlie classical editing and more specifically through sections on apparatus format and terminology.

I have tried to take nothing for granted and to regard no assumption or practice as self-evidently valid, but to subject all of them to scrutiny, which will often result in acknowledging their limitations. A recurring theme is the role played in textual criticism by non-objective factors. Textual criticism deals with relative probability and persuasiveness, not with demonstration, and as a result its conclusions must always be to a degree provisional.

This is a personal book, both in the sense of being written in a first-person style that reflects its origins in lectures and also in being rooted in my own editorial experiences: many of my examples of textual problems are drawn from Ovid's *Metamorphoses*. One of the pleasant consequences of writing it has been the opportunity to reconsider my critical outlook and the scholars who have shaped it.

It is likewise a pleasure to thank the many colleagues and friends who have helped me in putting the book together. Denis Feeney and Stephen Hinds suggested the topic many years ago, persevered through long stretches in which progress was invisible, and offered acute and supportive responses when draft chapters at last began to appear. Gian Biagio Conte prompted the invitation to deliver the Comparetti Lectures in 2008 at the Scuola Normale Superiore in Pisa, which provided the stimulus needed to turn inchoate thoughts into the semblance of a book. Audience members in Pisa contributed helpful questions and comments; there are too many for me to thank them all, but I cannot leave out Giuliana Crevatin, Rolando Ferri, Glenn Most, Lisa Piazzi, Seth Schein, and Mario Telò. For advice and information of various kinds I am grateful to Archie Burnett, Cynthia Damon, Albertus Horsting, Bob Kaster, Tom Keeline, Dániel Kiss, Matt McGowan, James McKeown, Stephen Oakley, Christopher Parrott, Irene Peirano, Richard Rutherford, Justin Stover, Richard Thomas, Julian Yolles, and James Zetzel. Special thanks are due to the anonymous reader for Cambridge University Press, whose comments helped me to clarify my arguments at several points, to Gail Trimble, who read the manuscript at a late stage and improved it in many places, and to Michael Sharp, for his unfailing support and advice.

Chapter 6 has acquired its own set of benefactors. I am once again grateful to Gian Biagio Conte and the Scuola Normale for the opportunity to discuss some of the ideas in that chapter, also to the participants in a seminar on the text of Propertius at the 2010 meeting of the American Philological Association, and to Stephen Heyworth for his spirited response to the papers at that session.

When I began graduate work, I was quite unsure of my future direction; the one thing of which I felt certain was that I would never engage in textual criticism. Robin Nisbet gently led me to see that the only way I could write the dissertation I had undertaken – a commentary on Seneca's *Agamemnon* – would be to edit the text as well. In gratitude for that realization, for so much else that followed, and above all for his example, I dedicate this book to his memory.

Introduction

I

When I pick up a new novel or work of non-fiction, I do not expect to see an editor credited; I assume that I am in direct contact with a text created by an author and put into circulation by a publisher. In fact, matters may be more complicated if, for example, the publisher has employed a copy-editor to correct the author's manuscript, a practice once common but now increasingly rare outside academic publishing. Yet such behind-the-scenes activity is hardly ever acknowledged, which maintains the impression of an unmediated communication between author and reader.

So the presence of an editor implies that something has occurred that requires assistance from a third party in putting an author's work into the hands of readers. In the case of a contemporary work, the author may have died before the text had reached a final form, and the editor's task is to construct as far as possible the text that the author would have wished to see published. Such undertakings can involve extensive intervention, as with David Foster Wallace's novel *The Pale King*, left unfinished at his death in 2008 and published in 2011. The editor, Michael Pietsch, began with a manuscript of more than 1,000 pages and arrived at a version of roughly half that length.

An ancient parallel is Virgil's *Aeneid*, left unrevised at the poet's death and prepared for publication by his friend and fellow-poet L. Varius Rufus.[1] The biographical tradition reports that the emperor Augustus, in overruling Virgil's wish that the manuscript of the poem be burned, directed Varius to make as little change to the text as was necessary to render it publishable;

---

[1] L. Plotius Tucca is named as a co-editor, but since nothing is known of his literary pursuits it seems likely that Varius was principally responsible for the editorial work.

even if that account is accurate, we have no way of knowing how much of what we read as Virgil is in fact the work of Varius.

The other main function of an editor in the contemporary context is to bring together work that has been dispersed in separate publications or that has not been previously published. A recent example is Archie Burnett's edition of the poetry of Philip Larkin (2012), which has been criticized for including poems that Larkin never published and that he may not have wished to see in print. That activity as well has parallels in Antiquity: the corpus of Catullus' poetry in its transmitted form, a miscellany whose formal and generic diversity is unique in ancient literature, is more likely to be the product of posthumous editorial collecting than anything Catullus himself meant to publish.[2]

Although there are some similarities between what a contemporary editor does and what was done in the ancient world, the task of an editor of a classical text today differs from that of the editor of a modern text in a fundamental way. Editors of classical texts have no difficulty in defining their aim as that of reconstructing the author's original version, while at the same time recognizing that, given the evidence available, that aim can never be fully achieved. We have no authors' autographs of classical texts, and in most cases the earliest surviving copies are from the ninth century CE, separated by many hundreds of years from the original copies.[3] As a result, no classical text can be recovered in all its details; the most that can be hoped for is a close approximation to the original.[4] For many editors of modern texts, however, an abundance of evidence with a direct connection to the author can render the concept of an original text problematic.

The editor of a modern text must often decide *which* authorial version of a text to edit. An extreme case is Byron's poem *The Giaour*, which survives in versions that range from 344 verses in the holograph draft to 1,334 in the seventh printed edition.[5] But many other texts present similar problems on a

---

[2] The dedicatory poem to Cornelius Nepos puts it beyond doubt that Catullus published *a* collection of his poems, but I do not believe that it contained more than the first sixty poems in our corpus, if that much. This view is controversial; see, for example, Wiseman (1969), (1979) for a contrary hypothesis and Thomson (1997), 6–10 for a judicious summary of the issues. See also pp. 39–40.

[3] Only for some patristic texts do we possess manuscripts close in time to the original texts: e.g., Augustine's *De doctrina Christiana*, completed in the 420s, of which a fifth-century copy is extant (now in St Petersburg); the manuscript was once thought to have come from Augustine's own library.

[4] I will come back to this point from another direction in Chapter 2 (p. 40).

[5] McGann (1983), 59.

smaller scale. A notable example is Shakespeare's *King Lear*, of which the texts found in the First Quarto and the First Folio arguably reflect distinct authorial versions, Q1 a draft of the play before it was performed and F1 a text revised at some time after performance.

Confronted with situations of that kind, editors must choose between an eclectic approach that draws on multiple witnesses and constructs a text that is identical to none of them and what Gary Taylor has called a 'versioning' approach, that is, reconstructing or reproducing separate authorial versions of a text.[6] In recent years the versioning method has won more and more adherents: for example, the Norton Shakespeare prints *Lear* as found in Q1 and F1 as independent texts on facing pages; for good measure it also provides a text conflated from both sources, the form in which the play has traditionally been read.

Multiple authorial versions are also a recognized phenomenon in medieval vernacular literature: a conspicuous instance is Langland's *Piers Plowman*, which survives in at least three authorial forms (conventionally designated the A, B, and C texts), each of which has been edited as a separate entity and which have also been presented (along with a possible fourth version, Z) in a parallel-text edition.[7]

Similar questions can arise in the editing of musical scores, as is shown by the tangled editorial history of Anton Bruckner's symphonies. Bruckner revised many of his symphonies after their first performances, partly on his own initiative and partly in response to suggestions from friends and conductors. The first published editions also incorporated many unauthorized departures from Bruckner's autographs introduced by former students on whom he had relied for editorial help. Robert Haas, who was responsible for the first attempt at a critical edition, conflated wherever possible material from several versions to arrive at an 'ideal' synthesis; most performers today use the editions by Leopold Nowak, who attempted to keep those versions distinct.[8]

Such considerations are almost entirely absent from classical editing, because in nearly all cases the differences between manuscript copies of a classical text do not represent different versions of the work, but rather

---

[6] Taylor (2007), 847–8. He makes the important point that, depending on the documentary evidence available, a version may need to be reconstructed using an eclectic approach.

[7] For the parallel-text edition and a review of the poem's editorial history, see Schmidt (2008).

[8] Details in Hawkshaw and Jackson (2001), 467–71.

scribal attempts (more or less successful) to reproduce a single form of a text.[9] In a few texts (Ovid's *Metamorphoses* being one) the presence of authorial variants has been asserted, although in my view their existence has not been convincingly established. Even if all the alleged examples were accepted, they would amount only to minor retouching, not the kind of thorough revision that can be documented for many modern texts and musical scores. A number of classical texts were revised by their authors, but in no case do both the first and the revised version survive.[10] Ovid's *Amores* is the best-known example: the extant collection, comprising three books, is preceded by an 'epigramma', which states that there were once five books of poems but that the author preferred the shorter version. It is plausible that the revised text, with its explicit authorial approval, drove the earlier version out of circulation, although it is still somewhat surprising that no traces of the prior form made their way into the transmission.

For good reasons, then, the eclectic approach has been the dominant model in classical editing. That is likely to remain true, although in the last chapter I will mention the possibility created by digital technology of disseminating the individual transmitted forms of a text alongside an editorial reconstruction of the putative original.

In addition to modifying the notion of a single original text, modern textual criticism has also called into question the notion of the author as the unique source of texts. Jerome McGann has emphasized instead the collaborative nature of text production, in which the author is one component – admittedly an indispensable one – in a chain of agents that may include friends of the author, publisher's readers, copyeditors, printers, and proofreaders, all of whom may be responsible for alterations of the author's original text. It is often difficult to disentangle the contributions of these agents, and, McGann would argue, the attempt to do so places the author's manuscript in an unduly exalted position and ignores the realities of how texts (in the sense of what reaches readers) are created.[11]

---

[9] A rare exception is the *Historia Apollonii Regis Tyri*, which survives in two recensions, RA and RB; for parallel-text editions see Kortekaas (1984), (2004). This work might be called 'semi-classical' both in its date (late fifth or early sixth century CE) and in the extensive Christian influence it displays.

[10] Cicero recast his *Academica*, originally in two books, into a four-book form. The original second book survives, as does part of the first book of the second edition. See Brittain (2006).

[11] McGann (1983).

McGann's stress on the role played by figures other than the author fits what is known or can be surmised for a number of classical texts. The *Aeneid* and Catullus have already been mentioned. Friends of Ovid may have been instrumental in putting the *Metamorphoses* into circulation after he went into exile. Friends of the author could also become involved before a work reached its final form: the Younger Pliny describes an elaborate process of reading a work-in-progress first to himself, then to two or three listeners, then giving the text to others for their comments, and finally reading to a larger audience, making changes at every step of the way.[12] The transmitted texts of the comedies of Plautus and Terence almost certainly incorporate changes made by actors and producers in both the original performances and in subsequent revivals, as well as readings arising from ancient scholarly study of the texts.[13] Medieval manuscripts of Horace's *Odes* include material that is certainly non-authorial (e.g., metrical analyses) and other elements that are probably non-authorial (such as titles for individual poems, e.g., *Ad Pyrrham* for *C.* 1.5).[14] Our texts have also been affected by processes that are now impossible to reverse, such as changes in orthography. It seems very likely from the evidence of inscriptions that Cicero employed such forms as *caussa* for *causa*, and the Qasr Ibrim papyrus of poetry by Cornelius Gallus from the late first century BCE uses *quom* instead of *cum* and the older *ei* where we are accustomed to *i* (e.g., *deiuitiora tueis = diuitiora tuis*). On the whole, however, the extant manuscripts of Latin authors employ a 'modernized' orthography (i.e., that prevalent in late Antiquity), which is in turn the orthography of most modern editions of classical texts.

Classical texts were, one imagines, no less the product of a collaborative process than are modern ones; the difference is that in the classical sphere the collaborators are either too close to the author for their contributions to be discernible (e.g., Varius and the *Aeneid*) or else too distant from the author to be given weight in the editorial process (e.g., medieval scribes, who can only affect a text by miscopying it).[15]

---

[12] *Epist.* 7.17.7. Being a friend of Pliny was obviously no joke.

[13] Marshall (2006), 257–79 argues that any given performance of a Plautine comedy contained a certain amount of improvisation by actors; he thinks it is possible that some originally unscripted moments were incorporated into later performing texts (261).

[14] On titles, see Schröder (1999).

[15] In an intermediate position are the interpolators, especially of the kind I call 'collaborative' (see Chapter 5). My use of the term is independent of McGann's, but fits well with his emphasis on the communal nature of text production.

Classical editors' fixation on the author's original does not necessarily betoken ignorance of or hostility to the questioning of that concept in other areas of textual criticism, but is rather the result of the circumstances in which classical literature has been preserved.

II

In order to survive into the ninth century and to have some chance of being copied subsequently, an ancient text had to pass through two bottlenecks, each resulting from an advance in the technology of script or book production. The first was the transition from the papyrus roll to the parchment codex, a process that probably began in the second century CE and was substantially complete by the fifth century.[16] Because papyrus lasts for a relatively short time unless accidentally preserved, it seems safe to conclude that any text that had not been recopied on parchment by the end of the fifth century would have been lost by the time of the second great transition, from the scripts of antiquity to the Caroline minuscule that was developed in the last decades of the eighth century. Surviving the first of those two transitions did not guarantee that a text would survive the second: parchment, although far more durable than papyrus, was also much more expensive and more limited in quantity, and in the centuries of cultural and economic constriction following the breakup of the Roman Empire in the West, book production often entailed painful choices – shall it be Cicero or St. Augustine? – or else a sort of zero-sum situation in which new books were created by reusing the scrubbed-off ('palimpsested') leaves of earlier codices.[17] Extant palimpsested manuscripts contain fragments of several classical texts that have been otherwise lost, but that had survived the transition to the codex. The best-known example is Cicero's *De re publica*, of which substantial sections were discovered in 1819 by Angelo Mai in a Vatican manuscript.[18] A single palimpsest, Vat. Pal. lat. 24, put together in southern Italy in the late sixth or early seventh century, contains portions of ten earlier manuscripts, with texts including Seneca's lost *De amicitia* and *De vita patris*, Livy Book 91, and Hyginus' *Fabulae*, as well as works of Cicero, Lucan, and Aulus Gellius that survive in medieval copies.[19] It would be natural to assume that the monastic copyists responsible for palimpsesting manuscripts were animated by a bias

---

[16] For a brief account, see my article 'Codex' in Thomas and Ziolkowski (2014).
[17] See Reynolds (1983), xiv–xvii; for a list, see Lowe (1964).
[18] Facsimile by Mercati (1934); see Reynolds (1983), 132.
[19] Full study by Fohlen (1979).

against pagan texts, but in fact utility rather than ideology seems to have been their overriding concern, as can be seen from the fact that the text most often palimpsested was the early Latin translation of the Bible (the *Vetus Latina*), which had been rendered obsolete by Jerome's 'Vulgate' version.

Few texts seem to have survived into the late eighth or early ninth century only then to disappear. A possible instance was described in heart-rending terms by A. E. Housman:

> [O]ne day toward the end of the eighth century the scribe of cod. Paris. Lat. 7530 ... began to copy out for us, on the 28th leaf of the MS, the *Thyestes* of Varius. He transcribed the title and the prefatory note ... Then he changed his mind: he proceeded with a list of the *notae* employed by Probus and Aristarchus, and the masterpiece of Roman tragedy has rejoined its author in the shades.[20]

Housman's scenario is probably too melodramatic, since it seems likely that the text of Varius' play had already disappeared by this time, leaving its *titulus* behind, like the Cheshire Cat's grin.[21]

The transition from manuscript to print, which for most of the Latin classics took place between about 1475 and 1525, did not entail the kind of winnowing experienced at the earlier two stages. In a few instances, such as Velleius Paterculus' *Roman History* and the *Fabulae* of Hyginus, the unique manuscript used for the printed edition seems to have been discarded and lost, but I know of no text that survived in manuscript form to the age of printing that did not eventually reach print.

The passage from manuscript to print does, however, have some points in common with the earlier salvaging of classical texts after the collapse of the Roman Empire. Neither process was planned or coordinated so as to produce optimal results. Classical texts survived in the first place because they had the good fortune to be copied at critical moments, and the quality of those copies determined the character of the later transmission; that explains why, for example, Ovid's *Fasti* is relatively well preserved while the text of his *Heroides* is much more corrupt and interpolated. Texts entered print in a similarly haphazard fashion, sometimes on the basis of good manuscripts but probably more often on the basis of indifferent or bad ones, and the nature of those first printed editions also had a powerful influence on the character of later editions.

A form of evidence that is important for editing classical texts but that has no exact counterpart in the modern period consists of quotations in ancient

---

[20] Housman (1917), 42.

[21] Also, to be precise, a one-line fragment that survives as a quotation in Quintilian.

sources. Seneca, for example, in his *Epistulae morales*, cites almost fifty Greek and Latin authors. Along with well-attested canonical figures such as Virgil and Horace are a few otherwise lost texts; perhaps the most remarkable of Seneca's quotations are several eye-popping specimens of the mannered writing of Maecenas, the patron of Virgil and Horace.[22] But it is the grammarians, with their habit of illustrating forms or usages with citations from a wide range of authors, who offer the richest troves of indirect tradition. A single book of Priscian's *Institutiones grammaticae* (Book 6, which deals with the nominative and genitive cases) contains citations from fifty-three authors, thirty of whom lack direct manuscript attestation. Among the highlights are a dozen fragments each from Ennius' *Annales* and Sallust's *Histories* and quotations from seven plays by the Republican tragedian Accius.

In addition to preserving fragments of lost works, quotations can also harbour potentially original readings that have disappeared in all manuscripts. In Propertius 4.5.47 *ianitor ad dantes uigilet; si pulsat inanis* ('let the doorkeeper stay awake for those with gifts; if someone knocks empty-handed'), the entire manuscript tradition reads *pulset*, an unwanted subjunctive form influenced by the preceding *uigilet*; the correct *pulsat* is found in a graffito on a wall in Pompeii.[23]

Although quotations in ancient sources constitute evidence much older than the medieval manuscripts of the author being quoted, they are not immune to corruption, whether from cross-influence of manuscripts of the quoted text or simply from the usual processes of scribal error. Ovid's account of the weaving contest between Arachne and Minerva in *Metamorphoses* 6 contains the splendidly alliterative line *percusso pauiunt insecti pectine dentes* (58 'as the comb beats <the weft> the notched teeth tap <it> into place'). The rare but certainly correct verb *pauiunt* (from *pauire*, a technical term for tamping down the weft) has been replaced in most of the Ovid tradition by easier synonyms, *feriunt* or *quatiunt* (both verbs for 'striking'), which may have originated as glosses on *pauiunt*;[24] a trace of the original reading lingered in one older manuscript, which had a nonsensical *pauent* ('they fear') before it was 'corrected' to *feriunt*. Ovid's line is quoted by Seneca in *Epist.* 90.20, where again *pauiunt* has been corrupted, this time to *pariunt* ('they give birth') in the oldest manuscript, with *feriunt* common in later manuscripts. Jan Gruter (1560–1627) conjectured *pauiunt* in the Seneca passage, and the conjecture has been adopted by all

[22] *Epist.* 19.9, 92.35, 101.11, 114.4–8.
[23] See Heyworth (2007b), 455.
[24] The lexicon of Festus contains the entry *'pauire* est *ferire'* (p. 244 M.).

modern editors of Ovid.[25] Another source of error in indirect transmission is the habit of ancient authors of quoting from memory rather than after consulting a text. As a result their citations may contain readings due entirely to the faulty recollection of the quoting author: Seneca's citation of *Met.* 6.58 reads *quod lato* for *percusso*.

III

Scribal error is an inevitable component of a manuscript medium of transmission. That ancient scribes were as fallible as their medieval successors, and that they fell prey to many of the same types of error, can be clearly seen from the small number of ancient copies that survive. Ancient and medieval scribes alike had to deal with a wide range of pitfalls. Some were inherent in the material they copied, which often confronted them with unfamiliar names, recondite vocabulary, complex syntax, and baffling metrical patterns. Others were posed by the particular form in which the scribe encountered the text: the exemplar might have been damaged, or was for other reasons difficult to read; the script might be an unfamiliar one, and letters or abbreviations might be incorrectly interpreted; punctuation and/or word division might be inconsistent, faulty, or absent; marginal notes or glosses might be mistaken for parts of the text (in Seneca's *Epist.* 42.4, most manuscripts have the syntactical direction *subaudi si*, 'understand *si*', in the text); if the scribe was copying from dictation, auditory confusions might arise.[26]

A beautiful example of an error produced in part by palaeographical factors occurs in Catullus' epithalamium for Manlius Torquatus, when the poet calls for the traditional banter directed at the newly married couple: *ne diu taceat procax | Fescennina iocatio* (61.119–20 'let the ribald Fescennine jesting not be long silent'). The manuscripts read *locatio*, 'renting out', which makes no sense in the context; an Italian humanist, Coluccio Salutati, corrected to *locutio* ('utterance, expression'), but a much better correction, *iocatio* ('jesting'), was made by Heinsius. There is an excellent palaeographical explanation for the error: in the ancient Roman script called 'Rustic Capital', the letters I and L closely resemble each other and so are easily confused. Even in this case, however, the palaeographical element is

---

[25] Nicolas Heinsius thought of the same conjecture in Ovid, but declined to alter the common reading *feriunt*, in part because he thought *feriunt* was the reading of the Senecan quotation.

[26] For a useful collection of errors of various kinds, see Reynolds and Wilson (2013), 223–35.

only one factor, others being the greater familiarity of the combination LOC vis-à-vis IOC (because of the frequency of words such as *locus*) and the scribe's lack of acquaintance with the ancient custom in question. Confusion of letters is most likely to occur when ignorance of the content removes the control that would otherwise prevent a scribe from writing what he knows is nonsense.

Errors could occur even when the text posed no particular challenges of reading or comprehension. Some were produced by inattention, such as copying the same word(s) twice (dittography), failing to copy a repeated word or words (haplography), or skipping from one occurrence of a word to another in the same context, omitting the intervening words (*saut du même au même*; sometimes called homoeoarchon or homoeoteleuton if the similarity lies in the beginning or end of the respective words). Others appear to result from slips in eye–brain–hand communication, such as transpositions of letters or syllables that produce nonsense: for example, Virgil *Georgics* 3.166 *criclos* for *circlos* (M), *Aeneid* 11.711 *rapu* for *pura* (M¹), Valerius Flaccus 2.268 *falamuribus* for *famularibus* (V). Still others may have been caused by the scribe's speaking the text to himself as he copied (what Alphonse Dain called 'dictée intérieure') and altering the form to suit his pronunciation: so perhaps Quintilian 6.3.93 *pane et aqua uiuo > bibo*, Horace *Carm.* 1.25.20 *Euro > (H)ebro*.[27]

Another large class of errors can be called 'psychological' in that they arise from the scribe's mental interaction with the text he is copying. So, for example, the text may be altered because it evokes some association in the scribe's mind. The change may be the simple substitution of a synonym, such as *ferrum* for *telum* or *labores* for *dolores*, or it may replace a word with another of similar shape, but different meaning, as often happens with dactylic words (*tempore/corpore, nomine/sanguine, uulnera/pectora*, etc.). If the scribe is attempting to make sense of the text as he copies, he may rearrange word order for easier comprehension; and since scribes often construe small strings of words rather than entire sentences, they may unconsciously alter a form to fit what they wrongly believe is its syntactical function. The oldest recorded scribal error in a Latin literary text, in the Qasr Ibrim papyrus with verses by Cornelius Gallus, is probably of that type: in the phrase *quom tu | maxima Romanae pars eris historiae* ('when you will be the greatest part of Roman history'), addressed to a 'Caesar' (probably Julius), the papyrus

---

[27] For collections of verbal confusions, see Housman (1903), liv–lix (on transposition of letters and syllables), Havet (1911), Courtney (1970), xxxii–xlvi.

gives the third-person form *erit* for *eris*. T and S are not particularly similar in the scripts likely to have been used in the exemplar; it looks as though the scribe, having copied *pars* and forgetting the preceding *tu*, assumed that *pars* was the subject of the verb and therefore wrote *erit*.

A particular type of association is religious. Until the thirteenth century, almost all scribes were Christian monks, and from time to time words with scriptural or other religious resonances triggered subconscious alterations. In Caesar *BC* 1.40.3 some manuscripts turn *legiones* into *religiones*; in Valerius Flaccus 3.76 *galeae* ('helmet') becomes *galileae* ('Galilean'); in Ovid *Met.* 15.836 *prolem sancta de coniuge natam* ('the offspring born of his chaste wife', said of Augustus' stepson Tiberius), the Nativity-like language seems to have prompted one twelfth-century scribe to write *uirgine* for *coniuge*, making Livia an unlikely avatar of the Madonna; and in Manilius 4.422 *laudatique cadit post paulum gratia ponti* ('in a short while the charm of the admired sea vanishes') the substitution of *Christi* for *ponti* (probably owing to the theological associations of *gratia*) transforms a statement about the changeability of the elements into a critique of St Paul's role in the evolution of Christianity.[28]

Many errors arise from the interaction of more than one factor in the form and content of the text and the mental state of the scribe. One of the nicest examples of apparent *error Christianus*, the misreading in Petronius' *Satyricon* 43.1 of *ab asse creuit* ('he has grown from a penny' or 'he started out with only a penny') as *abbas secreuit* ('the abbot has hidden it away'), was almost certainly prompted as much by absence of word division in the exemplar and the scribe's lack of familiarity with the coin term *as, assis* as by any grievances he may have harboured against his superior.

Finally, I cannot resist mentioning a slip for which I was responsible when editing the Canadian classical journal *Phoenix*. The Spring 1980 issue included a review of the edition of a text on military surveying, *De metatione castrorum* ('On measuring camps'). In typing up the table of contents, I rendered the title as *De metatione castorum*, which could mean either 'On measuring chaste men' or 'On measuring beavers'. An alert reader who adopted the second interpretation wrote to congratulate me on perpetrating such a quintessentially Canadian error.

---

[28] As Housman drily comments: 'gratiam Christi post Paulum cecidisse tam uerum quam generi humano luctuosum est, sed nunc de mari agitur' ('that the grace of Christ declined after Paul is as true as it is calamitous for the human race, but at the moment we are concerned with the sea'). On such so-called 'monastic corruption', see Ogilvie (1971), Willis (1972), 100–2.

Scribal error is for obvious reasons the bane of classical editors, but it can also be a powerful diagnostic tool. Miscopyings can provide valuable clues to a manuscript's history. In most of the Latin scripts used in antiquity and the early Middle Ages, certain letters are more readily confused than others (some examples: in 'Rustic Capital', E/F, I/T, C/G; in Uncial, C/G; in Half-uncial, r/s; in some pre-Caroline and early Caroline minuscule, a/cc); if a manuscript contains a significant number of errors traceable to particular letter shapes, one may hazard a guess about the script in which its exemplar (or a more remote ancestor) was written.

Even more useful are scribal errors that can reveal a manuscript's relationships to other copies of the same text; the analysis of such indicative errors is the basis of the genealogical method, sometimes called 'stemmatics' and often, if inaccurately, associated with the name of Karl Lachmann (1793–1851). The underlying rationale begins with the assumption that errors cannot stem from the original but must have arisen at some later point in the tradition. That axiom might appear open to question in that even the fair copy of a classical author's text could have contained copying mistakes, but the objection is not powerful enough to invalidate the method; in addition, 'error' in this context includes not only textual readings but also other kinds of non-original elements, such as chapter headings or poem titles.[29] If, therefore, two copies of a text, A and B, agree in an error not found in other copies, A and B must have some relationship to each other in addition to their common descent from the original. Either the error originated in A and found its way into B, in which case A is the direct or more remote source of B, or vice versa, or A and B independently inherited the error from a common source. The same principle can be used to link larger groups of manuscripts, with more specific relationships within the group determined by subsequent steps in the analysis. For such conjunctive errors to have full value in a stemmatic analysis, the readings or features in question must be as securely non-original as possible, and they must be of a kind not likely to have occurred independently more than once. Perhaps the earliest, and one of the most convincing, applications of this type of analysis was made in the fifteenth century by Angelo Poliziano with regard to the manuscripts of Cicero's *Epistulae ad familiares*. Poliziano observed that in a fourteenth-century copy of the letters a group of folios had been misplaced in binding, producing a dislocation of the text at that point, while

---

[29] Focusing on securely non-authorial readings and other features is a way to minimize the risk of circularity entailed in appealing to a lost original in order to categorize departures from it as errors. See also pp. 50–2. (Chapter 3).

in a number of other copies the same textual dislocation occurred with no physical damage to account for it; he correctly inferred that the copy with the misplaced gathering was the source of all other copies containing the same error.[30] The other side of the same analytic coin is the use of errors to separate manuscripts: if A contains errors that do not appear in B, A cannot be the source of B. Here the proviso is that the errors in question should not be ones that a reasonably intelligent scribe could correct for himself.

Some errors are both conjunctive and separative: many lacunae (omissions of text), for example, provided that the omitted material is securely genuine and not an interpolation, that there is no obvious cause for omission (which could induce more than one scribe to make the same error), and that the content of the omission could not be reconstructed by a scribe based on information in the surrounding text. Conversely, some errors have little value either conjunctively or separatively, for example, the Gallus papyrus' *erit* for *eris* (pp. 10–11): the shape of the sentence could lead more than one scribe to make the same alteration, while the error, once made, could be easily corrected by an alert scribe in a subsequent copy.

Conjunctive and separative errors can be used in combination to define more precisely the relationship of our A and B: if A shows separative errors vis-à-vis B – that is, A has errors not found in B – but the reverse is not true, then B is probably the source of A; if each contains separative errors vis-à-vis the other, they are likely to be independent of each other.[31]

The network of affiliations connecting manuscripts of a text, if recoverable with sufficient clarity, can be represented by a schematic diagram, or stemma.[32] Stemma is Greek for 'wreath' or 'garland'; in Latin it carries the metaphorical sense 'family tree', immortalized in Juvenal's *stemmata quid faciunt?* ('what's the point of family trees?'), a tag that has led a second life in discussions of text-critical method. The link between the senses may be provided by Roman wall paintings in which portraits of ancestors were connected by garland-like decoration.

In theory, the entity at the head of the stemma could be the author's original text, and that is the case in some medieval traditions. In all classical transmissions known to me, however, there are some errors common to all witnesses that cannot derive from the original; they must therefore have been present in a source of all extant manuscripts. That common source is called the archetype: looked at from the perspective of the original, the archetype

---

[30] Grafton (1983), 28–9, Reynolds and Wilson (2013), 145.

[31] The classic treatment of the logic of stemmatics is Maas (1958).

[32] See pp. 53–4, for sample stemmata.

represents the latest stage of the transmission attested to by all surviving witnesses; from the perspective of the extant witnesses, it represents the earliest stage of the transmission that can be reconstructed from them. The archetype can be an extant manuscript, as it is with Seneca's *De beneficiis* and *De clementia*, Statius' *Siluae*, and Tacitus' *Annals* 11–16 and *Histories*, but it is usually a hypothetical construct.[33]

Stemmatic analysis is often seen as an attempt to emulate scientific procedures, and some early celebrations of the method do ascribe to it the aura of infallibility sometimes associated with the sciences, but the underlying model is better thought of as mechanical. The ideal stemma is both a sorting device and a calculator, at the lower end weeding out derivative manuscripts (*codices descripti*) and at the upper end yielding the readings of the archetype. For the stemmatic machinery to function at peak efficiency, however, the scribes themselves need to have behaved more like machines than human beings, faithfully perpetuating the errors of their exemplars while conveniently generating new errors in every fresh copy, and studiously refraining from attempts to improve the text either by their own wits or by consulting another copy. Unfortunately, few scribes and readers at any time can have adhered to such an austere code of conduct.

There is, in fact, clear evidence from both Antiquity and the Middle Ages that shows copyists or owners attempting to correct manuscripts by consulting a source other than the manuscript's exemplar. A number of owners' *subscriptiones* in Latin manuscripts from the late fourth through the early sixth centuries CE illustrate this process at work.[34] Some notes specify the source of correction, like the one found at the end of Livy's first pentad: 'Nicomachus Dexter u. c. emendaui ad exemplum parentis mei Clementiani' ('I, Nicomachus Dexter u. c., corrected against the copy of my parent [or relative?] Clementianus'). A few record attempts at correction with no second copy available (e.g., Flavius Julius Tryphonianus Sabinus corrected Persius 'sine antigrapho'), perhaps suggesting a departure from standard practice. The Carolingian scholar Lupus of Ferrières (*c.*805–862) describes a similar procedure in more explicit terms: thanking a monk from Prüm for sending him a copy of Cicero's *Epistulae ad familiares*, Lupus says

---

[33] Cicero (*Att.* 16.3.1) and Martial (7.11.4) use *archetypus* to refer to an author's original copy. On the various meanings of *archetypus* in Humanist Latin ('author's copy', 'official copy', 'source of all other copies'), see Rizzo (1973), 308–17; for its use in modern critical parlance, see Reeve (1986).

[34] For a good discussion, see Reynolds and Wilson (2013), 39–43.

that he will have it collated against his own copy, 'so that from both of them the truth may be dug out if possible'.[35]

The entering into a manuscript of readings that derive from a source other than its exemplar has acquired the name 'contamination'; the sinister connotations of the term reflect the seriousness of the threat it can pose to stemmatic analysis. A term such as 'horizontal' or 'lateral' transmission would be both less prejudicial and more usefully descriptive of the process, but 'contamination' is probably too firmly established in text-critical discourse to be dislodged.[36]

If we assume that most owners and copyists had at least some interest in improving the quality of their manuscripts, it would seem reasonable to conclude that contamination was a common phenomenon; one might even suspect that it was the norm, and purely vertical transmission the exception. Contamination would have been impossible only in the case of rare texts, where a second copy might not be available, or for texts circulating in geographically disparate regions.

The effects of contamination can vary considerably, depending on when it took place and how thoroughly it has affected the tradition. Contamination prior to the archetype (such as that suggested by some of the *subscriptiones*) need not hamper a stemmatic treatment of the extant manuscripts, provided that the archetype itself was relatively free of variant readings. If the archetype did contain numerous variants, contamination in its descendants is almost inevitable.

Contamination lower down in the stemma can also vary in its effect. Contamination that is limited to a single manuscript family need not invalidate stemmatic analysis of a tradition as a whole. The real danger arises when the source of contamination is another branch of the stemma; in such a case the application of standard stemmatic arguments could result in misconstruing the actual relationships of manuscripts.[37]

Thoroughgoing contamination can make a manuscript's place in a stemma unrecognizable, but few scribes or owners are likely to have carried out the task in the spirit of a modern editor collating manuscript witnesses on a word-by-word basis. As a result, it may be possible to discern a manuscript's

---

[35] *Tullianas epistolas quas misisti cum nostris conferri faciam, ut ex utrisque, si possit fieri, ueritas exculpatur* (*Epist.* 69); see Reynolds and Wilson (2013), 105.

[36] My Harvard colleague James Hankins has observed that in another context this activity would be called 'scholarship'.

[37] West (1973), 35–6 illustrates the potential for misunderstanding with a hypothetical example.

underlying affiliation even if it displays evidence of contamination.[38] Two
provisos, however, are in order. The first is that the choice of errors must be
made with particular care to distinguish readings probably inherited from an
exemplar from those likely to have been introduced by lateral transmission.
The other is that, even when a stemma can be drawn in a tradition where
contamination is known to be present, the stemmatic calculus of variants can
only be employed with great caution, if at all.

The essential principles underlying stemmatic analysis were grasped as
early as the fifteenth century, but more than 300 years passed before classical scholars began to apply them to the study of entire manuscript traditions.
One obstacle was practical, the difficulty of gaining access to large numbers
of manuscripts in a time before train travel and photography. A more subtle factor was the effect of printing: as unsatisfactory as many of the earliest printed texts of classical authors were, they long remained the point of
departure for subsequent editions; new manuscript readings or conjectures
were patched onto the received text (the *textus receptus*), but the underlying
fabric escaped examination.

Caesar's *Bellum ciuile* furnishes a striking example of the persistence of
readings found in early printed editions and also of the utility of stemmatic
analysis in assessing the authority of manuscript evidence.[39] In a justificatory
message to Pompey, Caesar wrote that his *dignitas* had always been his highest priority, dearer than life itself (*BC* 1.9.2 *sibi semper primam fuisse digni-
tatem uitaque priorem*). That, at least, is how the text runs in all but one of the
manuscripts regarded as fundamental by modern editors. The one exception
is a Paris manuscript (T in editions), which inserts *PR* between *primam* and
fuisse. The abbreviation *PR* normally stands for *populus Romanus*; T.'s reading would therefore make Caesar say that he had always placed the dignity
of the Roman people first – a more flattering, but considerably less honest
statement. No other extant manuscript agrees with T, but the *editio princeps*
of 1469 has a possibly related insertion, *primam rei publicae fuisse*; now
it is the dignity of the Republic that comes first in Caesar's eyes.[40] Though
often discredited, the addition held on tenaciously to its place in the text until
the manuscripts of the *BC* received a stemmatic treatment, which showed

[38] The point is made in perhaps overly optimistic terms by Reynolds and Wilson (2013),
293: 'It must be stressed that in many traditions the amount of contamination that has
taken place is not sufficient to prevent the useful application of stemmatic theory'.

[39] I am grateful to Cynthia Damon for unravelling this story.

[40] *Res publica* is often abbreviated *RP*, which makes a connection to the reading of T (or a
kindred source) seem plausible.

that a reading unique to T (a *lectio singularis*) was extremely unlikely to represent the reading of the archetype. At that point both T's reading and its *Doppelgänger* disappeared from critical editions of the work.[41]

The genealogical study of manuscript transmission began in New Testament criticism toward the end of the eighteenth century and took root in classical circles between about 1815 and 1840, a process traced by Sebastiano Timpanaro in his classic work *La genesi del metodo del Lachmann* (*The genesis of Lachmann's method*).[42] The title has an ironic aspect, since Timpanaro's main contribution was to show that Lachmann, whose name had long been associated with stemmatic criticism, was in fact not its founder or even its most thorough practitioner. Lachmann's celebrity as a proponent of stemmatics was owing above all to his edition of Lucretius (1850), which brilliantly employed the new method to conjure up, as if by magic, not just the existence but also the physical appearance of the archetype, a manuscript that had been lost for more than a thousand years.

Stemmatic analysis as exemplified by Lachmann was essential to the image of what I call the 'heroic editor', the subject of the next chapter.

---

[41] Unfortunately, the most recent reprint of the Loeb edition (2006) retains the reading *primam rei publicae fuisse*. A bibliographical addendum of 1990 lists the principal twentieth-century editions, but the text itself remains that of A. G. Peskett in 1914, based on the edition of H. Meusel (1906).

[42] Timpanaro (1963) (2005 English translation by G. Most).

CHAPTER

I

Textual criticism in a post-heroic age

In the year 1816 Karl Lachmann published at Leipzig the first scientific recension of Propertius. As for the textual criticism of his predecessors, it resembled nothing so much as the condition of mankind before the advent of Prometheus.   (Housman (1893), 102)

Textual criticism today finds itself in a paradoxical situation. It is still recognized as a basic discipline within the study of Classics, or at least within that part of Classics that concerns itself with textual and literary evidence. Classical editing also continues to be a vigorous area of publication. The principal British and European series of critical texts, the Teubner, Oxford, and Budé, are all highly active, both in publishing new editions and in replacing earlier volumes. In the United States, the Loeb Classical Library has been enjoying a renaissance for the past two decades; many of the older editions have been succeeded by editions of much higher quality, and a number of new texts have been added to the series.

At the same time, however, textual criticism is becoming increasingly arcane to most professional classicists, and even many of its practitioners have lost a common sense of its aims and methods.

Explaining this situation calls for a brief historical excursus. From the mid nineteenth century to the first decades of the twentieth, textual criticism enjoyed a privileged status in classical studies, especially in Germany, which at the time was the acknowledged leader in classical scholarship. Much of the prestige of the subject was owing to the work of certain charismatic and influential critics, representatives of what I will call here the 'heroic editor'. In the century that followed, the methods and assumptions that underpinned the authority of such figures have been called into question, which has in turn altered the standing of textual criticism and contributed to a lack of consensus among critics.

In 1858 the University of Jena was celebrating its tercentenary. Among the congratulatory messages from other universities was one from the University of Bern that contained, apart from the formulaic salutations by the Rector and Academic Senate, a disquisition on the text of Virgil by Otto Ribbeck, his *Emendationes Vergilianae*. It is hard to imagine a similar choice being made today, but at the time a piece of technical writing on the text of Virgil was considered an appropriate expression of the highest intellectual work being done in the university.

The prototype of the heroic editor was Karl Lachmann. Some critics of earlier centuries – Richard Bentley being a good example – possessed many of the same traits, but Lachmann was the first textual critic to be seen in heroic terms by his contemporaries, hailed as a Prometheus of criticism by his biographer Martin Hertz and seen in similar terms by succeeding generations, as in my opening quotation from Housman.[1] A profile of the heroic editor could be drawn by generalizing from the characteristics of Lachmann himself: acute intelligence, total dedication to editorial work on a wide range of texts, quickness to suspect the text as transmitted in manuscripts, fertility in conjecture, confidence in judgement, and authoritativeness in expression. Lachmann also displayed the sort of precocity shown by Hercules when he strangled the serpents in his cradle: his edition of Propertius appeared when he was aged twenty-three.[2] Lachmann can even be called an eponymous hero, in having given his name to the set of editorial practices developed by several other scholars in the first decades of the century. The method of determining the relationships of manuscripts on the basis of shared errors was for a long time referred to as the 'Lachmann method', because Lachmann had used it in a spectacular way in his 1850 edition of Lucretius to reconstruct the long-vanished archetype.

Like ancient Greek heroes, Lachmann acquired a talismanic aura in the decades following his death. To be a classical textual critic at the end of the nineteenth century was to be, or at least to pretend to be, an admirer of

---

[1] Hertz (1851), 167. The connection between Hertz and Housman was noted by Kenney (1974), 106.

[2] Other critics at the time were similarly precocious: Franz Buecheler published his *editio maior* of Petronius in 1862 at the age of twenty-five and Friedrich Leo was twenty-six when he produced his groundbreaking edition of Seneca's tragedies in 1877. For another example, see p. 71.

Lachmann. A. E. Housman, always quick to sniff out cant in other scholars' writing, in a review of the Catullus edition of Robinson Ellis mocked the editor for his professed admiration for Lachmann:

> [W]hy does Mr Ellis esteem Lachmann's criticism? His own criticism is pre-Lachmannian and anti-Lachmannian, and his apparatus is just what an apparatus used to be before Lachmann and his contemporaries introduced their reforms. Lachmann, who had none but bad MSS, was content with five of them; Mr Ellis, who has two good MSS, is not content with fewer than twenty bad ones into the bargain.[3]

Some of Housman's own rhetoric has contributed nonetheless to the heroizing process, by suggesting a superhuman character in the greatest critics, as in his portrayal of Scaliger and Bentley as 'toiling giants': 'in Manilius, an author both corrupt and difficult ... it is no cause for wonder that even after Scaliger and Bentley there remains as much to explain as to emend, and that these toiling giants, amidst loads of rubbish, have carted away some fragments of the fabric.'[4] More generally, Housman's many references to critics of the past have helped to create a Pantheon of greats that begins with Scaliger, includes Heinsius and Gronovius, then Bentley and Lachmann, and implicitly culminates in Housman himself.

To display their superior qualities, heroes need to vanquish villains, or, even better, monsters, and so a natural consequence of the heroization of the editor is an approach to the history of editing that produces lurid narratives of colossal obtuseness or dereliction among predecessors. Samuel Johnson's *Preface to Shakespeare* is an early and distinguished example, but the most notorious specimens of the genre are Housman's prefaces to his editions of Manilius, Juvenal, and Lucan, which have provided generations of readers with what Housman called a 'low enjoyment'. Indeed, it is impossible to resist the appeal of such set pieces as the following:

> If a man will comprehend the richness and variety of the universe, and inspire his mind with a due measure of wonder and of awe, he must contemplate the human intellect not only on its heights of genius but in its abysses of ineptitude; and it might be fruitlessly debated to the end of time whether Richard Bentley or Elias Stoeber was the more marvellous

---

[3] Housman (1905b), 122. Housman's reference to 'Lachmann and his contemporaries' suggests that he was aware of the important role played by other critics in the evolution of the genealogical approach.

[4] Housman (1903), xl.

work of the Creator: Elias Stoeber, whose reprint of Bentley's text, with a commentary intended to refute it, saw the light in 1767 at Strasbourg, a city still famous for its geese ... Stoeber's mind, though that is no name to call it by, was one which turned as unswervingly to the false, the meaningless, the unmetrical, and the ungrammatical, as the needle to the pole.[5]

Delightful as it is, that passage and others like it create a misleadingly clear-cut impression of textual scholarship, in which the heroes are exalted to an almost godlike status, while the objects of scorn sink to the level of dumb beasts.[6]

After their deaths, ancient heroes became the objects of cult. The heroes of textual criticism have likewise received, and continue to receive, honours denied other scholars. Modern editors of Ovid's *Metamorphoses*, myself included, have instituted the custom of signalling in their critical apparatuses the readings preferred by their seventeenth-century predecessor Nicolas Heinsius, especially when they have made a different choice. (In his Teubner edition of Horace, D. R. Shackleton Bailey has done something similar for readings preferred by Bentley.[7]) A reviewer of my edition has called this practice 'excessive', and I am inclined to agree.[8]

Today, however, the heroic critic is an endangered species, possibly even one on the verge of extinction.[9] One of the last was D. R. Shackleton Bailey, who died in 2005, certainly heroic in the quantity of his editorial work – editions of all of Cicero's letters, Horace, Lucan, Statius, Martial, the pseudo-Quintilianic declamations, and the Latin Anthology – and in his fertility as an emender (more than 2,000 original conjectures, by his own count), also in his concentration on editing and emending to the exclusion of literary criticism and in his admiration for Bentley and Housman, of

[5] Housman (1903), xix.

[6] See also Housman's reference to Buecheler's dog-like students (p. 23) and the description of the 'editor of no judgment' who 'cannot but feel in every fibre of his being that he is a donkey between two bundles of hay' (1903), xxxi.

[7] The editor of the Budé *Metamorphoses*, Georges Lafaye, went a step further and regularly cited Heinsian readings with their own *siglum* (H), as if Heinsius were a witness to the text of Ovid.

[8] Richmond (2006), 132.

[9] A similar phenomenon is visible in the area of Middle English. Derek Pearsall, reviewing A. V. C. Schmidt's parallel-text edition of *Piers Plowman*, described it, and the editorial work of George Kane on the same poem, as 'a monument to an intellectual rigor, physical stamina, and self-belief that mark the climax and maybe the conclusion of a heroic era of textual scholarship' (2010), 703.

whom he might well be seen as the intellectual descendant.[10] Shackleton Bailey's early work on Tibetan texts parallels Lachmann's edition of the *Nibelungenlied* in its mastery of texts far removed from classical Latin.

As such figures have become rare, scepticism about the value of their work has been increasing. Here, for example, is Antonio La Penna already in 1982, reviewing Rudolf Hanslik's Teubner text of Propertius:

> [I]n [Hanslik's] tendency to introduce excessive innovations and to place too much confidence in conjecture I see the clear influence of the English tradition of Bentley and Housman, a tradition still strong and currently, if I am not mistaken, in a phase of vigorous growth: I refer to scholars like Shackleton Bailey or <George> Goold. The tendency extends to scholars of German origin such as O<tto> Skutsch or G<eorg> Luck. While I am happy to acknowledge that these are outstanding Latinists and brilliant and elegant emenders, I think it appropriate to say candidly that their conjectures are rarely necessary or highly probable; their textual criticism is often an elegant pastime, perhaps pardonable, or even enviable, if one considers how few diversions professors have.[11]

None of the scholars mentioned by La Penna is still alive. Many brilliant textual critics are at work today, and there is even evidence of a neo-sceptical movement represented by scholars such as David Butterfield, Stephen Heyworth, and John Trappes-Lomax in Britain, Hans-Christian Guenther in Germany, Gautier Liberman in France, the late Giancarlo Giardina in Italy, and Antonio Ramírez de Verger in Spain. While some of their endeavours approach heroic proportions (e.g., Heyworth's OCT edition of Propertius, which will be discussed in Chapter 6), rather than setting the agenda for the field these scholars must struggle to avoid being seen as radicals or extremists.

A critic who continues to operate in the heroic mode today risks seeming at odds with the times. A case in point is Otto Zwierlein, a scholar of enormous learning and acuity (and one for whom I have a high personal regard), described with justice by Don Fowler as 'one of the few modern scholars able to bear the weight of sustaining the German Great Tradition'.[12] Zwierlein's OCT edition of Seneca's tragedies (1986), preceded by numerous articles and accompanied by an extensive textual commentary, is an achievement

[10] For an assessment and reminiscence, see Thomas (2008).

[11] La Penna (1982), 521. Here and elsewhere translations from modern languages are my own. La Penna echoes a description by Timpanaro (1953), 96 of hypersceptical critics who produce 'frivolous conjectures, at best elegant variations, at worst an idle pastime'.

[12] Fowler (1991), 236.

of great and lasting value. In his subsequent work, however, a tendency to diagnose interpolation on a large scale has become increasingly pronounced. In four volumes of Plautine studies (1991–2, preparatory to an edition not produced), Zwierlein argued that Plautus was much more like Terence in his fidelity to his Greek originals and concern for dramatic coherence than is generally thought; consequently he ascribed any passage that seemed to depart from that image to a later revision. His approach (which explicitly recalls that of nineteenth-century predecessors such as Friedrich Ritschl and J. L. Ussing) provoked reactions ranging from outright dismissal to partial acceptance.[13] Zwierlein's most radical project of this nature was an attempt to show that significant portions of the works of Virgil and Ovid are the result of a revision undertaken during the reign of Tiberius by the rhetor-poet Julius Montanus.[14] This enterprise manifests in an extreme form the confident scepticism displayed by many of the great nineteenth-century German textual critics, and shows what such scepticism can lead to if it is unrestrained by considerations of plausibility. If the work had been published in the 1860s or 1870s it might have received a warmer reception, although even in that more sceptical age Zwierlein's hypothesis might have seemed too extreme; appearing at the end of the twentieth century, it has found adherents only among Zwierlein's own students.[15]

The loyalty of Zwierlein's students is also reminiscent of the heroic age in Germany, when the highest-ranking classicists could be distinguished by the number and fidelity of their ἑταῖροι. The influence exercised by German professors on their students was caricatured by Housman in several places; for example, in his sneering reference to 'the troop of little dogs which trotted at <Buecheler's> heels';[16] as usual, Housman's picture is a cruel exaggeration, but it captures a genuine aspect of late nineteenth-century German classical scholarship. It is now rare to find a textual critic whose approach has such a defining influence on a significant number of younger scholars.

In addition to the near-disappearance of the heroic editor as a personality type, developments on the methodological level have also affected the tone in which textual criticism is practiced. The confidence (sometimes spilling over

---

[13] For the former, see Gratwick (1993b); for the latter, Jocelyn (1993), (1996), who disputed many of Zwierlein's excisions but welcomed them as antidotes to textual complacency.

[14] Zwierlein (1999), (2000).

[15] It is a pleasure to note that Zwierlein's most recent work, an edition of two early Christian martyr-acts, has been hailed as 'an exemplary work of scholarship' and 'a masterpiece'; see Kraus (2015).

[16] Housman (1926), xvii.

into arrogance) displayed by post-Lachmannian critics was fuelled in part by the belief that they had in their possession powerful analytical tools for the study of manuscript evidence and the reconstruction of the archetypes from which they descend: principally, of course, the stemmatic method. In the course of the twentieth century, however, stemmatic method was dethroned; not refuted, because the various theoretical assaults on stemmatic method have not invalidated its basic assumptions. They have shown, however, that its applicability to specific transmissions varies greatly, and that if it is inappropriately employed it may be more damaging than helpful.[17]

Parallel to the reduced scope accorded to stemmatic analysis has been the increased attention devoted to the transmission of texts (often called *Überlieferungsgeschichte*), which considers manuscripts not merely as vehicles for the preservation of texts, but as evidence of a text's historical and cultural afterlife.[18] The study of transmission shifts attention from the editorial functions of recension and emendation and highlights the role played by scribes and readers; perhaps for that reason it has held little appeal for editors such as Shackleton Bailey, to whom it might seem essentially irrelevant.[19]

Another striking feature of the current state of textual criticism – which seems plausibly related to the passing of the heroic age of editing and the certitude that characterized it – is the absence of consensus on how classical texts should be edited. This situation is in marked contrast to certain periods in the past that displayed a marked tendency of one sort or another, for example, the heyday of scepticism in the mid to late nineteenth century followed by the pendulum swing towards conservatism in the decades that followed.

The present lack of consensus can be illustrated with reference to the house of Teubner in recent decades. For a long time, 'a Teubner text' was not only a synonym for a reliable text, but also suggested a particular approach to editing. To be sure, the style in question would have varied with changing fashions, and at any time there could be deviations from the prevailing

---

[17] For further discussion, see pp. 61–4 (Chapter 3). I am restricting myself to criticisms that have arisen within the sphere of classical scholarship. The objections raised by medievalists who question the validity of all eclectic reconstructions are of a different order.

[18] See Tarrant (1995a), 115–17 for a sketch of the main actors and developments. Reeve (2011) is a collection of work by the most distinguished living exponent of *Überlieferungsgeschichte*.

[19] On Housman and *Überlieferungsgeschichte*, which he notoriously derided as 'a longer and nobler name than fudge', see Reeve (2009). Housman's scorn was principally directed at products of pseudo-history, such as hypothesizing the existence of ancient editions on the basis of little or no evidence.

norms: K. P. Schulze's revision of Baehrens's Catullus was carried out, in Housman's unforgettable words, with 'Oedipodean piety'.[20] But the point of Housman's criticism lay precisely in Schulze's edition being a disgrace to the name of Teubner. The bifurcation of the Teubner firm generated by the post-Second World War division of Germany set off a first phase of breakdown in the Teubner house style: in the 1970s and 1980s there was often a noticeable difference of editorial approach between Teubner–Leipzig volumes and Teubner–Stuttgart products, with the latter on the whole superior in technique to the former. Sometimes the difference also maps neatly onto an East (conservative) versus West (sceptical) divide, as in the case of Horace (Borzsák vs. Shackleton Bailey), but sometimes the opposite is true, as with Propertius (Hanslik vs. Fedeli). Today's Teubner editions display a vast range of styles and approaches, as can be seen from the various editions of Ovid that have gradually replaced the early twentieth-century Teubner editions of Rudolf Ehwald. (It is another aspect of the development I am tracing that a century ago a single scholar could edit all of Ovid's works, a task that would now seem beyond the capacity of even the most gifted and industrious editor.) The current Teubner Ovids range from the conservative Anderson *Metamorphoses* through the middle-of-the-road *Fasti* (Alton–Wormell–Courtney) and *Epistulae ex Ponto* (Richmond) to the sceptical, even radical, *Tristia* of J. B. Hall. Style and presentation are also widely divergent, for example, Anderson's parsimony in recording variants versus Ramírez de Verger's maximalist approach.[21]

As a natural consequence of the breakdown in consensus on how best to edit texts, we also see a tendency towards non-communication between editors and critics of differing outlooks. To adopt a term from Stanley Fish, instead of a coherent 'hermeneutic community' of textual scholars we have several almost independent communities, each with its shared assumptions, methods, and standards of assessment. The point can be exemplified by citing two reviews of the same edition, Renato Badalì's 1992 text of Lucan.

First, Sebastiano Timpanaro:

> This edition of Lucan's epic is commendable for the accuracy of the apparatus criticus and for balance and methodological rigor in constituting the text … We have therefore a solid, reliable, and even healthily problematic

---

[20] Housman (1894), 252.

[21] For further discussion of differences in apparatus style, see Chapter 5.

edition: the editor often leaves the transmitted reading in the text and in the apparatus signals one or more conjectures with a 'fortasse recte'.[22]

Then, John Hunt:

> Its regressions are many and blatant, and fairly overwhelm the few signs of progress; the number of places where emendation is needed but abstention is offered is, in particular, hard to take. The desire to edit Lucan was simply not enough. Nor was industry in the collation of Lucan's MSS any substitute for critical judgment in the construction of Lucan's text ... The apparatus criticus contains simultaneously too much and too little. B. is the sort of editor who, while energetically conserving the text against certain and probable conjectures, thinks nothing of crowding the apparatus with conjectures of every stamp, and of telling us, quite gratuitously, which editor 'has approved' which conjecture ... His apparatus is the creation of an editor unwilling to waste the fruits of his labors in collation; hence its frivolous superfluities.[23]

Reading Timpanaro's evaluation on the one hand and Hunt's on the other, one would hardly believe that the two are referring to the same edition. The divergence in their views is not limited to the text and the editor's choices among variants and conjectures, which would seem to be the obvious locus of disagreement, but extends as well to such features as the *apparatus criticus*, which might have been expected to be relatively straightforward in the reactions it prompts.

The Modern Language Association of America has a Committee on Scholarly Editions that confers an actual seal of approval (an emblem with the words AN APPROVED EDITION, printed on the verso of the title page) on editions that meet specific standards; among the criteria are 'accuracy with respect to texts, adequacy and appropriateness with respect to documenting editorial principles and practice, consistency and explicitness with respect to methods'.[24] It does not seem likely that a body of that kind with the authority to certify the quality of editions could be established in the field of Classics.

It is not surprising that a field no longer led by charismatic figures and often at odds with itself should find its standing within the larger discipline of Classics altered; signs of that change are visible in many quarters.

One indication of current attitudes towards textual criticism is the attention paid to the subject in the burgeoning genre of companion volumes. To

[22] Timpanaro (1995), 218–19 and 220.   [23] Hunt (1998), 497, 502, 504.
[24] www.mla.org/cse_guidelines.

my knowledge, none of the numerous volumes in the *Cambridge Companion* series contains an article on the textual history and editing of the author in question, while many volumes in the series published by Brill and Blackwell do contain such articles. Since the Cambridge series aims to offer 'fresh and provoking perspectives',[25] one might infer that textual criticism is seen as irrelevant to that purpose.

A change of a different sort is harder to document, but I believe it is true, at least in the English-speaking sphere: a reduction in the attention paid to new editions in the form of critical reviews.[26] James Willis's Teubner Juvenal (1997) is a striking example: as far as I can determine, that edition received precisely three reviews.[27] Although an extreme case, it is not an isolated one: a decade earlier, J. B. Hall's 1985 Teubner text of Claudian, arguably a much more important edition than Willis's Juvenal, also attracted few serious reviews.[28] Several explanations are possible, not necessarily contradictory: there are fewer competent scholars available to review editions, but perhaps also a sense that such scholarship is of less interest to the general classical readership than other kinds of work.

To test this impression in a somewhat more systematic way, I have tabulated the number of reviews in *Classical Review* devoted to editions, commentaries containing original editions, and other works relating to textual criticism and palaeography in two five-year periods, 1966–70 (the time at which I first took an interest in reviews of editions) and 2001–5. Table 1 presents the results.

In each year of the more recent period, the absolute number of reviews devoted to those subjects shows a decrease in comparison with the earlier period, but the difference in percentage is even greater, because the overall number of reviews has greatly increased, reflecting the increased volume of publication in the field. *CR* now reviews much more widely than previously, and while it has not abandoned an interest in textual criticism, that field of study is much less prominent now than in the recent past.

At the institutional level, there has been a dramatic change in the place occupied by textual criticism and editing. An edition or a work of textual

---

[25] From the publisher's blurb for Harrison (2007).

[26] For a similar complaint in the area of Hispanic studies, see Ayerbe-Chaux (1992), 22.

[27] The volumes of *L'Année philologique* covering the years 1997–2006 register only Kissel (1999), Astbury (2000), and Desy (2003).

[28] A similar search of *L'Année philologique* for the years 1985–95 yielded, in addition to a couple of brief notices, reviews by Green (1987), Savon (1987), Consolino (1988), and Verdière (1988).

Table 1. *Reviews in* Classical Review *of works relating to textual criticism*

Year	Editions	Commentaries	Other	Total	All reviews	Percentage
1966	26	4	10	40	228	17.5
1967	26	5	2	33	222	14.8
1968	17	10	3	30	199	15.0
1969	26	4	4	34	210	16.2
1970	26	3	6	35	233	15.0
2001	21	2	0	23	356	6.5
2002	14	5	2	21	286	7.3
2003	15	11	1	27	328	8.2
2004	12	11	4	27	323	8.3
2005	11	12	5	28	412	6.8

character is no longer seen as a desirable form of training for a beginning classicist; in many graduate programmes, Ph.D. candidates are discouraged from undertaking work of that kind on the grounds that doing so might brand them as 'textual critics' and so blight their chances of finding a position. As a result the most promising young classicists rarely devote themselves to textual scholarship. That is certainly the case in the United States and to some extent in Britain. It does not seem to be as true for European countries; some European institutions, such as the Scuola Normale in Pisa, have continued to train large numbers of talented critics and editors. The situation is not entirely bleak, however. In recent years, a number of classicists in Britain and the United States have followed a dissertation or first book on a literary or cultural-historical topic with a commentary – the Cambridge 'green and yellow' series has been particularly popular in this regard[29] – and have thereby been potentially exposed to issues of text as part of the task of a commentator.

I say 'potentially' because writing a commentary does not necessarily entail establishing a text, although I do find it surprising that the word-by-word scrutiny called for in a commentator would not naturally result in the formation of a text.[30] Probably the most egregious instance of a commentary

[29] Examples include Thomas (1988), Hardie (1994), Mankin (1995), Knox (1995), Damon (2003), Ash (2007), Myers (2009), and Gowers (2012).

[30] Volumes in the Cambridge Classical Texts and Commentaries series (familiarly known as the 'orange' series) were originally required to include an independently constructed text. That stipulation has been waived, and recent volumes have in general devoted less attention to textual issues than earlier ones. See Gibson (in press).

that bases itself on existing editions is Franz Bömer's seven-volume commentary on the *Metamorphoses* (1969–86), one of the longest (and dullest) commentaries ever written on a classical author, which began by taking Rudolf Ehwald's Teubner text as its basis and switched its allegiance to William Anderson's successor Teubner partway through. Bömer's first volume appeared when I was a graduate student; I was still innocent and self-righteous enough to be shocked that a scholar could embark on a commentary on such a grand scale and be content to derive his textual information at second hand.

Many of the developments I have been describing could be characterized as indications of decline, and there can be no doubt that textual criticism as a discipline within classical scholarship no longer occupies the exalted position it held at the time of Lachmann. But to speak in terms of decline would be a highly inauspicious beginning, and in fact there are good reasons to adopt a more positive outlook. For one thing, the heroic style of criticism had its faults as well as its virtues, and its passing provides an opportunity to reframe the goals and procedures of textual scholarship in a more satisfactory form.

To give an example, one hallmark of the heroic mode of editing is the drive towards certainty, or even the confident assertion of certainty. Our time is one that finds such claims suspect, and if we reflect on the nature of the problems with which textual criticism deals and on the character of the evidence available to it, it becomes clear that certainty is hardly ever within the critic's grasp. Despite what some of its practitioners may seem to believe, textual criticism deals not in proofs or demonstrations, but in probabilities and persuasion. Since persuasion is fundamentally a rhetorical activity, a suitable next focus of attention is the place of rhetoric in textual criticism.

CHAPTER

2

The rhetoric of textual criticism/ textual criticism as rhetoric

> It is not easy to discover from what cause the acrimony of a scholiast can naturally proceed ... The various readings of copies, and different interpretations of a passage, seem to be questions that might exercise the wit, without engaging the passions ... Perhaps the lightness of the matter may conduce to the vehemence of the agency; when the truth to be investigated is so near to inexistence, as to escape attention, its bulk is to be enlarged by rage and exclamation.
>
> (Johnson, *Preface to Shakespeare*)[1]

For centuries one of the most striking characteristics of textual criticism has been its fondness for strongly coloured rhetoric. In the first part of this chapter I want to examine that rhetoric and ask what it implies about textual criticism as an activity. The penchant for denunciation that Johnson so effectively deflates will play a part in the discussion, but I am even more interested in the metaphors that textual critics employ, often without conscious reflection, in the course of their work. The second section focuses on the absence of proof in textual criticism and the central role played by persuasive argument, or rhetoric in another sense.

I

Areas of study characterize themselves by their preferred rhetorical modes. Particle physics is a good example, a field in which equations can be described as 'beautiful' or 'elegant' and where 'quarks' (a term derived from Joyce's *Finnegans Wake*) come in 'flavours' including 'charm' and

[1] Johnson (1968), 102.

'strange'. The terminology evokes an atmosphere of aesthetic pleasure touched by whimsy.

Textual criticism, by contrast, has gravitated towards images of crime and disease. Some of those images are so pervasive that their metaphorical character is largely forgotten, such as describing erroneous manuscript readings as 'corrupt' or calling manuscripts 'witnesses'. But we also find more exuberant uses of such imagery, as in the following quotations from F. A. Wolf and Lachmann portraying textual difficulties as sites of illness or infection: Wolf *Iusta recensio ... emplastis solutis ulcera nudat* ('a true recension ... takes off the bandages and lays bare the sores'); Lachmann *Illa pestis ingruit, quae ... pro uulneribus emplastra et foedissimas cicatrices reliquit* ('that plague breaks out which ... leaves bandages and disgusting scars in place of wounds').[2] When the text is thought to be beyond repair, the language of mortality is invoked, as in references to a *locus conclamatus* or *locus desperatus*, assimilating the afflicted passage to a person on the point of death. The term 'contamination', used to describe the insertion into a manuscript of readings from an unrelated source (a process engaged in by scribes wishing to improve the text), carries a suggestion of contagious disease; before it became standard usage, Otto Keller employed the even blunter term *Gebrechen* ('malady') in speaking of the phenomenon in the manuscripts of Horace.[3] Error-prone copyists are 'convicted' of textual wrongdoing[4] or are found guilty of 'scribal delinquency'.[5] The study of interpolation has generated its own subdivision of such imagery: the terms for allegedly interpolated material carry overtones of illegitimacy, such as *uersus spurii* or (even more pejorative) *adulterini*, while the shadowy figure of the interpolator is often depicted as a would-be forger (*falsarius* in older parlance).[6]

Corresponding to those images of textual error are metaphors that cast the critic in a variety of flattering roles: healer (error as disease), sleuth (error as crime), judge or arbitrator between competing claimants. In its juridical aspect the language casts the critic as investigator, prosecutor, and judge all in one.

---

[2] For both citations, see Timpanaro (2005), 77 n. 12.

[3] 'Jede ohne Ausnahme ... leidet an diesem Gebrechen' ('Every <manuscript> without exception ... suffers from this malady', Keller (1879), viii.

[4] See, e.g., Tarrant (1978), 359–60: when the manuscripts of Aurelius Victor's *De Caesaribus* can be compared to an independent branch of tradition in another text, they 'can often be convicted of bold interpolation'.

[5] Kenney (2004), 369; see pp. 35–6.

[6] In Chapter 5 I suggest an alternative model for understanding interpolation.

The most flamboyant examples of this kind of rhetoric belong to the heroic age; its most conspicuous and artful exponent was A. E. Housman. Here is a well-known specimen, from the Preface to Manilius I: '*Lucida tela diei:* these are the words that come into one's mind when one has halted at some stubborn perplexity of reading or interpretation, has witnessed Scaliger and Gronouius and Huetius fumble at it one after another, and then turns to Bentley and sees Bentley strike his finger on the place and say *thou ailest here, and here*.'[7]

I had always assumed that the expression 'thou ailest here, and here' was a scriptural quotation, but it comes from Matthew Arnold's verses in memory of Wordsworth, in a passage on the death of Goethe:

> When Goethe's death was told, we said:
> Sunk, then, is Europe's sagest head.
> Physician of the iron age,
> Goethe has done his pilgrimage.
> He took the suffering human race,
> He read each wound, each weakness clear;
> And struck his finger on the place,
> > And said: Thou ailest here, and here!
> > > (Matthew Arnold, 'Memorial Verses' for Wordsworth)[8]

Housman's rhetoric, especially his use of quotations and imagery drawn from poetry and scripture, deserves a fuller study; here I will touch on some of its aspects.[9] Sometimes the effect seems straightforwardly elevating, as when in the passage just cited Housman enhances Bentley's stature by allusively equating him with Goethe. In polemical contexts, the results can be more ambiguous. In another passage from the Preface to Manilius I, Housman speculates on the reaction of a conservative, but intelligent, scholar to the work of a less gifted student: 'indeed I imagine that Mr Buecheler, when he first perused Mr Sudhaus' edition of the *Aetna*, must have felt something like Sin when she gave birth to Death'.[10] Housman here evokes both scripture (James 1.15 'when

---

[7] Housman (1903), xvi.

[8] I learned the source of the quotation through an internet search, but it had been previously identified by Brink (1986), 207 n. 55.

[9] Such a study should include places where Housman's language has a scriptural colouring without making a specific allusion. The tirade against the *Thesaurus linguae latinae* in the Preface to Juvenal ((1931), lv–vi) contains two direct quotations ('well done, thou good and faithful servant' and 'the sluggard is wiser in his own conceit than seven men who can render a reason') but also such phrases as [the soul that believes] 'that its own flimsy tabernacle of second-hand opinions is a habitation for everlasting'. On that passage, see p. 74.

[10] Housman (1903), xliv.

lust has conceived, it gives birth to sin; and when sin is accomplished, it brings forth death') and Milton's dramatizing of that text in *Paradise Lost* (2.781–9); but the awful grandeur of the comparisons makes the two German scholars, introduced with their honorific 'Mr', look puny and ridiculous.[11]

Housman's propensity for scorn and invective has exerted a pernicious influence on subsequent generations of textual scholars; Housman's own motives, though, need not have been discreditable. Paul Naiditch suggests that invective was a way for Housman to express the affront he felt at ignorant or mistaken assertions and also a means by which he hoped to intimidate inferior scholars, as he wrote that mediocrities had been 'cowed and kept under' in nineteenth-century Germany as long as there were Madvigs and Lachmanns around to make them aware of their inferiority.[12] Naiditch's first point is supported by Housman's frequent use of 'you lie' or 'liar' in his marginalia; he seems to have acknowledged no distinction between honest error and mendacity, which heightened his indignation when confronted with statements he knew to be false.

Today such an idiom seems overblown and affected; speaking of Housman in particular, E. J. Kenney used the adjective 'febrile'.[13] It is found mainly in the work of critics who convey by it a certain nostalgia for the heroic age of criticism.

This mode of speaking is also found in medieval studies, where it is probably an inheritance from the classical sphere. Derek Pearsall writes, with reference to the use of terms such as 'corrupt' or 'degenerate' to characterize manuscripts: 'it is interesting to observe how the language of moral approbation and disapprobation hangs around textual criticism and to speculate on the influence it may have on editorial attitude'.[14] Pearsall turns the editor-as-physician metaphor against editors who impose an eclectic method that aims to produce an 'ideal' text onto medieval genres such as popular verse romances, where each manuscript represents an act of recomposition: 'instead of the noble ideal of the editor as the physician who is restoring the body of the text to its original whole and healthy state, we have the reality of the fanatical surgeon who cuts away dead and living tissue indiscriminately in his desire to demonstrate the truth of his diagnosis'. He also writes that 'we should not be content to confine our experience of medieval poetry within the sterile operating theater (or terminal intensive care unit) of the modern critical edition'.[15]

---

[11] Housman's qualifying 'something like' may signal an awareness of his own extravagance.

[12] Naiditch (1996), 147–9, quoting Housman (1903), xli–ii.

[13] Kenney (1974), 71.   [14] Pearsall (1985), 103.

[15] Pearsall (1985), 101 and 105.

Employing a similar tactic, Bernard Knox used the critic-as-doctor motif to mock hunters of interpolations in the texts of Greek tragedy: if *Antigone* 905ff. were to be judged an interpolation, Knox wrote, 'we must even give our late and reluctant blessing to the shade of August Nauck, who, acting on a principle somewhat like that of the English provincial dentist – "If you won't miss it, why not have it out?" – gave the ungrateful world a text of Euripides some four hundred lines shorter than any it had seen before'.[16]

James Zetzel has advanced a historical explanation for classical textual criticism's fondness for a morally tinged vocabulary of disease and corruption. He locates its origin in the Protestant need for a secure text of sacred scripture, which, he argues, has influenced both the desire among classicists to retrieve the lost original and also the rhetoric used to describe departures from that original.[17] The explanation may be essentially correct, although the phenomenon in question long antedates Protestantism. Before Luther was born, Italian humanists had deployed a rich vocabulary of moral opprobrium in describing textual error, including terms such as *uitium, corruptio*, and *deprauatio*.[18] Furthermore, in their rhetoric the humanists were reflecting much earlier practice. It may have been Saint Jerome, with *his* need for a secure text of sacred scripture, who first used morally tinged words such as *falsare, deprauare, peruertere*, and *corrumpere* to describe unintentional scribal error.[19]

Similar metaphors have crossed over into the digital world: we speak of 'corrupt' files or data, and our computers can be infiltrated by 'viruses' and 'worms'. There may be something about the preservationist focus of textual criticism – and indeed of any activity that concerns itself with the accurate transmission of data – that explains why incorrect transmission is described in highly pejorative and moralizing language.

The persona of the critic as judge also has its roots in Antiquity, specifically in characterizations of eminent scholars such as Aristarchus in Greek and Probus in Latin. Horace's depiction of the good critic in *Ars Poetica* 445–50 is pervaded by imagery from the legal sphere:

---

[16] Knox (1966), 105. Knox is using a rhetorical style more often associated with sceptics to support a conservative position, probably with deliberate irony.

[17] Zetzel (2005), 157–61. [18] See Rizzo (1973), 219–26.

[19] See Arns (1953), 180–2. As far as I can tell, *deprauare* and *peruertere* are not so used in classical texts, and when *corrumpere* or *falsare* is applied to documents it denotes deliberate tampering or falsification.

uir bonus et prudens uersus <u>reprehendet</u> inertes,
<u>culpabit</u> duros, incomptis allinet atrum
transuerso calamo signum, ambitiosa recidet
ornamenta, parum claris lucem dare <u>coget,</u>
<u>arguet</u> ambigue dictum, mutanda <u>notabit</u>;
fiet Aristarchus.

an upright and sensible man will <u>censure</u> lines that are lifeless
and <u>condemn</u> those that are harsh; opposite the unpolished
he will smear a black mark with the stroke of his pen;
he will prune back showy ornaments, <u>compel</u> you to shed light
on the unclear, <u>expose</u> doubtful expressions, <u>mark</u> what needs to be
changed;
he will become an Aristarchus.

As Niall Rudd points out, Horace endows his critic with the authority of a prosecutor, censor, and judge.[20] Other references to ancient critics are less flattering, as when Cicero portrays Aristarchus' obelizing of Homeric lines he considered spurious as merely capricious (Cicero *ad fam.* 3.11.5 *Aristarchus Homeri uersum negat quem non probat*, 'Aristarchus denies to be Homer's any verse he doesn't like').[21] Another indication of the ancient image of the critic as an incessant fault-finder is the motif of 'a poem so good – or with such powerful supporters – that it need not fear even the criticism of a Probus/Cato/Viscus'. So with all likelihood in the final lines of the Gallus papyrus, and explicitly in Martial 3.2.12 *illo* [sc. *Faustino*] *uindice nec Probum timeto.*[22]

Illness can befall even the innocent, but the rhetoric of criminality requires a perpetrator, and that person is usually the scribe. To my knowledge, the denunciation of scribal incompetence is not a prominent motif in classical literature. Cicero, for example, refers matter-of-factly to the correction of copyists' errors as the final stage before a text was put into circulation.[23] A more vitriolic style has been enshrined in classical circles at

---

[20] Rudd (1989) *ad loc.*

[21] A similar indictment of editorial caprice is found in Thomas Edwards, *The Canons of Criticism* (1748) (prompted by contemporary editing of Shakespeare): 'I. A Professed Critic has a right to declare that his Author *wrote* whatever He thinks he *ought* to have written, with as much positiveness as if He had been at his Elbow. II. He has a right to alter any passage which He does not understand'. Cited by Taylor (1987), 54.

[22] On Martial's poem, see Holford-Strevens (2008).

[23] *Att.* 13.23.2 *libri ad Varronem non morabuntur … tantum librariorum menda tolluntur.* ('The books for Varro won't be long now … it is just a matter of removing copyists' errors').

least from the time of the Renaissance, and is of a piece with the humanist feeling of superiority to all things medieval.[24] There is a seamless progression from Poggio's reference to the scribe of M, the archetype of Statius' *Siluae*, as *ignorantissimus omnium uiuentium* ('the most ignorant of all living creatures') to Michael Reeve's description of the *editio princeps* of the same work, 'printed from a remote and corrupt descendant of M emended with breath-taking ineptitude'.[25]

Just as Bentley, in Housman's phrase, 'treats his MSS much as if they were fellows of Trinity',[26] Bentley's successors have often used the same slashing rhetoric in speaking of their fellow-editors as when berating scribes for their incompetence. A distinctive subtype of this sort of polemic is the criticism levelled by British textual critics against their continental counterparts. I first became aware of this phenomenon as a graduate student in Oxford in the late 1960s, reading reviews of editions in *Classical Review* with a mixture of *Schadenfreude* and 'there-but-for-the-grace-of-God-go-I' dread. A typical opening sentence: 'few editions of a classical author come one's way in which performance falls so far short of pretensions as here'.[27] Savaging Budé editions in particular has long been a popular blood sport among British scholars.[28] One finds phrases such as 'blind trust in the manuscript tradition', 'mistakes of every kind, many of them flagrant and betraying appalling ignorance of the Latin language', 'misunderstandings … on every page', and, finally, 'the book is a disgrace to the Budé series'. All of those citations are drawn from a single review by W. S. Watt of the edition of Cicero's *De officiis* by the unfortunate Maurice Testard; this is an especially rich specimen of reviewer's venom, but it is typical of the criticisms found in other hostile notices.[29] References to more recent Budé editions in a review-article by Michael Reeve show that the game is still being played: see, for example, his quotations from Ted Courtney ('colossal incompetence') and Peter Marshall ('a disaster').[30]

---

[24] In that respect, the humanists have a modern descendant in James Willis, whose hostility to medieval copyists finds expression in such locutions as 'monastic blockheads', 'dunce monk', and 'cathedral-builder' – surely the strangest term of obloquy ever coined. (See Willis (1972), 12, 21, and 7 respectively.)

[25] Reynolds (1983), 398.   [26] Housman (1903), xviii.

[27] Kenney (1965), 55.

[28] For my own contribution to this less than noble pursuit, see Tarrant (1978); also p. 108 n. 7.

[29] Watt (1968). The second edition of Testard's *De officiis* (1974) corrected some of the misprints noted by Watt, but made no reference to his review.

[30] Reeve (2000), 202–3, citing Courtney (1999), 399 and Marshall (1999), 411.

The animus may be in part stimulated by the hollow assurances of quality with which Budé texts are offered to the world. H. D. Jocelyn makes that point explicitly: 'M.'s volume, like others in the collection, is prefaced with a boast about the supervision exercised by a "technical commission". The many faults of presentation ... show, however, that no very rigorous check of the submitted manuscript took place'.[31] Another reason is that many Budé editors practise, and pride themselves on doing so, a form of conservative criticism, often involving staunch adherence to a 'best manuscript', that 'flies in the face of six decades of northern European scholarship'.[32] This style of polemical criticism may have been perfected by British scholars, but it is not restricted to them, as can be seen from Alf Önnerfors's verdict on the edition of Vegetius by Leo Stelten: 'eine wissenschaftliche Katastrophe'.[33]

Conservative critics have not on the whole responded in kind,[34] although Paolo Fedeli did protest against the intemperate scorn displayed by reviewers in *Classical Review* towards editions produced by non-British scholars (principally himself).[35] Amused dismissal rather than head-on attack is a popular tactic, for example, La Penna's 'elegant pastime' (p. 22), or Timpanaro's description of Shackleton Bailey as 'this ingenious but unrestrained maker of conjectures'.[36] Perhaps because it is difficult to impugn the intelligence or learning of the best sceptics, an appeal to some shared concept of taste or good breeding is a useful strategy.

What is most relevant for my purpose is not the vehemence of such assessments but the assumption of certitude that underlies them. The critics who write in this vein are confident of their ability to discern truth from falsehood. One of the favourite terms for transmitted readings of which they disapprove is 'nonsense'; here, for example, is Shackleton Bailey reviewing Leighton Reynolds's edition of Cicero's *De finibus*: 'I think R. as an editor might fairly be described in a now [i.e., in 2001] topical phrase: a compassionate conservative. Not a dedicated upholder of traditional nonsense, though occasionally

---

[31] Jocelyn (1991), 82.   [32] Dewar (1991), 333.

[33] Önnerfors (1993), 494. Not even Michael Reeve has escaped the wrath of Önnerfors: see (2006).

[34] A notable exception is Flores (2006), (2012a), who lashes out ferociously at critics of his edition of Lucretius.

[35] Fedeli (1986).

[36] Timpanaro (1995), 220. Timpanaro ((1953), 96) had spoken of Housman in almost identical terms as 'an ingenious maker of conjectures, but at times too daring'. The similarity would have given Shackleton Bailey great pleasure.

letting it lie unmolested.'[37] For an extreme example of this confidence see J. B. Hall's review of Anderson's *Metamorphoses*, in which Hall lists some thirty passages and tells us in how many of them Anderson made the wrong choice (which was most of the time).[38] One is tempted to think that, if Hall was so certain of the right choice at all times, it is a shame that he did not produce his own edition and spare the rest of us much effort.

The assumption of certitude also underlies the habit of commending conjectures in the language of prizes and competition. The highest category of commendation for a conjecture is the term 'palmary', an older equivalent of 'first-prize winning' or 'gold medal'. George Goold similarly refers to a transposition in Propertius 2.28 proposed by Stephen Heyworth as 'prize-winning'.[39] But one can only award prizes for conjectures if one knows what goal they are aiming at.

It is useful to examine the language of critical praise and blame because that language reflects in a more explicit form an assumption that also underlies the rhetoric of textual disease and corruption with which I began, namely, the assumption that there was once an original text, intact and unblemished, represented in a master copy from which all other copies descend; in the course of transmission that original has been in various ways distorted, and the critic's task is to uncover the distortions and restore the original. The truth may not be recovered without a struggle. The disease may resist treatment, and the criminal may go to great lengths to escape capture. But if the doctor or the detective is sufficiently skilful, the malady or the offense will in the end be traced and brought to light. I would call this the myth of the recoverable original.

In his *Storia della tradizione*, Giorgio Pasquale provocatively asked 'was there always an archetype?' In a similar vein, one could ask 'was there always an original text?' If by an original text one means a version incorporating the author's final intentions, then it is clear that in some cases there was never an original text. To refer again to the best-known example, we may say that there was an original text of Virgil's *Eclogues* and *Georgics*, but not of the *Aeneid*. The situation appears similar with Lucretius' *De rerum natura*, where the transmitted text seems to contain a number of passages to which the author had not given a final form or location. Lucan's *Bellum ciuile* is another likely example of a text left unfinished at the author's death which in its circulated form probably

---

[37] Shackleton Bailey (2001), 48.
[38] Hall (1980), 63.   [39] Goold (1989), 112.

contains some editorial intervention. Ovid's *Fasti* appears to have been abandoned halfway through; the six books that survive have been incompletely revised. Other examples could be cited.

At the other end of the spectrum are cases where there are solid reasons to believe that a text was placed in circulation with its author's knowledge and, presumably, approval. One such instance is Horace's *Epistles* I, which ends with an *envoi* addressed to the *libellus* as if it were a slave leaving home to seek its fortune in the big city. Ovid's *Ars Amatoria* is another. Ovid may have later regretted publishing the poem, which furnished one of the causes for which Augustus banished him to the shores of the Black Sea, but for that very reason there can be no doubt that he was fully aware of the poem's public appearance.

Between those two poles lie the majority of cases, in which we have no information about the circumstances in which a text began to circulate.

Whether or not there was an original text in the sense defined earlier, it is unrealistic to hope that with the available evidence we can ever fully recover the original or first form of any classical text. The first form of the *Eclogues* eludes our grasp as does that of the *Aeneid*. Even if we *could* succeed in completely reconstituting an original, we would have no way of knowing that we had done so.

It was at one time fashionable to postulate ancient editions of texts on flimsy or even non-existent grounds; so, for example, the editions of various authors supposed to have been produced by Valerius Probus, or the recensions of Lucan and Juvenal hypothesized on the basis of subscriptions that some late antique readers entered in copies of their texts.[40] The ghosts of those editions have long been exorcized, but there is no reason to doubt that editions of classical texts were produced in late antiquity, and those editions may have affected – or even created – the manuscript traditions that we have inherited.[41] Our manuscripts of Horace, for example, contain titles and metrical analyses that probably derive from a late antique edition. That edition may also have been responsible for gathering works originally circulating separately into an *opera omnia*; in the case of Ovid's *Amores, Medicamina, Ars amatoria*, and *Remedia amoris*, an edition brought together a number of works of a related kind within an author's larger corpus.[42] No modern editor of Ovid's amatory works hesitates to

---

[40] For the subscriptions, see p. 14.

[41] On late antique editions, see Tarrant (1995a), 99–103.

[42] In the opening poem of *Tristia* I, Ovid instructs this latest collection of his poetry on how to conduct itself when it arrives in Rome; when it reaches Ovid's house it

publish them in the collected form that they acquired in late antiquity; in that respect there is not even a pretence of reconstructing the authorial versions of the works.[43]

The activity of a critic or editor is sometimes compared to that of a restorer of a work of art, who seeks to undo the damage produced in the course of time and to uncover the work's original beauty. That appealing image is the perfect embodiment of the myth of the recoverable original. Whether it accurately describes the work of an art restorer is for others to say; it certainly does not describe the work of an editor of classical texts. Our editions are syntheses of manuscript evidence and conjecture, none of which has any direct connection with the original text. The editor is like someone attempting to reassemble a jigsaw puzzle some of whose pieces (which ones or how many is not known) have lost their original shape, while others (which ones or how many is not known) are entirely missing. In such circumstances the result cannot claim to be a restoration, or even a reconstruction; at best it will be an approximation of the original.[44]

Although the ideal of the recoverable original is impossible to achieve, the concept still has a useful part to play. One of its benefits is psychological: it seems unlikely that scholars would be willing to devote themselves to editorial projects that often span decades if they were not sustained by the hope of recovering the author's text. It may also be necessary for critics to operate as if a single recoverable original existed, in order to avoid a bedlam of competing reconstructions.[45]

From what has been said it follows that the notion of a definitive edition is even more a myth than the concept of the recoverable original. No edition of a classical text can be definitive, in part because the possibility of new and convincing conjectures can never be ruled out, but also because in any text of some length there will be places where different editors can reasonably make

is told to join its 'brothers' but to hold itself aloof from the disgraced *Ars*. The passage shows clearly that Ovid had no conception of the uniting of the *Amores* and *Ars* that took place at some point before the archetype of those works was produced – although had he foreseen it he might well have rejoiced at the posthumous rehabilitation of the *Ars*.

43 As regards Horace, however, a case can be made for presenting the works in chronological order rather than following the arrangement by genre found in the manuscript tradition.

44 Similar remarks at a theoretical level in Longo (1981).

45 I am grateful to the anonymous reader for that point, as well as for incisive comments on this entire section.

different choices, either by preferring one manuscript reading to another, or by adopting a conjecture instead of the transmitted reading(s), or by judging the text corrupt and using the obelus. There is also the fact that almost no edition of a classical text so far published cites the manuscript evidence in a comprehensive manner. (I will return to that issue in Chapters 7 and 8.) At the moment, therefore, the most that an edition can aim to accomplish is to report accurately the essential manuscript evidence and faithfully to reflect the present state of understanding of the text, in order to serve as an instrument of research and as a basis for further discussion. To fulfil the latter purpose it will signal the places where the text is most in doubt, in the hope of stimulating new attempts at solution. As a result, every important edition is at the same time a point of arrival and a point of departure. In Gian Biagio Conte's elegant formulation, 'a critical edition is only a working hypothesis'.[46]

In arguing against a manner of speaking that exaggerates the certainty to which textual criticism can aspire, I may have substituted another that overemphasizes uncertainty. Some overcompensation of that kind may be permissible to right the balance, but considering what textual criticism can realistically achieve, I believe it is preferable to err on the side of diffidence rather than confidence. That diffidence, however, operates in two directions: it encourages distrust of the transmitted text as much as it might make one wary of attempts to emend it.

II

To classify textual criticism as a form of rhetoric is a way of highlighting the fact that its arguments depend on persuasion rather than demonstration. Textual critics cannot prove that their choices are correct; the most they can hope to do is lead their readers to believe that those choices are the best available ones.

Facts do, of course, play an important part in textual arguments. But in the end the facts cannot yield a definitive answer, only a relative probability, which is where the critic needs to employ rhetorical argument. As an example let us consider a small textual problem in the *Aeneid*. In the last book of the poem Aeneas is wounded by an arrow from an unseen assailant and forced to leave the battlefield; as he is carried back to camp he orders his companions to take the swiftest measures

---

[46] Conte (2013), 52.

to treat him: *ense secent lato uulnus telique latebram | rescindant peni-tus, seseque in bella remittant* (12.389–90 'that they should cut open the wound with a broad sword to lay bare the arrow's deepest hiding place, and send him back to the fight'). In line 389 *latebram* ('hiding place') is the reading of most manuscripts, but the late antique Medicean codex (M) and a few Carolingian manuscripts have the plural *latebras*. Since either form is acceptable in this context, one might reasonably opt to follow the majority of witnesses, but matters are complicated by the fact that this would be the only occurrence of the singular in Virgil, against eleven instances of the plural (either the accusative *latebras* or the dative/ablative *latebris*), all of them unanimously transmitted. Modern editors are divided: Mynors and Conte print *latebram*, but Geymonat (like Sabbadini before him) adopts *latebras*. In my commentary, I sug-gested that the singular was better suited to the metaphorical sense the word carries here, but that argument is weakened by another passage in which the metaphorical sense appears with the plural form, *Aen.* 10.601 *tum latebras animae pectus mucrone recludit* ('then with his sword he opened [Liger's] breast, the hiding place of his spirit'). Furthermore, if, as I also suggested, the use of *latebra* in this passage alludes to the Trojan Horse, twice called a hiding place (*latebras, Aen.* 2.38 and 55), the allusion might be more readily perceived if the plural appeared in both passages. The facts of the case leave the decision in doubt. I pre-ferred *latebram* because it seemed to me more likely that M and the other manuscripts that read *latebras* were influenced by knowledge of Virgil's usual preference for the plural than that a majority of manuscripts would have gratuitously introduced an anomalous singular. Such calculations of probability are always attempts to persuade (first oneself, and then oth-ers); they are often phrased in a way meant to enhance their persuasive force (here the adverb 'gratuitously').

One consequence of seeing the arguments of textual critics as essentially rhetorical is that questions of proper or legitimate method can be more appro-priately recast in terms of persuadability. Moritz Haupt said that, if the sense seemed to require it, he was prepared to conjecture *Constantinopolitanus* where the manuscripts offered the monosyllabic interjection *o*;[47] the ques-tion raised by his hypothetical alteration is not whether it would be proper

---

[47] Belger (1879), 126; quoted by Housman (1922), 77. Haupt made the remark as an exception to the precept that a conjecture should not contain more syllables than the manuscript reading it seeks to replace.

or legitimate, but whether he could convince any other scholar that he had acted reasonably.

Granted that an appeal to rhetoric is an essential component of text-critical argument, is there a particular rhetorical mode appropriate to a post-heroic practice of textual criticism, specifically one that acknowledges the limits of what that criticism can achieve? Some years ago, I made a comparative study of the rhetorical styles of two eminent textual critics, Heinsius and Bentley, using as a basis their printed notes on the *Metamorphoses* and Horace respectively.[48] Some of the results are relevant to the present discussion.

Heinsius' critical vocabulary is weighted more heavily towards commendation than denunciation. The manuscripts he cites most often are described as excelling by their age (they are *antiqui* or *ueteres* or *uetustiores*), by their overall superiority (*meliores* or *melioris notae* or *optimi*) and by their relative 'correctness' (*castigatiores*). Heinsius' terms of praise for manuscript readings include generalized expressions of approval or attraction such as *bene* ('good'), *non* (or *haud*) *male* ('not/not at all bad'), *probe* (expressing general approval), *quod placet* ('pleasing'), *quod arridet* or *quod omnino arridet* ('attractive/highly attractive'), and *sequor* ('I follow') or *amplector* ('I embrace'), as well as a variety of more specific approbations: *uenuste* ('charmingly'), *argute* ('wittily' or 'cleverly', often of a pointed or epigrammatic phrase), *uerius* ('closer to the truth'), *rectius* (i.e., in better accord with normal syntax or usage), *concinne* or *concinnus* (usually connected with avoidance of repetition, to which Heinsius was excessively sensitive), and *elegans* or *eleganter*. Considered singly, none of those terms is unusual, but the accumulation of laudatory language creates an atmosphere of refined appreciation.

Negative terms for manuscript readings are relatively uncommon and on the whole not highly charged. *Frustra* ('in vain') and *perperam* ('wrongly') are used of variants judged to be unnecessary or misguided, and a transmitted reading that Heinsius finds linguistically intolerable may be called *uix* (or '*non*') *Latinum*. But the emotionally charged terms with which Bentley often stigmatizes manuscript readings – terms such as *ineptus*, *puerilis*, *inficetus* ('uncouth'), *putidus* ('disgusting'), and *absurdus* – are conspicuously rare in Heinsius' language.

Bentley, by contrast, is a master of denunciation, a true ancestor of Housman and the scourges of the *Classical Review*. Examples of rhetorical coercion can be found on every page of his Horace. Using superlatives,

[48] Tarrant (1999).

indignant questions, irony and sarcasm, and morally loaded terms such as *prauus* and *peruersus*, Bentley seeks to inflame or intimidate his reader.

2.4.23 Suspicionem tamen meam dissimulare non possum, irrepsisse nempe librariorum seu incuria siue audacia *claudere* pro *condere* ... Quis in Latinis litteris adeo hospes est, ut receptissimam hanc locutionem nesciat? ('I cannot conceal my suspicion that *claudere* has crept in, through the negligence or audacity of the scribes, in place of *condere* ... Is anyone so unfamiliar with Latin literature as not to know that this expression is extremely common?')

3.19.24 *uicina seni non habilis Lyco*] Sed tuam fidem, uir clarissime! an quia *tamquam uicina* uiuit rei familiaris uxor, ideone *uicina* absolute *uxorem* significauerit? ('But I ask you, my good man, because a wife lives *tamquam uicina*, does it follow that *uicina* by itself could mean "wife"?')

3.21.5 Vix alius est locus, in quo infelicius se gesserint Interpretes ... [On *pia testa*] Quomodo enim *pia*, si *querelas* forte uel *rixas* gesserit? Hoc tamen patienter admiserunt nimis aequi Interpretes. Tu uero uerba accipe, quasi sic interpungerentur, *seu facilem pia, Testa, somnum.* ('There is hardly annother passage in which the commentators have performed so wretchedly ... How can it be *pia*, if it has produced *querelas* or *rixas*? But this has been tolerated by the complaisant commentators. You, however, should understand the words as if they were punctuated *seu facilem pia, Testa, somnum.*')

3.24.6 *Durum* et *dirum* in MStis ubique fere confunduntur; ut mirum sit tam praue et peruerse hic congruere in peiore scriptura. ('*Durum* and *dirum* are almost always confused in manuscripts, so it is amazing that the manuscripts here so wickedly and perversely agree on the worse reading.')

Heinsius' notes are nearly devoid of such rhetorical fireworks, and can seem at first oddly impersonal by comparison. A conjecture may be introduced with nothing more dramatic than *scribendum fortasse* ('perhaps one should write', 4.224) or *uidetur tamen scribendum* ('but it seems that one should write', 11.363), and when Heinsius does call attention to his activity as an emendator the language used is more likely to imply diffidence than to claim victory, as in the conditional form used at 15.624: *scripserat Naso, si genius eius mihi perspectus est* ('if I have rightly grasped his thought, Ovid wrote ...') or the double negative at 4.86: *nec uero absimile Nasonem scripsisse septa* ('it is not implausible that Ovid wrote *septa*'). Bold suggestions may be introduced apologetically, as though the reader's indulgence had to be secured for such audacity, cf. 11.134 *ut tamen, quod res est, dicam, opinor Nasonem dedisse* ... ('but to say what is the case, I think that Ovid wrote ...'), 433 *timide dico, sed dico tamen, uideri scriptum a Nasone* ... ('I say it hesitantly, but I say it nonetheless, that it appears that Ovid wrote ...'). Heinsius also presents some of his innovations as acts of restoration, 'giving back' to the poet a choice word or pointed phrase of which he had been deprived, cf. 15.546: *eleganti et proprio uerbo, quod etiam Nasoni redonauimus Met.* 3.691 ('an elegant and well-chosen word, which we have returned to Ovid as well at *Met.* 3.691'), 11.701 *redde Nasoni suum acumen et scribe*, sine me me pontus habet ('give Ovid back his point and write *sine me me pontus habet*'); the trope deflects attention away from the critic onto his beneficiary, Ovid.

Although Heinsius had more right than any previous editor of Ovid to compliment himself on original insights, he generally does so with only a mild gesture of amazement that a point had not already been seen, for example, 8.313 *miror hoc fugisse doctos interpretes* ('I am surprised that this has escaped the learned commentators'), 8.605 *miror interpretes hoc non vidisse* ('I am surprised that the commentators have not seen this'). References to other scholars by name, when not laudatory, are generally neutral, and Heinsius' harshest judgements are usually couched in non-specific terms.[49]

There is no trace in Heinsius' writing of the unseemly spectacle Bentley so often evokes, of eminent critics falling into absurd or grotesque errors; see, for example, 2.9.1 *Barine*] *Vitiosum uidetur illud nomen Barine, ut acute obseruauit Tan. Faber ... Immaniter tamen lapsus est idem Faber, cum, et testante et laudante hoc Dacierio, reposuit ... Earine* ('The name *Barine* appears to be corrupt, as Tan. Faber shrewdly noticed ... But Faber grievously blundered in substituting *Earine*, an error recorded and praised by Dacier'), 4.4.15 *Nam quod uiri clarissimi Xylander et Chabotius adiectiue hoc accipiunt, lacte ubere siue copioso, id absurdius est, quam ut refelli mereatur* ('As for the fact that those distinguished scholars Xylander and Chabotius take this as an adjective, *lacte ubere*, i.e., abundant, this is too silly to deserve refuting'). This melodramatic personalizing is one obvious way in which Bentley's critical rhetoric foreshadows that of Housman, although

---

[49] Heinsius' demolition of Tanaquil Faber (in his note on *Ars* 2.660) is not a genuine exception, since it was motivated by Faber's aspersions on the honesty of Heinsius' father (cf. Kenney (1974), 67 n. 6). What Heinsius says there about having chosen to praise Faber rather than criticize him seems generally true of his treatment of other scholars: *silentio plerumque inuolui, quae reprehensionem merebantur; quae laude digna judicabam, praedicaui ingenue* ('I often shrouded in silence things that deserved rebuke; what I judged worthy of praise I candidly proclaimed').

Bentley's references to other scholars have a generosity not often visible in Housman.

For the present discussion, the most intriguing characteristic of Heinsius' notes is a willingness at times to entertain two or more solutions to a textual problem. That is not a consistent policy: there are hundreds of notes in which Heinsius argues energetically for a single answer. The exceptions are therefore all the more remarkable in a critic who can be so often both decisive and independent.

The following are examples of notes in which Heinsius commends two or more variants or conjectures:

8.839 *plura cupit*] '*Petit* cum melioribus. alterum jam praecessit. nisi *capit* reponis cum uno Vossiano et altero Erfurt<ensi> ... sed forte paulo ante [834] legendum: *plusque capit* ... Nam ita Graeuianus aliique nonnulli.' ('[Read] *petit* with the better manuscripts, since the other word [*cupit*] has appeared just before [i.e., 834 *plusque cupit*]. Unless you put in *capit* as in one of Vossius' manuscripts and an Erfurt manuscript. But perhaps in the earlier line one should read *plusque capit*, which is the reading of Graevius' manuscript and several others.')

11.393 *arce locus summa, fessis loca grata carinis*] 'Quam inconcinnum *locus* et *loca* in uno eodemque uersu! Scribo igitur, *arce focus summa*. Pharon designat, seu turrem, ex qua nocturni ignes in usum nauium lucebant. Hanc conjecturam postea primus Vaticanus confirmauit ... an *pharus* scripserat Naso? ut apud Val. Flaccum 7.83 ... Sed *focus* praestat. nisi *faces* mauis. Potest et *foci*. nam sec<undus> Palat<inus> et Urbin<as> *loci*, quod in suis Constantius etiam Fanensis inuenerat.' ('How clumsy to have *locus* and *loca* in the same line! I therefore write *arce focus summa*. He is referring to a lighthouse or tower, from which fires shone at night to guide ships. This conjecture was later confirmed by the first Vatican manuscript ... Or perhaps Ovid wrote *pharus*, as in Valerius Flaccus 7.83 [other parallels cited from Statius, Juvenal, and Rutilius Namatianus]. But *focus* is better, unless you prefer *faces*. *foci* is also possible, since the second Palatine manuscript and the Urbinas manuscript have *loci*, which Constantius Fanensis had found in his manuscripts as well.')

15.492–3 *quoties flenti Theseius heros | 'siste modum' dixit*] 'Pro *siste modum*, quod Latinum uix est, repono, *sit modus o, dixit*. Certe Zulichemianus, *siste modo* ... bene etiam unus Vossianus, *flendi*' ('In place of *siste modum*, which is hardly Latin, I print *sit modus o, dixit*. At least Zulichemius' manuscript reads *siste modo*. Also worth commending is *flendi* in one of Vossius' manuscripts.')

15.603 *succinctis*] '*Peliacis* unus Leid<ensis> eleganter. ut Catal. [i.e., Catull.] 64 *Peliaco quondam prognatae uertice pinus*. Sed nec uulgatum damno lib. 10.103 *et succincta comas hirsutaque uertice pinus*. Zulich<emianus> non male, *substrictis*. quomodo *substricta ilia* libro 3.216 de cane, et *substricta crura* lib. 11.752.' ('One Leiden manuscript elegantly reads *Peliacis*, as in Catullus 64.1 *Peliaco quondam prognatae uertice pinus*. But I do not fault the common reading, cf. *Met.* 10.103 *et succincta comas hirsutaque uertice pinus*. Zulichemius' manuscript has *substrictis*, which is not bad, as in 3.216 of a dog's *substricta ilia* and 11.752 *substricta ilia*.')

In some of these cases, one can infer from Heinsius' language which reading he prefers (e.g., 15.603, where the words *nec uulgatum damno* imply that he would retain the common reading *succinctis*), but others leave the question unresolved. The note on 11.393 is especially instructive. It begins with an exclamation of disgust at the 'inconcinnity' of *locus* and *loca* in the same line, and everything that follows takes it for granted that this repetition is intolerable. But Heinsius contemplates no fewer than four replacements for *locus* (*focus, pharus, faces, foci*), and while *focus* is explicitly preferred to *pharus*, the other two possibilities seem to be left open.

Two other recurring moves in Heinsius' notes suggest a similar openness about the final choice of reading. In one, Heinsius explicitly presents the reader with a second option by using an expression like *nisi mauis* ('unless you prefer'): this phrase is used to introduce the conjecture *faces* in the note just mentioned, and appears often elsewhere. In the other, Heinsius voices a preference for or an attraction to a reading – most often with a word such as *malo* or *malim* ('I prefer/would prefer') – but does not act on it by placing it in the text. The most appealing expression of this kind is the lovely phrase *quod parum abest quin amplectar* ('which I am very close to embracing', 4.168), describing an impulse that many editors have felt but that few have so vividly portrayed.[50]

If there is a rhetoric appropriate to a post-heroic textual criticism, I believe it will resemble the style of Heinsius more than that of Bentley. In fact, from this point of view, Heinsius could be called, paradoxically, a post-heroic hero, since his emphasis on multiple possibilities foreshadows the current move away from dogmatic certainty. There is an analogy

---

[50] See also p. 142 (Chapter 7).

to Heinsius' position with regard to stemmatic method. His treatment of manuscript evidence is pre-Lachmannian in that he never attempted to work out the relationships of manuscripts using genealogical principles, but at the same time it could be described as post-Lachmannian in the sense that his eclectic approach to variants now appears to be more productive than a stemmatic analysis for traditions such as that of Ovid's *Metamorphoses*.

Determining the approach that best suits the nature of a particular manuscript tradition is at the heart of recension, which is our next topic.

3

Establishing the text 1: recension

> In so many respects objectivity is an illusion, and the margin of discretion is at once appealing and agonizing for the philologist. If the critical editor is not an arrogant rewriter of the text, he is constitutionally a desperate man. Philology lives by hypotheses more than by certainties, nothing but hypotheses, more or less judicious.
>
> (Gorni (2003), 54)

The Latin noun *recensio*, the corresponding verb *recensere*, and their English counterpart 'recension' have in the course of time conveyed a variety of meanings. These may be divided into two categories, one of which relates to the product of editorial work and the other to some part of the editorial process.

The first set of usages denotes establishing a text or creating a particular version of a text. In pre-modern contexts the term is often applied to some putatively influential form of a text, such as the so-called 'Peisistratean recension' of the Homeric poems (the form in which they were allegedly standardized in sixth-century Athens), or the 'Varronian recension' of Plautus (a product of Roman textual scholarship that involved distinguishing genuine plays from plays attributed to Plautus). In English one might similarly refer, for example, to 'Bentley's recension' of Horace, that is, the text of Horace created by the totality of Bentley's editorial choices, although expressions of that sort now sound rather old-fashioned.

The other usages single out particular aspects of an editor's activity. One describes the basis on which the text is established in any given place. In this sense *recensio ope codicum* ('recension on the basis of manuscripts') is distinguished from *recensio ope ingenii* ('recension on the basis of conjecture').

Recensio or 'recension' also relates to a prior stage of the editorial process, the method by which a critic or editor analyses the manuscript witnesses to determine how best to employ them in reconstructing the original form of the text.[1] The most important method employed by editors of classical texts has itself gone under a variety of names: 'genealogical analysis' because it aims to sort manuscripts into affiliated groups and to map their descent, or 'common error method' because of it uses shared error to carry out that task; it is often more loosely referred to as 'stemmatic analysis' or 'stemmatics and associated with the name of Karl Lachmann.

This chapter concerns itself with recension in the sense of genealogical analysis and with *recensio ope codicum*; *recensio ope ingenii* is treated in the following chapter.

An essential procedure of recension is the tabulation and examination of shared errors to see if genealogical connections can be established among manuscripts, with the twin aims of eliminating derivative manuscripts (*codices descripti*) and of reconstructing the lost manuscript(s) from which the surviving witnesses descend. The principles underlying that analysis have been set out in the Introduction (pp. 12–17); now it is time to see how they are applied. Here is a relatively straightforward example, from Catullus' ironic salute to Cicero (poem 49, lines 4–7):

> Gratias tibi maximas Catullus
> agit pessimus omnium poeta,
> tanto pessimus omnium poeta
> quanto tu optimus omnium patronus.

> Catullus, worst of poets,
> gives you his warmest thanks,
> as much the worst of poets
> as you are the best advocate of all.

> 7 patronus O: patronum GR

In line 7, the sense requires *patronus*, in agreement with *tu* and *optimus*. Of the three oldest manuscripts, O, G, and R, O reads *patronus* but GR have *patronum*, which is syntactically impossible. GR are therefore in agreement in error. Now we must ask whether it is more likely that the change from *patronus* to *patronum* took place only once, in a common ancestor of G and R, and then passed into both manuscripts, or that the error was independently made twice, in G and in R. In the first case, we would have the beginnings of

---

[1] Hereafter I use 'editor' as shorthand for 'critic or editor'. A textual critic may engage in the activities described in this chapter without producing an edition, but the issues involved have their ultimate rationale in the context of editing texts.

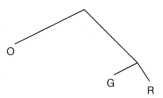

Stemma 1 Bipartite stemma with O comprising one branch and GR the other

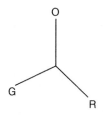

Stemma 2 Single branch stemma with GR deriving from O through an intermediary

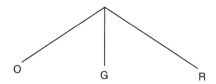

Stemma 3 Tripartite stemma with each of O, G, and R comprising an independent branch

an argument for postulating a common source of GR that is not a source of O. That source could be O itself or a source independent of O. (See Stemma 1 and Stemma 2.)

In the second case, we would have no reason for affiliating G and R, and Stemma 3 could be entertained.

Considered in isolation, the question cannot be answered. Stemmatic reasoning favours the most economical hypothesis, that the error was made only once, a presumption based on relative probability. In this passage, however, the change from *patronus* to *patronum* was probably caused by assimilation to the ending of the previous word, *omnium*. Alterations of that kind are a frequent form of scribal error, a fact that complicates the calculus of likelihood.

A prudent editor will therefore require a number of instances in which G and R agree in error before concluding that they are stemmatically related. One such case is of interest because it illustrates exactly the same form of error in GR. In the poem dramatically set at his brother's grave site (101), Catullus asks his brother to 'accept these <offerings>, which have been handed down by ancestral custom as sad gifts for the dead' (7–9): *haec, quae prisco more parentum | tradita sunt tristi munere ad inferias, | accipe*. For the accusative *haec* in O, which is required by syntax as the object of *accipe*, GR read *hoc*, by anticipation of the following ablative *prisco more*. Taken by itself, each agreement of GR could be accounted for by the hypothesis of independent scribal error; seen together (along with numerous other agreements), they create a strong presumption that GR have a common source that is not a source of O.

We must now ask whether GR derive from O or whether they are independent of it. Here the relevant evidence will consist of passages in which O contains an error not found in GR and not easily corrected. One potential example comes from poem 23, where Catullus jokingly lists some of the blessings enjoyed by Furius in his poverty (lines 15–16): *a te sudor abest, abest saliua, | mucusque et mala pituita nasi* ('you don't have sweat, don't have spittle, or phlegm or a bad head cold'). In line 15 the second *abest*, required by metre, is missing in O but present in GR; it would take an alert scribe to notice the metrical flaw and arrive at the correct solution, but that scenario is not impossible, and so we need additional proof. Another passage, from poem 13, offers a more subtle, but also more persuasive argument for GR's independence from O. After telling his friend Fabullus that he will dine well with him if he brings the entire dinner himself, Catullus begins to reveal the other side of the bargain (line 9): *sed contra accipies meros amores* ('but in return you will receive undiluted affection'). In place of *meros* O reads *meos*, which yields a possible sense ('you will receive my affection'), but which lacks the point of *meros* and its hint of *merum*, unmixed wine. It is a fair bet that, if *meos* had been the original reading, not one scribe in a thousand would have thought of changing it to *meros*. We are therefore on firm ground in granting GR independence from O, and in confirming the accuracy of Stemma 1.[2]

That example shows that using shared errors as a means of determining manuscript affiliations calls for judicious calculation of probabilities and close attention to all potentially relevant factors.

---

[2] For simplicity's sake, I have not introduced the steps that would show that G and R are independent of each other, and have omitted several other details of the early Catullus transmission. For a fuller discussion, see McKie (1977) and Thomson (1997), 22–43.

The application of this type of analysis to a manuscript tradition can lead to a variety of conclusions. It is theoretically possible that the position of every witness could be represented stemmatically. That may indeed be the case with texts for which only a small number of independent witnesses survive, such as the late antique poem known as the *Peruigilium Veneris*.[3] Some other traditions also lend themselves to a high degree of stemmatic plotting: in a forthcoming study of Porphyrio's commentary on Horace, Stephen Oakley convincingly argues that twenty-two of the twenty-three extant manuscripts derive from a single ninth-century codex (Vat. lat. 3314); he also divides the fifteenth-century manuscripts and early printed editions into five distinct groups.[4] In more populous traditions, however, it is not possible to assign every manuscript a place in a stemma, usually because of contamination in part or all of the tradition.[5] Sometimes part of the tradition (usually the oldest part) can be analysed stemmatically, while the later witnesses do not yield to stemmatic treatment: some examples are Seneca's tragedies, Catullus, Propertius, and the *mutili* of Sallust.[6] In such cases the fact that later manuscripts cannot be plotted on a stemma may not have much relevance to establishing the text.

Stemmata come in a wide variety of shapes and sizes. The simplest sort of stemma could be represented by Tacitus' *Annals* 1–6, which survives in a single manuscript; the stemma would be a straight line from Tacitus to the 'First Medicean' manuscript (Laurentianus 68.1), with an unknown number of intermediate points separating them. This example is a useful reminder that stemmata can only represent witnesses that survive or that have left some trace in the tradition: there must have been many other copies of the *Annals* in existence between the second and the ninth centuries, but there is no way to represent their relationship to the one copy that survives.

As an example of a more complex stemma I offer my attempt to depict the relationships of the oldest manuscripts of the *Metamorphoses* (Stemma 4). (Dotted lines are used to represent the direction of contamination.)[7]

---

[3] See Reynolds (1983), 9–13.

[4] I am grateful to Stephen for allowing me to see his work in advance of publication.

[5] For the concept of contamination, see pp. 14–16 (Introduction).

[6] Reynolds (1983), 343: 'the *mutilus* tradition can be represented in stemmatic form if confined to the earlier and less contaminated witnesses'.

[7] The stemma shown here incorporates corrections to the one in Tarrant (2004), xxvii. See also n. 22.

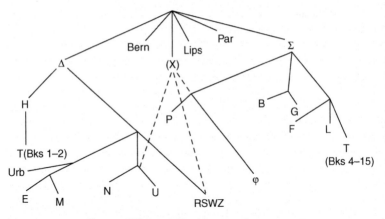

Stemma 4 From Tarrant (2004), xxvii, with corrections

Manuscript traditions are often categorized as either 'closed' or 'open'. The terms were coined by Pasquali, who intended them to signify whether the archetype could or could not be reconstructed on mechanical grounds. If 'open' and 'closed' are used in that sense, it is possible and even likely that the same tradition could be 'closed' in some places and 'open' in others, as in Catullus (first stemma depicted earlier), where the agreement of O with G or R should yield the reading of the archetype ('closed' recension) while the agreement of GR against O would be a case of 'open' recension.[8]

Owing to the ambiguity inherent in Pasquali's usage and the different senses that the terms have acquired in subsequent discussions, any writer who wishes to retain them needs to provide a definition. I use 'closed' and 'open' to refer to traditions that can or cannot be analysed stemmatically.

Examples of closed traditions include Quintilian's *Institutio oratoria* ('a striking example of a tradition where extant Carolingian manuscripts can be shown to have generated the host of later codices'[9]), Cornelius Nepos, and Seneca's *Apocolocyntosis*.

One tradition that is almost completely open is that of Lucan, of which Housman wrote that 'the manuscripts group themselves not in families but in factions; their dissidences and agreements are temporary and transient, like the splits and coalitions of political party; and the utmost which can be

---

[8] On Pasquali's use of the terms and their subsequent history, see Alberti (1968).

[9] Winterbottom in Reynolds (1983), 332.

done to classify them is to note the comparative frequency of their shifting alliances'.[10]

In most cases, our present view of a tradition needs to be treated as provisional, since the tradition has not yet been fully explored. In a fully closed tradition, no reading not attested in the oldest strata of the tradition should be archetypal. But that conclusion can only be reached after investigating the later manuscripts to determine whether they contain readings probably inherited from the archetype that cannot be accounted for on stemmatic grounds. Until now, though, very few manuscript traditions of any size have been exhaustively studied. The absence of such studies is a recurrent motif in the essays collected in *Texts and Transmission*: 'a large number of later manuscripts have not in fact been inspected';[11] 'further exploration is overdue';[12] 'large reaches of the later tradition have not been explored';[13] 'this question still remains to be answered definitively';[14] 'no one yet knows whether none, some, or all of the other manuscripts are independent of <A>'.[15] A notable exception is Claudian's *De raptu Proserpinae*, of which J. B. Hall collated almost all the extant manuscripts (132 of 134), concluding that the tradition is completely contaminated.[16] It seems likely that some traditions that are now thought to be closed may need to be reassessed if and when more study of their later representatives is carried out.[17]

As the foregoing remarks show, determining how fully to investigate the manuscripts of a given text is an issue with important methodological implications. From a logical standpoint, complete collation is the only defensible approach, but in most cases that is a counsel of perfection rather than a feasible policy. For the *Metamorphoses*, I decided to collate in full all extant manuscripts

---

[10] Housman (1926), vii. Gotoff (1971) convincingly established the basic affiliations of some of the oldest manuscripts, but pervasive contamination rules out any recourse to stemmatic reasoning; see Tarrant in Reynolds (1983), 215–18, but see also n. 35 this chapter.

[11] Reynolds (1983), 172 n. 6, on Frontinus' *Strategemata*.

[12] Reynolds (1983), 199, on Justin's epitome of Trogus.

[13] Reynolds (1983), 316, on Pliny the Elder.

[14] Marshall in Reynolds (1983), 355, on the status of the fifteenth-century manuscripts of the *Historia Augusta*.

[15] Reeve in Reynolds (1983), 424, on Tibullus. None of the three critical editions published since then (Luck (1988), Bauzá (1990), Della Corte (1989)) attempts to resolve that fundamental issue.

[16] See Hall (1969), 61–4.

[17] The fragility of some current views is brought out by Winterbottom's statement about the tradition of Curtius Rufus: 'there are a large number of later manuscripts, virtually unexamined and therefore classed as *interpolati*' (in Reynolds (1983), 148).

written before 1200 (which happens to be the cut-off point of Birger Munk Olsen's indispensable catalogue[18]), and to rely on samplings for manuscripts after that date; in all I looked at nearly 300 manuscripts, most of them in a highly selective way.[19] But in dealing with popular authors such as Horace or Lucan or Juvenal, even collating all manuscripts up to 1200 would require more time and effort than most editors are willing to devote to an activity that they think is not likely to yield much benefit in establishing the text. In practice, therefore, editors generally cross their fingers and hope that the manuscript evidence they have assembled contains all or almost all potentially archetypal readings.

An editor attempting to survey a large number of later manuscripts may reasonably employ selective collation, but the choice of passages to examine needs to be carefully considered. It is not sufficient, for example, to look only at places where the earlier manuscripts disagree: that might help to determine where a later manuscript fits in the tradition (although in an open tradition stable affiliations are not likely to be visible), but it is no way to turn up evidence of good readings that have bypassed the early witnesses. It would be potentially more useful to examine places where the text currently rests on conjecture, along with a randomly chosen stretch of the text that could offer evidence of a manuscript's independence.

Even in a closed tradition, later manuscripts may have value as sources of conjecture (*fontes coniecturarum*, as they are designated in some editions). Finding a reading previously regarded as a conjecture in a manuscript does not alter its status, if it seems likely to be a successful correction by a scribe rather than a bit of inherited tradition, but it does provide an earlier attestation and may help refine our sense of what kinds of correction medieval scribes were capable of, which is currently one of the largest gaps in our knowledge.[20]

Once the manuscripts (or those chosen for investigation) have been collated and their relationships plotted to whatever extent seems feasible, the editor's next task is to establish the oldest form of the text attested by the tradition, which will usually be the text of the archetype. Where all manuscripts agree, their consensus yields the text of the archetype. Difficulties arise when the editor must choose between two or more manuscript readings. The editor

[18] Munk Olsen (1982–9); see also Munk Olsen (2007) for the last of six supplements and references to the previous five.

[19] I was also able to supplement my reports of a number of manuscripts by consulting Heinsius' collations, preserved in the Bodleian Library in Oxford and the Deutsche Staatsbibliothek in Berlin.

[20] Hall (2008), 3.394 comments on 'how frequently the conjectures of modern scholars coincide with the readings (mostly, if not entirely, conjectural) of medieval copyists. From this inferences may be made about the quality of medieval textual scholarship'.

will sometimes be able to establish the text of the archetype by a simple calculus of shared readings; in such cases, the tradition usually consists of three
or more independent branches, and the agreement of the majority will give
the archetypal text. But tripartite and pluripartite stemmata are less common
than bipartite stemmata, such as that of Catullus. There the reading of the
archetype can be determined by the agreement of O and G against R or by the
agreement of O and R against G, but when G and R agree against O, the two
readings have equal stemmatic value, and the reading of the archetype can
only be ascertained by weighing the relative merits of the readings.

The frequency of bipartite stemmata in classical textual criticism has been
a source of controversy. Critics of stemmatic analysis have seized on what they
allege to be an over-representation of such stemmata as an indication either
of a flaw in the method itself (usually thought to involve insufficient attention
to contamination) or of a misapplication of the method by editors. The methodological objections have been successfully parried,[21] and the proportion of
bipartite stemmata does not in fact seem high enough to justify suspicion.[22]
Furthermore, historical factors may help to account for the greater frequency
of bipartite stemmata. Since pluripartite stemmata are not rare in classical traditions consisting largely of fifteenth-century manuscripts – nor are they rare
in the transmission of medieval Latin texts – it seems likely that traditions
represented by Carolingian manuscripts are more often bipartite than pluripartite because early copies perished before propagating their lines.[23] The labour
involved in transcribing an ancient codex into minuscule script may also have
been a factor in limiting the number of copies made directly rather than from
apographs in minuscules.

When choosing between or among equally well-attested variants, the editor may have recourse to a variety of potentially relevant factors: considerations of sense and style, of grammar, diction, metre or prose rhythm, and

---

[21] See primarily Reeve (1986), responding to Timpanaro. For a brief summary, see Tarrant
(1995a), 112–13.

[22] Grier (1988), 276 notes that, of the forty-five traditions for which stemmata are offered in
Texts and Transmission, twenty-seven or 60 per cent are bipartite and ten or just under a
quarter are tripartite or pluripartite. To the latter figure could be added Donatus' commentary
on Terence (for which a tripartite stemma is a possibility), Ovid's *Fasti* (where a third branch
is postulated to account for contamination), and the Fourth Decade of Livy (which has two
independent but fragmentary witnesses in addition to the main stream of transmission).

[23] My stemma of the *Metamorphoses* tradition (mentioned earlier, p. 54) appears to be
pluripartite, but several branches are represented by Carolingian fragments that have no
known descendants. The tradition is essentially bipartite, with possible traces of a third
branch.

so on. Even after all pertinent evidence has been assessed, the decision is often not obvious. Hall admitted with rare candour that he often found himself forced to choose between variants that seemed to possess equal intrinsic merit; he concluded that 'on many occasions one might as well toss a coin to decide which reading to print'.[24] Such a situation surely calls for its own *siglum* in the apparatus.[25]

It is worth noting that such precepts as *lectio difficilior, lectio potior* ('the more difficult reading is the preferable reading') are not actually rules, but statements of relative probability, and are therefore to be used with caution. Another such expression, *usus scribendi* ('the practice of the author'), bears closer examination. It encapsulates an analogical argument, namely, that every author has certain preferred modes of expression, and that the reading that more closely corresponds to the author's customary practice is therefore to be preferred. There is clearly some validity to this principle, but its risks are no less obvious. For one thing, authors are not automatons who repeat themselves without variation; for another, copyists too can become aware of the stylistic preferences of the authors whose works they transcribe, and can replace a word that strikes them as anomalous with a more typical variant.[26]

As a consequence, appealing to parallels within an author's work as a criterion for deciding between variants calls for the exercise of judgement; what appears to be a parallel could result from a scribal reminiscence of a similar passage in the same text or elsewhere. The text of the *Metamorphoses* contains at least one certain example of such a scribal reminiscence. In Book 12.103 *cum sua terribili petit inritamina cornu* ('as when <a bull> rushes at what enrages it with its fearful horns'), instead of *inritamina cornu* one group of manuscripts reads *inritamenta malorum* ('incitements to evil'), which makes no sense in the context and which must be an echo of Book 1.140 *effodiuntur opes, inritamenta malorum* ('riches are dug out <of the earth>, incitements to evil').[27] The text of the *Aeneid* also contains an error

[24] Hall (1969), 65.

[25] Donaldson (1970), 116 made a similar proposal: 'perhaps we ought to devise a new symbol, to be placed prominently in the text when authority is being docilely followed, one that means "Editor has no idea what to read here, and hence is taking refuge, as usual, in dear old MS Pf". A small ostrich, with head in the sand, might do'.

[26] For a possible example, see the earlier discussion of *Aeneid* 12.389 (pp. 41–2).

[27] This is an excellent example of a conjunctive error in stemmatic terms, since it is very unlikely that the same recollection would have occurred to more than one scribe. It is therefore almost certain that any manuscripts that read *inritamenta malorum* are genealogically related.

almost certainly induced by recollection of a passage elsewhere in the poem: 4.24 *sed mihi uel tellus optem prius ima dehiscat* ('but I would wish that the earth's depths would first gape open for me'), where after *optem* the scribe of F at first wrote a nonsensical *dimittere*; the only plausible explanation is that he was prompted by the verb *optem* to think of 5.29 *quoue magis fessas optem dimittere nauis* ('or where I would rather wish to beach our weary ships'), the only other occurrence of the form *optem* in Virgil.

In my opinion, some other variants in the text of the *Metamorphoses* may be explained in this way. For example, in Book 6, after the petrification of Niobe her fellow-Thebans are prompted to recall similar occurrences from the past: *utque fit, a facto propiore priora renarrant* (6.316 'and, as often happens, starting with the more recent event they retell earlier incidents'). All older manuscripts read *renarrant*, but some thirteenth-century manuscripts have the variant *retractant*, a verb that appears several times in Ovid and once in a very similar context in Book 4, when Cadmus and Harmonia are reflecting on their earlier lives: *iamque malis annisque graues, dum prima retractant│fata domus releguntque suos sermone labores* (4.569–70 'and now, weighed down with years and misfortunes, as they relate the original fate of their house and rehearse their tribulations in speech'). In my apparatus entry on 6.316, I cited the passage from Book 4 and suggested that it might have been the source of the variant *retractant*, but the situation is actually more complicated. Apart from *Met.* 6.316, the verb *renarrare* appears only once more in Ovid, in *Met.* 5.635–6, where Arethusa is relating to Athena her escape from the river Alpheus: *et citius quam nunc tibi facta renarro,│in latices mutor* ('and, sooner than I can retell the event to you now, I was changed into water'). It seems, therefore, that *renarrant* and *retractant* each has one close Ovidian parallel. Hence the editor's decision cannot turn simply on parallels, and I opted for *renarrant* as the reading of the preponderance of manuscripts. But whichever reading is the original, the other appears to be an 'echo-variant' inspired by a passage elsewhere in the poem.

I had not thought that my interpretation of some apparent parallels as scribal reminiscences was controversial, and so was surprised to read that it 'threatens to undermine the system of parallels on which textual criticism relies'.[28] I do not wish to downplay the importance of parallels – it would be impossible to edit any classical text without reference to them – but rather

---

[28] Luck (2005a), 187.

to insist that they do not possess a fixed value, and that, like other forms of textual evidence, they must be assessed on an individual basis.

Particular problems of recension are posed by bipartite transmissions in which one witness or one branch of transmission offers a text that is on the whole superior to the other. Seneca's tragedies are a clear case; others would include the satires of Persius and Juvenal. (Often the superior witness or group is said to be 'purer' and the inferior one 'interpolated', a holdover from Lachmannian terminology, where 'interpolated' does not refer to inserted material but rather to alterations that replace difficult or obscure readings with more easily grasped equivalents.) The methodological issue raised by such transmissions is how far to privilege the better witness or witnesses. One extreme is the 'best manuscript' approach, which follows the superior branch in all cases where its readings are potentially correct. The flaw in that method was exposed by Housman in one of his most powerful statements:

> Chance and the common course of nature will not bring it to pass that the readings of a MS are right wherever they are possible and impossible wherever they are wrong: that needs divine intervention; and when one considers the history of man and the spectacle of the universe I hope one may say without impiety that divine intervention might have been better employed elsewhere.[29]

In this case, Housman's rhetoric is not standing in for logic but strengthening the impact of a logically cogent argument, which ultimately rests on an appeal to probability. There are, to be sure, circumstances in which adopting the reading of the generally better manuscript or group of manuscripts is the most reasonable course of action, most notably when there is no way to evaluate competing readings on their intrinsic merit. Here is Housman again, from the preface to Juvenal: 'since we have found P the most trustworthy MS in places where its fidelity can be tested, we infer that it is also the most trustworthy in places where no test can be applied ... A critic ... when he employs this method of trusting the best MS, employs it in the same spirit of gloomy resignation with which a man lies down on a stretcher when he has broken both his legs'.[30] There are also times when it may be reasonable to follow the readings of a single manuscript systematically, as when the form or style of a work makes it difficult to distinguish scribal from authorial readings (a situation more likely to be found in a medieval than a classical text); in those conditions following a manuscript with few obvious copying errors would be a defensible method. But in the majority of cases, trusting in a single witness or group will be vulnerable to Housman's objection, and the editor should consider the readings of both families on their merits.

In open transmissions, where stemmatic analysis can play at best a limited role, all the uncertainties of recension are greatly magnified.[31] For example, the distinction between older manuscripts (*codices uetustiores*) and more recent manuscripts (*codices recentiores*) may become so blurred as to have no value in arbitrating between or among variants. It is worth noting that, while the designation *codex recentior* ('later manuscript') is a matter of fact that can be verified on palaeographical grounds, the description *lectio recentior* ('later reading') is contingent on the absence of an older witness and is therefore susceptible to revision in the light of fuller evidence. A remark I once made with reference to the tradition of the *Metamorphoses* can be applied to any open transmission: every *lectio recentior* is potentially a *lectio uetustior* for which an older witness happens not to survive.[32] That point was epigrammatically expressed in the heading to one of the chapters of Giorgio Pasquali's *Storia della tradizione*: *recentiores, non deteriores* ('later <witnesses>, not inferior ones'); the chapter itself presented numerous examples of authentic readings preserved only in later manuscripts, even manuscripts of the fifteenth century or later.[33]

The danger of neglecting readings found in later manuscripts is illustrated by cases in which the discovery of an earlier witness has given those readings an older attestation. Seneca's *Epistulae morales* provides an example. In 1913, Achille Beltrami drew the attention of scholars to a hitherto unstudied tenth-century manuscript in the Biblioteca Queriniana in Brescia. This *codex Quirinianus* (known as Q) contained many clearly correct readings that had previously been known only from *recentiores*; it also contained whole phrases and sentences that had been regarded as interpolations found only in late manuscripts. The accession of Q required

---

[31] Deciding whether or not one is facing such a situation is itself a matter of judgement; determining the degree of openness in a given transmission may be beyond what can be proven, even given the less than absolute criteria of proof that obtain in this field.

[32] Tarrant (1995b), 114.

[33] Pasquali (1952), 41–108. If there were a prize for famous last words in textual criticism, a strong contender would be the following, written by Eduard Fraenkel in 1951 (350): 'we are not still living in the age of eclectic textual criticism'. Fraenkel was reviewing Franco Munari's edition of Ovid's *Amores* and criticized him for having considered the quality of readings in *recentiores* rather than asking whether they were stemmatically independent. When the review appeared, Fraenkel's good friend Pasquali was about to publish the second edition of the book that would in large measure bring back the age of eclectic textual criticism.

not only a reassessment of the authority of those readings, but also of the place of the *recentiores* in the tradition as a whole. In his study of the tradition of the *Epistulae morales*, Leighton Reynolds cited the case of Q to support the proposition that 'recension is an essential preliminary for critical evaluation and no scholar, however acute, can be expected to distinguish constantly and consistently between true and false readings unless he knows something of the authority of the manuscripts which offer them'.[34] He argued that only that principle can explain why the discovery of Q caused such a stir, given that two *recentiores* (one of the fourteenth century and one of the fifteenth century), which had been known for some time, offered substantially the same text. He concluded, surely correctly, that 'their evidence was neglected because they were *recentiores* and, by implication, of lesser "authority" than the older manuscripts'. But I wonder if the story of Q does not also show that it is always questionable to assign value to readings based on the age of the manuscripts that contain them. Suppose that Q had not survived, or that it had not been noticed by Beltrami. The readings that its discovery vindicated would have had just as much intrinsic merit without Q's support as they do with it; would editors be justified in ignoring those readings simply because they lacked an authoritative witness? Another thought: in the absence of Q, acknowledging the presence of good readings in two later manuscripts would have required redrawing the stemma to explain how they got there, or else called for an admission that the tradition was not entirely closed. It therefore seems likely that inertia and excessive confidence in the correctness of the stemma help to explain why the merit of those readings was not recognized sooner.

Consider another example (which I owe to James McKeown), Ovid *Amores* 1.2.21–22:

nil opus est bello: pacem ueniamque rogamus;
   nec tibi laus armis uictus inermis ero.

there is no need for war: I ask for peace and mercy.
   nor shall I bring you glory, an unarmed man conquered by arms.

21 pacem ueniamque *Yς*: u. p. *Sς*

Until McKeown's 1987 edition, all modern editors had printed *ueniam pacemque*, the reading of the *uetustiores* – or rather of a single *codex*

---

[34] Reynolds (1965a), 66–7.

uetustior, S, since of the four older manuscripts used by editors, RPSY, only S and Y are present and legible at this point (R is illegible and P's text begins thirty lines later, at 1.2.51). The remaining *uetustior*, Y, Berlin Hamilton 471, does indeed read *pacem ueniamque*, but its importance was not realized until 1965, when Franco Munari redated it from the fourteenth century to the eleventh.[35] As McKeown shows in his commentary, *pacem ueniamque* is superior on internal grounds; his most compelling argument is that Ovid is evoking a formula found in prayers and appeals for peace, in which the order is consistently *pacem–ueniam*, never *ueniam–pacem*. Subsequent editions – Kenney's second edition and Ramírez de Verger's Teubner – duly print *pacem ueniamque*. But I suspect that, without the support of the Berlin manuscript, that superior reading would have continued to languish: McKeown tells me that he would have printed it even if it were only a reading of the *recentiores*, but he also admits that he only began to search for it among later manuscripts – where it is widely attested – after its appearance in the Hamilton manuscript had been recorded. Neither Kenney in his first edition nor Munari in his edition had even recorded it as a variant.[36]

Deciding when to adopt a reading from later manuscripts is one of the most difficult choices an editor makes. In an open tradition, any reading found in later manuscripts that is not impossible on grounds of form or sense must be regarded as potentially authentic and evaluated on its merits.[37] That being said, in the case of a text represented by a large number of early manuscripts (i.e., manuscripts from the ninth to the eleventh centuries), it seems reasonable to require that a reading attested only in later witnesses should be arguably superior to the reading(s) of earlier sources in order to be adopted. A clear-cut measure of superiority is whether the editor would be willing to adopt the reading in question if it were a conjecture rather than a manuscript variant.[38]

---

[35] Munari (1965).

[36] Munari's edition was first published in 1951. The preface to the fourth edition (1964) anticipated a thorough revision to take account of the Hamiltonianus, but this never took place, for 'motivi editoriali e professionali' (preface to 1970 reprint).

[37] I stated the point too narrowly when I wrote *à propos* the tradition of Lucan that 'an editor must regard any reading or variant not an obvious blunder that is found in one or more of the ninth- and tenth-century manuscripts as potentially ancient' (Tarrant (1983), 218). Reeve (2009), 151 correctly speculated that 'the restriction of date probably reflects ignorance of the many later manuscripts rather than anything established or assumed'.

[38] Another relevant factor is how often the *recentiores* offer superior readings; the more often that happens in a given tradition, the stronger will be the *prima facie* case for accepting a reading from the *recentiores* in any particular instance, provided that the reading or readings in question satisfy the criterion stated earlier.

A reading that seems to me to meet the required standard is found at *Met.* 8.876, in the grisly *dénouement* of Ovid's story of Erysicthon, when the hunger-maddened king has exhausted all sources of food and is about to begin devouring his own flesh. All older manuscripts read *uis tamen illa mali postquam consumpserat omnem | materiam dederatque graui noua pabula morbo* ('but when the power of the disease had used up all sustenance and had furnished new nourishment to his illness'). Taken literally, the clause beginning *dederatque* is in blatant contradiction to the previous statement; it can only stand if *dare pabula* is interpreted metaphorically ('furnish food', i.e., 'make a situation worse'), which seems hard to accept in a context where actual food is central. The problem is solved if we read *deerantque* for *dederatque*, making the second phrase a consequence of the first: 'but when the power of the disease had used up all sustenance and new nourishment was now lacking to his illness'. I was ready to print *deerantque* as a conjecture by Burman (which is how it had appeared in previous editions), but then it turned up as a correction in one twelfth-century manuscript and as the reading of several thirteenth-century manuscripts.

On the other hand, I consider the later reading *retractant* for *renarrant* in *Met.* 6.316 (discussed earlier, p. 59) arguably equal in plausibility to the earlier one, but not clearly superior to it. Applying a criterion of that kind calls for fine discrimination on the editor's part; such decisions are ones that a subsequent editor would probably want to revisit.

Even in the most orderly of traditions, the application of stemmatic reasoning is an exercise in judgement, not a set of mechanically determined steps; in less tidy traditions the recourse to editorial judgement becomes still more important. For all its uncertainties, however, recension is the part of an editor's work on which agreement is easiest to secure; much more controversial is the next stage, *emendatio*, to which we now turn.

Establishing the text 2: conjecture

'Till I have a letter from Colonel Campbell', said she, in a voice of forced calmness, 'I can imagine nothing with any confidence. It must be all conjecture'. 'Conjecture – aye, sometimes one conjectures right, and sometimes one conjectures wrong. I wish I could conjecture how soon I shall make this rivet quite firm'.

(Jane Austen, *Emma*, ch. 28)

In the subject of conjecture, several themes that have emerged in previous chapters – the absence of certainty in textual studies, the lack of consensus among critics, and the role played by persuasion – reach a joint culmination. No other aspect of textual criticism divides scholars so sharply. Unlike the disagreements I discussed in Chapter 1, which relate specifically to the present state of classical studies, divergent views of conjecture and its practitioners have been held for centuries.

To begin, a terminological note. Some writers use 'conjecture' and 'emendation' interchangeably, whereas others distinguish conjectures, which may be thought correct or not, from emendations, defined strictly as successful conjectures. I prefer 'conjecture' for the sake of transparency, and also because 'emendation' implies that there is a textual flaw that needs correction, which is often precisely the point at issue.[1]

---

[1] The distinction that is sometimes made between *emendatio ope codicum* (emendation on the basis of manuscripts) and *emendatio ope ingenii* (emendation on the basis of conjecture) only applies in a pre-stemmatic environment where what is being emended is a *vulgata* the sources of which are not subject to analysis. If an editor believes that a manuscript reading is both authentic and preserved as part of the paradosis, then adopting it is an act of *selectio* rather than *emendatio*; if, on the other hand, an authentic reading found in a manuscript or manuscripts is thought to be a conjecture, then there is no significant difference between it and a conjecture made by a modern scholar.

Outstanding ability in conjecture has usually been a necessary qualification for heroic status, with the notable exception of Lachmann, whose
achievements in the area of recension would have earned him a place of
honour in the history of classical scholarship even if he had never made
a conjecture. In the case of other heroic critics such as Scaliger, Bentley,
Housman, or Shackleton Bailey, what has impressed their admirers
above all else has been their ability to generate striking conjectures in
abundance.

Among connoisseurs, the qualities of conjectures and their authors are
debated with something of the same passion and familiarity that baseball
fans or opera buffs bring to their favourite performers. A. S. Gratwick in
his commentary on Plautus *Menaechmi* 867 speaks of 'an untypically poor
conjecture of Dousa sen<ior>', as one might refer to 'an uncharacteristi-
cally dull rendition by Callas'.[2] Michael Reeve, in a memoir of the late Josef
Delz, recommends a number of conjectures that in his view give 'the flavour
of Delz in top form'.[3] Underlying such appreciations is the fact that all the
great conjectural critics have a distinctive style: Scaliger is characterized by
brilliance, Heinsius by elegance, Bentley by clarity and strong good sense,
Madvig and Housman by subtlety. But Shackleton Bailey makes the good
point that the most successful conjectures transcend individuality, and that it
is more often precisely in their shortcomings that we can recognize the individual traits of a critic, for example, Madvig's want of elegance, Heinsius'
excessive elegance, and so on.[4]

But the image of the hyperconfident maker of conjectures has also
provoked resistance and mockery. A classic example is Pope's attack on
Bentley in *The Dunciad* in the figure of Martinus Scriblerus, who cites
the opening three lines of the *Aeneid* as an occasion to propose three ludi-
crous conjectures. 'First, *oris* should be read *aris*, it being, as we see in
Aen. ii.513, from the *altar* of *Jupiter Hercaeus*, from which Aeneas fled
as soon as he saw Priam slain. In the second line, I would read *flatu* for
fato, since it is most clear it was by *Winds* that he arrived at the *shore* of
Italy. *Jactatus*, in the third, is surely as improperly applied to *terris*, as
proper to *alto*; to say a man *is tost on land*, is much at one with saying *he
walks at sea. Risum teneatis amici?* Correct it, as I doubt not it ought to
be, *vexatus'*.[5]

Even conjectural critics' own accounts of their work have their alienating
features, such as the obvious pleasure they take in their mysterious gift ('the

---

[2] Gratwick (1993a), 219. [3] Reeve (2008), 381.
[4] Shackleton Bailey (1982), 105–6. [5] Note on *Dunciad* 1.1.

secret of divination'[6]) or the assurance with which they divide scholars into sheep and goats, critics and non-critics.

For that reason, it is refreshing when a conjectural critic speaks about the enterprise in plain language. A fine example of this rare type is Robin Nisbet's 'How Textual Conjectures Are Made', a down-to-earth retrospective by an outstanding critic (or, in his own modest description, 'one textual critic, some of whose conjectures have been accepted by some people other than himself').[7] Nisbet claims no theoretical basis for his account and makes no pretence of being comprehensive, but he does provide an insight into a critic's thinking, and by reconstructing the background to several of his own proposals he sheds light on what is probably the most mystifying element of conjecture for an outsider: how a critic comes to believe that a text is corrupt. He recalls, for example, that a student on an exam paper, faced with the phrase *quo iure, quo ore?* from Cicero's second *Philippic* (2.103), translated it as 'by what right, by what authority?' Nisbet realized that, while 'authority' was an impossible rendering of *ore*, it did supply the sense needed to balance *iure*. At that point, 'it took only a few seconds to think of *quo more*, "by what precedent"', and a look at Merguet's lexicon to Cicero turned up five passages in which *quo more* is combined with *quo iure* or *quo exemplo*, or both.[8] Nisbet published the conjecture in 1960; I would regard it as a virtually certain emendation, but it is not even mentioned in Shackleton Bailey's edition of the *Philippics*, published in 1986.[9]

No archetype of a classical text is free of readings that cannot be attributed to the author. Conjecture is therefore not an arbitrary intervention on the part of critics, but is essential if we are to advance beyond the archetype in the direction of the lost original. The first six books of Tacitus' *Annals*, transmitted in a single manuscript that is therefore also the archetype, furnish hundreds of examples of readings that cannot be original: nonexistent forms such as *nuina* for *numina* or *deformides* for *deformis*, or garbling of securely attested proper names such as *Vipstania* for *Vipsania* or *Vibimus* for *Vibius*. Even the most conservative editor would not hesitate to accept the corrections of those and similar errors made by sixteenth-century critics.

---

[6] Shackleton Bailey (1982), 108.

[7] Nisbet (1991), 67.   [8] Nisbet (1991), 68.

[9] The reading *quo iure, quo ore* found in most editions is attested by only one of the two branches of the manuscript tradition; the other branch, represented by the oldest manuscript, has the obviously corrupt *quo iure quore*. The most recent editor of the *Philippics*, Giuseppina Magnaldi, brackets *quore*, leaving *quo iure* uncomfortably isolated.

It is one thing to show in general terms that some degree of conjecture will always be needed. One can also secure agreement that the transmitted texts of some authors are in greater need of conjectural emendation than others: all critics would admit that the manuscripts of Catullus, being late and probably deriving from a single ancient copy, are more corrupt than those of Horace. One cannot edit Catullus without either adopting several hundred conjectures or littering the text with obeli; one can edit Horace with virtually no recourse to conjecture, as Istvan Borzsák did in his Teubner edition, although it might not be advisable to do so.[10] But the specific level of conjecture required will always be an area of contention; even more so will be deciding whether conjecture is called for in a particular case. In the words of Gary Taylor, co-editor of the Oxford Shakespeare, 'we know that every early printed edition of Shakespeare's plays is more or less diseased; every compositor and every scribe commits errors. Corruption somewhere is certain; where, is uncertain'.[11]

Scholars leery of conjecture can point to the fact that, of the uncountable conjectures that have been made in the texts of the Greek and Latin classics since the Renaissance, only a minute proportion have found support from anyone except their makers. Roger Dawe's repertory of conjectures on Aeschylus records about 20,000 proposals made between the 1890s and the early 1960s. How many of them have a chance of being correct? Dawe's own guess was that 'I suppose 20 (0.1%) might be the estimate of a man who allowed cheerfulness to enliven a normally austere judgement'.[12] That minuscule success rate lends support to such pessimistic statements as Pasquali's dictum, '*emendatio* can only succeed in exceptional cases'.[13]

---

[10] It would not be unjust to say of Borzsák, as Housman said of an editor of Manilius, that he has 'a relish for the uncouth and is not dismayed by the hideous' (1903), xxii; instances of the latter are the forms *gragi* (for *cragi*) and *dragmis*. The fact that a description published in 1903 fits an editor a century later casts light on Housman's practice of storing up denunciations of editorial vices for which he did not have particular targets in mind.

[11] Taylor and Wells (1987), 60. Although the scope for conjecture is obviously more limited when dealing with printed material than with texts preserved only in manuscripts, even editors of modern texts have to grapple with some of the same issues as their classical counterparts. McCue (2012) provides a lucid account of the factors to be weighed in considering conjectures in the poetry of T S. Eliot. He surveys a number of specimen cases and for each one calculates a score of probability based on the relative weight of arguments for and against the proposed change.

[12] Dawe (1965), 3. [13] Pasquali (1932), 479.

On the other hand, the number of successful conjectures in classical Latin texts is in the thousands, probably the tens of thousands. Three texts alone – Catullus, Propertius, and *Annals* I–VI of Tacitus – account for well over a thousand generally accepted corrections to the archetype made by scholars from 1500 onwards. A comprehensive tally would also include the corrections made by copyists before a text reached print; for example, the hundreds of good readings in Propertius or Catullus attributed anonymously to '*Itali*' or '*recc.*' (i.e., the scribes of fifteenth-century manuscripts).

In the foregoing paragraphs I have been using the term 'successful' to describe conjectures that have obtained wide agreement. Since no conjecture can ever be proven correct, the closest approach to proof is acceptance by the 'hermeneutic community' (in Stanley Fish's term), that is, subsequent editors of the author in question, also commentators and interpreters of that author over a substantial period of time. Even that degree of acceptance does not show that the conjecture is correct, only that it represents the most convincing attempt yet made to solve what is agreed to be a genuine textual problem. In principle, even the most long-established conjecture can be superseded by a superior suggestion or can be rendered superfluous by a persuasive defence of the transmitted text.

When it comes to individual conjectures, every critic will have her favourites.[14] Here are a few that in my opinion display the conjectural faculty at its most persuasive.

(1) In his speech of thanks to the emperor Julian at the start of his consulship in 362 CE, Claudius Mamertinus details the vices of Julian's predecessor:

> Ad fores eorum qui regiis cupiditatibus seruiebant <u>ternos</u> patriciae gentis uiros cerneres ab huiusmodi dedecore non imbri, non gelu, non amaritudine ipsius iniuriae deterreri; demissi iacentesque uix capita supra eorum qui precabantur genua tollebant.   (*Pan. Lat.* 3 (11).20.4)

> At the doorsteps of those who ministered to the royal lusts you could have seen men of patrician descent [*ternos*], not deterred from such disgrace by rain, cold, or the very bitterness of the injury to their pride; stooping and prostrate, they scarcely lifted their heads above the knees of those whom they supplicated.

The transmitted reading *ternos* cannot be correct, since no disgrace attaches to appearing in groups of three. Of the many conjectures the passage has

---

[14] Conte (2013) is a collection of favourite conjectures, 'a repast of critical masterpieces that have elicited my admiration' (vii).

attracted,[15] the neatest and most convincing is Lipsius' *cernuos* ('head down', 'bending low'), a word rare before the fourth century; it coheres well with the later description (*demissi iacentesque*), and Mamertinus might have intended the sound play in *cernuos ... cerneres*. First adopted in modern times in Mynors's OCT text (1964), *cernuos* has been accepted in the subsequent editions of Fedeli and Paladini (1976) and Lassandro (1992).[16]

(2) Tacitus records a rumour that Titus had been sent to Rome in order to be adopted by Galba.

> Augebat famam ipsius Titi ingenium quantaecumque fortunae capax, decor <or>is cum quadam maiestate, prosperae Vespasiani res, praesaga responsa, et inclinatis ad credendum animis loco ominum etiam <u>fortuna</u>.
>
> (*Histories* 2.1.2)

> The report gained a readier hearing from the nature of Titus himself, which was equal to any fortune, from his personal beauty and a certain majesty which he possessed, as well as from Vespasian's prospering affairs, from prophetic oracles, and even from <u>good fortune</u>, which by minds inclined to credulity was regarded as equivalent to omens.

Thus the transmitted text, with the correction of *decoris* to *decor oris* by Beatus Rhenanus. Hugo Grotius drew attention to the closing words of the passage and proposed the small but telling change of *fortuna* to *fortuita*: once men's minds were inclined to believe in Titus' imperial destiny, even chance events were construed as omens of his coming rule. The alteration removes a somewhat awkward repetition of *fortuna* in different senses within the same sentence and supplies a pointed contrast to the *praesaga responsa* ('prophetic oracles'). All modern editions and commentaries adopt *fortuita*.[17]

(3) In *Aeneid* 10.703–6, Virgil narrates the death of the Trojan Mimas, a companion of Paris, 'whom Theano brought into the light fathered by Amycus, on the same night on which Cisseus' royal daughter [i.e., Hecuba], pregnant with a torch, gave birth to Paris; he lies in the city of his fathers, but the Laurentian shore holds Mimas, a stranger' (*una quem nocte Theano* | *in*

---

[15] For example, *crebros* (Baehrens), *celsos* (Fuchs), *intectos* (Arntzen). Novák deleted the word.

[16] The passage has special meaning for me because I can recall the excitement with which Roger Mynors spoke of Lipsius' conjecture and the pleasure he derived from having placed it in his text.

[17] Perhaps even more impressive is Grotius' conjuring of *similtudine* from *militum* in Tac. *Agr.* 46.2. On those and other Grotian conjectures in Tacitus, see Damon (2008).

lucem genitore Amyco dedit et face praegnas | *Cisseis regina Parim creat;*
urbe paterna | *occubat, ignarum Laurens habet ora Mimanta*). In the trans-
mitted text cited, the subject of *occubat*, who must be Paris, is not named,
an awkwardness already noted by ancient commentators. Among attempts
at conjecture the most brilliant and economical is Bentley's *Paris* for *creat*,
accepted by most modern editors. Line 705 would then read *Cisseis regina
Parim; Paris urbe paterna*, and the corruption would be explained as follows: by a common scribal error (haplography), the second occurrence of the
name Paris was omitted in an early copy, leaving the line metrically defec-
tive; the gap was then filled with the verb *creat* (to account for the accusative
Parim) by someone who failed to see that *dedit in lucem* ('brought into the
light') governed both *quem*, that is, Mimas, and *Parim*.[18]

Corruptions of this kind, resulting from the omission of a word or words
and their replacement to fill an obvious gap, are especially hard to emend,
since the lost word or words need bear no resemblance to the transmitted
text. (See further below, pp. 78–9.)

(4) A description of a rustic festival:

Cernis ut attrito diffusus cortice fagus
annua uota ferat sollemnesque incohat aras?   (*Ecl. Eins.* 2.15–16)

Do you see how the beech-tree, spreading with its well-worn bark,
bears its annual offerings and begins the accustomed worship at the altar?

Thus the unique manuscript that preserves the eponymously named
Einsiedeln Eclogues, plausibly dated to the reign of Nero. The image of the
beech tree approaching the altar with its gifts may have a Birnam Wood-
like charm, but it is not likely to be what the poet wrote. Baehrens[19] saw

---

[18] See also Conte (2013), 76–8. The passage bears on the question of whether the manuscript tradition of the *Aeneid* descends from an archetype later than Varius' edition.
If Bentley's restoration is correct, the transmitted text is the product of both omission
and interpolation; that text could not have stood in Virgil's manuscript, and it is hard
to attribute it to the text as edited by Varius, but is equally difficult to imagine several
ancient scribes or readers independently producing it. (It is noteworthy that the only two
places where modern editors agree that lines have been misplaced in all manuscripts
occur within a short distance of this passage, at 10.661–5 and 714–18.) Evidence like
this lends support to the hypothesis of descent from an archetype.

[19] Emil Baehrens (1848–88), an erratic but often brilliant conjectural critic, may be the
most striking example of the precociousness of heroic editors: by the time he was thirty,
he had published editions of the *Panegyrici Latini*, Valerius Flaccus, Statius' *Siluae*,
Catullus, and Tibullus. For an assessment, see Shackleton Bailey (1990).

that the context called for a description of the worshippers and consequently conjectured *pagus* for *fagus* and *caespite* for *cortice*: 'do you see how the villagers, spread out on the well-worn grass …?' Samuel Johnson wrote that 'The justness of a happy [i.e., successful] restoration strikes at once';[20] to my mind this is such a case. A subtlety of this conjecture highlights Baehrens's feeling for Latin: the meaning of *pagus* involved, 'the village' in the sense of its inhabitants (as in 'the whole village came to their wedding'), is not found before the post-Augustan period, with the exception of a stanza of Horace *Odes* 3.18 that has recently been called into question as a possible interpolation.[21]

As that example indicates, one of the challenges to conjecture in Latin is that the proposed change must not only yield an appropriate sense but must also be consistent with the idiom of the author, the genre, and the period in question. One of the strengths of Nicolas Heinsius as a conjectural critic was his intimate familiarity with Latin poetry from the Augustan period to the end of Antiquity, but that same wide range could sometimes lead him to propose corrections better suited to the writing of another time: some of his conjectures in Ovid, for example, seem somewhat too late in style to be convincing.[22]

Most conjectures entail some verbal alteration, but sometimes the original can be recovered simply by altering the punctuation. The episode of Baucis and Philemon in *Metamorphoses* Book 8 begins with a description of the devoted old couple and their humble dwelling. In recent editions, we read *parua quidem stipulis et canna tecta palustri,* | *sed pia Baucis anus parilique aetate Philemon* | *illa sunt annis iuncti iuuenalibus, illa* | *consenuere casa* (630–3 'a small <house> to be sure, thatched with straw and marsh reeds, but pious old Baucis and Philemon, in age equal to her, were joined in that house in younger years and in it grew old together'). The sense is tolerable, but *sed* seems to lack point, which ought to arouse suspicion. Rudolf Ehwald alertly introduced a semicolon after *pia*, giving the lines a new meaning: *parua quidem stipulis et canna tecta palustri,* | *sed pia; Baucis anus* etc. ('a small <house> to be sure, thatched with straw and marsh reeds, but pious; old Baucis' etc.). With this punctuation *parua quidem* is balanced by *sed pia* and the old age of both Baucis and Philemon is underscored by parallel descriptors (*anus – parili aetate*). At one point I was convinced that

---

[20] Johnson (1968), 109.

[21] See Cucchiarelli (2012); see also p. 91.

[22] Examples in Tarrant (1989).

Ehwald's conjecture was right, but I did not adopt it in my published text; I now regret that decision.[23]

The stylistic sensitivity required for successful conjecture can be honed by close study of Latin authors, but it also calls for a measure of innate talent. Conservatives and sceptics agree that conjecture has a creative aspect; in Nisbet's delightful epigram, 'textual critics are like poets on a very small scale'.[24] Timpanaro speaks of an intuitive, 'artistic' element for which no amount of linguistic or historical knowledge is an adequate substitute, citing Friedrich Leo and Eduard Norden as eminent Latinists who were nonetheless mediocre or poor conjectural critics.[25]

It is too soon to predict how many of Shackleton Bailey's 2,000 plus conjectures will find a place in the texts of the future, but I would be surprised if the number was much smaller than 200 (with many more destined to live on in various apparatuses).[26] A batting average of .100 will not get one into the Hall of Fame in Cooperstown, but for a textual critic in the second half of the twentieth century, making 200 successful conjectures is an extraordinary accomplishment.

A subset of conjectures consists of those which were later found to be the readings of manuscript witnesses. Thus many conjectural corrections were made to the text of Tacitus' *Histories* before the discovery of the oldest witness to the text, the 'Second Medicean' manuscript (Laurentianus plut. lat. 68.2). In such cases it is often said that the conjecture has been 'confirmed' by the manuscript evidence; I use scare quotes because 'confirm' seems too clear-cut a term, and also a potential question-begging one. Medieval scribes and readers were capable of correcting at least some errors, and so

---

[23] Conte (2013) devotes a chapter to conjectures of this kind (9–28; for this passage, see 15). Among his other examples, I especially like J. C. Jahn's repunctuation of *Am.* 3.9.37, usually given as *uiue pius: moriere pius. cole sacra: colentem*, etc., to read *uiue pius: moriere. pius cole sacra: colentem*. Kenney and Ramírez de Verger register Jahn's repunctuation, but neither adopts it. McKeown (1987) punctuates as does Jahn, but has no entry in his apparatus.

[24] Nisbet (1991), 68.

[25] Timpanaro (1953), 96; similarly Pasquali (1932), 479.

[26] Shackleton Bailey's conjectures in Cicero have fared well with several subsequent editors: Watt (1982) accepted twenty-nine of his proposals in the *Epistulae ad familiares*, Rizzo (1991) adopted fifty-five of his readings in just the first five books of the *Epistulae ad Atticum*, and the revision of his *Philippics* by Manuwald and Ramsey (2009) retains sixty-four of his conjectures. (Magnaldi (2008), however, accepts only eight, and in many places offers her own alternative solutions.) Especially striking alterations include *scire* for *Cicero* in *Fam.* 8.13.2 and *lacrimans* for *criminans* in *Att.* 4.15.4.

finding a reading in a manuscript does not in itself mean that the reading is traditional rather than the product of medieval conjecture. A persuasive example of a conjecture subsequently confirmed by a manuscript is Juvenal 15.7–8 *illic aeluros ... uenerantur* ('there' [i.e., in Egypt] 'they worship cats'). The word *aeluros* was conjectured by Jean Brodeau in 1555, and is a clearly correct solution to a corruption involving false word division combined with scribal unfamiliarity with the rare word *aelurus*: *illic aeluros* became *illicaeruleos* (the reading of the oldest manuscript, P), which was then 'corrected' to *illic caeruleos* (the reading of most other manuscripts). The word *aeluros* was later found in Vatican Urb. lat. 661, an eleventh-century manuscript in Beneventan script.[27] This reading is very unlikely to be a conjecture, since hardly any medieval reader would have known the word *aelurus*. It could, strictly speaking, be a lucky error, but to insist on that possibility would be carrying caution too far.[28]

Conjectures do not need to be successful to have value. Conjectures that point to a difficulty in the transmitted text without providing a fully convincing correction are sometimes called 'diagnostic' (a term coined by Paul Maas). The application of the term is a matter of perspective: what the author of a conjecture considers a sure cure may be thought of by others as no more than diagnostic. One of Robin Nisbet's examples strikes me as an excellent diagnostic conjecture. Catullus 22 describes one Suffenus, an untalented poet who publishes his wretched work in luxurious editions. Lines 6–7 appear as follows in most modern texts: *cartae regiae, noui libri,* | *noui umbilici ...* ('royal sheets [of papyrus], new books, new knobs'). Nisbet professed himself puzzled by *noui libri*, which refers to the work as a whole and is therefore not parallel to the surrounding phrases, which specify particular physical features. He conjectured *bibli* ('papyrus', genitive of *biblus*), a feminine noun which would seem to require a further change to *nouae* – except for the fact that V, the Catullan archetype, in fact reads *noue* (= *nouae*). With his conjecture, *cartae regiae nouae bibli* form a single phrase: 'royal sheets of new papyrus'. The proposal is highly intelligent, and it is easy to see how

[27] The Beneventan writing zone (which includes the abbey of Monte Cassino) is the source of a number of rare texts or forms of texts. Another Beneventan manuscript is the sole source of the Oxford fragment of Juvenal's sixth satire.
[28] The passage prompted Housman's diatribe against the *Thesaurus linguae Latinae* for not citing the Juvenal passage as an attestation of *aelurus* because 'in Germany in 1902 the inspired text of Juvenal was the text of Buecheler's second edition' (Housman (1931), lv–lvi). As Tom Keeline points out to me, according to the *TLL*'s own policies *aeluros* should have been cited as a variant. On this passage of Housman, see p. 32.

74

the rare *bibli* could have been altered to the more common *libri*, but doubts remain: *cartae regiae* in itself denotes writing material of the highest quality, after which a reference to 'new papyrus' seems not to add anything, and the point of *nouae*, that the papyrus is fresh and has not been previously written on, was already made in the words preceding the problem lines, *nec sic ut fit in palimpseston | relata* ('and not, as often happens, copied onto a reused surface'). But Nisbet's objection to the transmitted text is still valid, and one might add to the grounds for suspicion the inert repetition in *noui libri, noui umbilici*.[29]

Even a conjecture that is judged a failure can have a positive effect if the process of evaluating it results in an improved understanding of the text in question.[30] Paolo Fedeli has wisely observed that the harm done by a mistaken conjecture is less than that produced by accepting a text without reflection.[31]

On the methodological level, two diametrically opposed positions with respect to conjecture continue to be maintained.

At one extreme is the view that it is illegitimate to employ conjecture if the transmitted text can be made to yield an intelligible sense, or, in other words, that conjecture is only to be used when the transmitted text is obviously corrupt. That position is logically analogous to the precept that the best manuscript is to be followed wherever its readings make sense, and is therefore vulnerable to the same objection on grounds of probability.[32] But here it is, fresh as a daisy – as Housman might have said – in the pages of *RFIC* for 2005: 'I believe, though, that it is the common view that the intervention of textual criticism is justified only by its necessity; that is, that one should have recourse to it when, confronted by a certainly corrupt reading, it is absolutely necessary to intervene in order to make the text intelligible'.[33] In the light of an earlier discussion (see pp. 25–6), it is noteworthy that the writer not only

---

[29] Trappes-Lomax (2007), 76–7 advocates deleting lines 6–8, which he calls 'hopeless' and 'patently unworthy of Catullus'. With 6–8 removed, *nec sic ut fit in palimpsesto* is the only description of the physical appearance of Suffenus' publications, and that seems too unspecific to have the needed bite.

[30] For a recent example see Conte (2013), 53–4, rejecting my deletion of *Met.* 2.226.

[31] Fedeli (1998), 276.

[32] See pp. 60–1. The anonymous reader objected to my analogy on the grounds that 'identifying the "best MS" is inevitably subjective or question-begging; identifying a place where the transmitted text can only be construed through a brick wall is not'. But subjectivity is not so easily evaded: what a sceptical critic calls a brick wall could look like a picture window to a conservative.

[33] Salvadore (2005), 482.

subscribes to this position, but also speaks as though it were generally held; in fact, no English-speaking critic today could express such a view without incurring ridicule.[34]

Scholars averse either to particular conjectures or to the activity in general often describe a conjecture as 'unnecessary', a move that implies, even if it does not explicitly subscribe to, the position just mentioned. We may recall the example of Ovid *Am.* 1.2.21, where all modern editors had cheerfully printed *ueniam pacemque* – a reading that makes perfect sense – until an early witness appeared with a better reading, *pacem ueniamque*. It seems almost certain that if Heinsius, for example, had conjectured *pacem ueniamque*, conservative critics would have dismissed the proposal as elegant but unnecessary.[35]

Even some conservative critics would agree that there are times when it is legitimate to accept a conjecture, although the transmitted text is not obviously corrupt. Timpanaro adduces the presence of a close parallel, preferably in the same author, as a factor that can make a conjecture seem convincing. (He even speaks of parallels as providing confirmation or a guarantee, whereas I would prefer to say that they shift the calculus of probability in favour of a conjecture.[36]) An instructive example is Ovid, *Amores* 2.4.11–12, part of a passage in which Ovid says that he is equally attracted by modest and by forward women. Most manuscripts read *siue aliqua est oculos in me deiecta modestos,* | *uror et insidiae sunt pudor ille meae* ('or if some woman has cast her chaste eyes down at me, I am on fire and that modesty of hers lays a trap for me'). The general sense is acceptable, but *in me* prompts two reservations: first, a truly modest Roman maiden would not look at a man at all, and second, why are the woman's eyes 'cast down' (*deiecta*)? At least two manuscripts have the variant *in se* ('at herself'), which has been widely accepted and supported by Ovidian passages describing women modestly gazing into their lap (e.g., *Am.* 1.8.37 *cum bene deiectis gremium spectabis ocellis* 'when you look into your lap with eyes properly cast down'). That reading removes both objections to *in me*, and its only drawback is that it is not sufficiently specific: 'to look down at oneself' does not necessarily

---

[34] When E. J. Kenney incautiously stated that 'the transmitted text ... may be altered only when it is *demonstrably* faulty' (1974, 113–14, his italics), he was fortunate to get off with a mild reproof from Shackleton Bailey (1976b, 186 'the only point of critical theory in the book with which I cannot wholly agree'), who cited a lovely example from Cicero *Fam.* 9.16.8, where the transmitted reading (*matris tuae*) is not demonstrably faulty but a conjecture (*Matris tui*) is nonetheless clearly correct.

[35] West (1973), 55–6 cites a similar example from Euripides' *Hippolytus*.

[36] Timpanaro (1953), 98.

suggest looking down into one's lap. Timpanaro brilliantly conjectured *in humum* ('to the ground'), for which there are even closer parallels elsewhere in Ovid, among them *Am.* 3.6.67 *illa oculos in humum deiecta modestos* ('she, casting her chaste eyes towards the ground'). The conjecture was anticipated by Heinsius,[37] and while the fact that a conjecture has independently occurred to more than one critic cannot count as proof of its correctness, it may heighten its attraction.[38] The reception of the conjecture in subsequent editions of the *Amores* shows how hard it is to draw the line between an appealing, but unnecessary, change and a compelling alteration: Munari, who had defended *in me* in his first edition of 1951, adopted *in humum* in subsequent editions; Ramírez de Verger, an avowed admirer of Heinsius, also accepted *in humum*, while Kenney, as close to a true moderate in his editorial practice as it is possible to be, printed *in se* in both his 1961 edition and in the 1994 revision.

At the other end of the spectrum are critics who feel free to adopt any conjecture that in their view improves the text, even if the transmitted text makes good sense and has been generally regarded as sound.[39] That outlook has traditionally been associated with Anglo-Saxon critics such as Bentley and Housman and their more recent successors, for example, Shackleton Bailey, but some of the most freewheeling conjectural critics at the moment have emerged from scholarly traditions that had long been highly conservative: Gauthier Liberman in France, Giancarlo Giardina in Italy, and Antonio Ramírez de Verger in Spain. This position is not often stated openly, but Trappes-Lomax formulates an explicit policy in his guiding dictum: *si melius est, Catullianum est* ('if it is better, it is what Catullus wrote').[40] An extreme (and admittedly unfair) example of this neo-scepticism is the attempt by Giardina to emend *Veneris* to *Cereris* in Catullus 68A.9–10: *id gratum est mihi, me quoniam tibi dicis amicum,* | *muneraque et Musarum hinc petis*

[37] His note offers a fine specimen of Heinsian rhetoric (on which, see pp. 46–7): *argute et, si quid iudico, vere Iunianus cum Jureti Excerptis, in se deiecta … nisi quis hic quoque mallet,* oculos in humum deiecta ('Junius' manuscript and the excerpts of Juretus cleverly and, if I have any judgment, correctly read *in se deiecta* … unless someone might prefer to read *oculos in humum deiecta* here as well [as in *Am.* 3.6.67]'.

[38] Nisbet (1991), 88 goes a step further: 'such anticipations are a disappointment to all but the most generous temperaments, but they increase the chances that an idea might be right'.

[39] Nisbet himself in a rare rhetorical flight comes close to endorsing that position: 'even if it scans and makes a vague sort of sense, we must have a higher conception of classical perfection than what satisfied a fourth-century *grammaticus*' (1991), 90.

[40] Trappes-Lomax (2007), 1.

et Veneris ('this pleases me, because you say that you are my friend, and because you ask of me the gifts of the Muses and of Venus/Ceres').[41] With Giardina's conjecture, Catullus' addressee would have asked him for two favours, poetry (*munera Musarum*) and a piece of bread (*munera Cereris*). Somewhere Martinus Scriblerus is smiling in approval.[42]

Responsible critical practice falls somewhere between accepting the paradosis in all cases where it can be construed and making conjectures simply because an alternative can be imagined, but more specific guidelines are difficult to formulate. One criterion often applied in assessing conjectures is palaeographical plausibility, that is, whether the conjectured reading is close enough in appearance to the transmitted reading(s) as to make the postulated miscopying easy to explain. A conjecture that presupposes a frequent sort of scribal error will obviously be more persuasive than one requiring a more unusual or complex explanation, but scribes are not so obliging as to limit their mistakes to the most common and easily detected varieties, and so palaeographical plausibility can never be either an absolute requirement or a sufficient justification for a conjecture. One of the most plausible conjectures ever made from a palaeographical standpoint is Rossberg's *sancimus* for the transmitted *sanamus* in Propertius 4.7.69 *sic mortis lacrimis uitae sanamus/sancimus amores* ('so with the tears of death we heal/confirm the loves of life'): *ci* could very easily be misread as *a* in certain pre-Caroline and early Caroline minuscule scripts, and it is not at all implausible that the archetype of the Propertian tradition was written in a script of that type. Several recent editors have printed *sancimus*, but it seems to me both less euphonious and less meaningful than *sanamus*.[43]

A type of error that entirely negates the value of palaeographical factors is the omission of a word or words (often because of a repetition or other form of similarity) followed by their replacement with words of equivalent sense but quite different appearance. Housman amassed a large number of instances in the preface to his edition of Manilius I; one of his examples is Ovid *Met.* 6.374–6, describing the Lycian farmers after their transformation into frogs: *sed nunc quoque turpes | litibus excercent linguas pulsoque pudore, | quamuis sint sub aqua, sub aqua maledicere temptant* ('even now they exercise their foul tongues in quarrelling; with no shame, although they

---

[41] Giardina (2007), 182–3.

[42] Equally gratuitous is Giardina's proposal (2006) to emend *per amica silentia lunae* ('through the friendly silence of the moon') in *Aen.* 2.225 to *silentia noctis* ('the silence of the night') – a combination for which many parallels can, not surprisingly, be cited. Giardina's editions of Propertius will be discussed in Chapter 6.

[43] See pp. 118–19.

are under water, under water they try to utter curses'). Two major manuscripts read *linguis* ('with their tongues') in place of the second *sub aqua* ('under water'), which had been omitted by haplography. Here the correct reading is preserved in several older manuscripts, but if *linguis* were the unanimously transmitted reading, attempts to emend it with a word or words of similar appearance would be doomed to failure.[44] Housman wrote that 'Heinsius and Bentley would instantly have perceived that this superfluous and point-less *linguis* was not Ovid's, and they would both have conjectured … <sub aqua>'.[45] That may be placing too much confidence in their admittedly great powers of conjecture, but even a lesser critic might have realized that *linguis* was improbably flat after *linguas* in the previous line.

A related question is whether the proposer of a conjecture must be able to plausibly to account for the loss of the purported original reading. Here too the issue is best framed not in terms of legitimacy or validity, but of persuasion. Inability to explain how a given corruption occurred does not invalidate a conjecture, but it will usually make it harder for the conjecture to gain acceptance.[46]

A case in point: the extensive transpositions that have been proposed in the text of Propertius.[47] It is not at all unlikely that the Propertian arche-type – a manuscript copied with no great care or skill – contained a number of misplaced couplets, and that attempts to correct those dislocations in sub-sequent copies generated further displacements. James Butrica documented numerous transpositions in extant manuscripts: most are at short distances (within an elegy or between contiguous elegies), and the exceptions gener-ally involve the movement of larger blocks of text caused by a mistaken arrangement of folios. Hardest to explain are a few cases of a line or lines appearing far from their proper place. In one instance (3.1.2 inserted between 4.4.1 and 4.4.2) the link must be the appearance of *nemus* ('grove') in both passages; in the other two (1.16.11–13 between 2.3.26 and 27 and 4.9.31 between 1.5.2 and 3) there is no obvious cause.[48]

Some of the transpositions proposed by modern editors assume altera-tions that go far beyond what mere carelessness and botched efforts at cor-rection could be expected to produce.[49] The most conspicuous example is

---

[44] See also earlier text, pp. 70–1, on Virgil *Aen.* 10.703–6.

[45] Housman (1903), lx.

[46] Similarly West (1973), 58: 'a conjecture which presupposes an inexplicable corruption is not necessarily false, but it is not fully convincing'.

[47] Other aspects of the editing of Propertius will be considered in Chapter 6.

[48] Butrica (1997), 189–97.

[49] Butrica himself thought that 'any proposed transposition … should be explicable in terms of recognized types of dislocation' (1997), 195.

elegy 3.7 on the death by drowning of Paetus. In Stephen Heyworth's OCT edition, the sequence of lines is as follows: 1–8, 29–36, 19–20, 37–42, 47–50, 53, 52, 51, 54, 55–64, 17–18, 65–6, 43–6, 67–70, 13–16, 11–12, 9–10, 25–8, 71–2.[50] No fully worked out scenario is offered to account for the postulated shifts of couplets, and the only specific cause of dislocation adduced is the appearance of *Aquilo* at about the same point in the line in 13 and 71.[51] At the same time it must be acknowledged that the transmitted order of verses produces apparent breaks in continuity at several points. The alternatives to large-scale transposition are thus either to admit that the train of thought in this poem is disjointed to a degree unparalleled elsewhere in the author or to conclude that the poem is structured according to principles that have not yet been properly understood (e.g., Richard Thomas's hypothesis that Propertius is here stringing together a series of epigram-like units[52]).

In textual criticism as in jurisprudence, hard cases make bad law, and Propertius 3.7 may be too extreme an instance to provide a firm basis for broader methodological conclusions. As a general principle, though, one might suggest that, unless the progression of thought that results from transposition is so compelling as to appear unquestionably original, or unless the process by which the alleged dislocation(s) occurred is convincingly explained, or both, a critic who proposes numerous or extensive transpositions cannot expect to win widespread support.[53]

To conclude this chapter on an appropriately aporetic note, I will consider a few examples of a particularly thorny textual problem. In poetic texts, seemingly unemphatic repetition is a difficult phenomenon to weigh, both in choosing between manuscript variants and in deciding whether or not to adopt a conjecture: what is an acceptable repetition and what is the result of miscopying? One reason for the difficulty is that authorial attitudes towards repetition were not uniform; as Housman observed (oversimplifying somewhat), 'Horace was as sensitive to iteration as any modern; and those who choose to believe that he wrote *tutus bos etenim rura perambulat, nutrit rura Ceres*, which not even Lucan could have written, are as blind to truth as to beauty. Virgil was less sensitive, Ovid much less; Lucan was almost insensible, but not, like the scholars I speak of, quite'.[54]

---

[50] In addition to the transposed lines, Heyworth brackets 21–4 as either interpolated or belonging to another poem and posits a lacuna of one couplet between 16 and 11.

[51] Heyworth (2007b), 312.   [52] Thomas (2011).

[53] See also Tarrant (2006), 60–2.   [54] Housman (1926), xxxiii.

The passage of Horace (*Odes* 4.5.17–20) provocatively referred to by Housman provides a first test case. Horace is enumerating the blessings of Augustan peace:

> tutus bos etenim rura perambulat,
> nutrit rura Ceres almaque Faustitas,
> pacatum uolitant per mare nauitae,
> culpari metuit Fides

17 rura] prata *Faber*   18 rura] farra *Bentley*

The cow wanders safely over the fields,
Ceres and kind Fertility nourish the fields,
sailors speed over quieted seas,
Honor fears to incur blame.

The repetition of *rura* ('fields') in a conspicuous position does look awkward in a poet as careful about his choice of words as Horace; it also seems to mar the rhetorical structure of the stanza, in which each verse introduces a new aspect of peace. Shackleton Bailey retains the transmitted text, but expresses a measure of doubt by citing the conjectures *prata* ('meadows') and *farra* ('wheat'). The latter seems too specific, but *prata* is attractive for its sound in combination with *perambulat*, and its use to refer to cultivated land has a parallel elsewhere in the *Odes*, 3.18.11–12 *festus in pratis uacat otioso | cum boue pagus* ('the joyful villagers at ease in the meadows with resting oxen'), which can in fact be seen as a counterpart to the later passage.[55] The best defense I can think of for the repetition of *rura* is that its lameness is of a piece with the passage as a whole, arguably one of the most inert stanzas in the *Odes*.

Immediately before the remarks on poets' preferences quoted earlier Housman had described Bentley's attempt to weed out repetition in Lucan: 'he had conceived the design of expelling from the text those repetitions of the same word at a brief interval which are commoner in this poet than in any other; and, though he did his worst and waded knee-deep in carnage, he failed. They were too many for him; more than he could remove, more even than he could detect'.[56] Bentley's foiled efforts offer a useful guideline in weighing the need for conjecture: the more often conjecture will be required to remove a given phenomenon, the more carefully the critic

[55] Note, though, that these lines have been questioned as a possible interpolation by Cucchiarelli (2012).
[56] Housman (1926), xxxiii.

should consider the possibility that the phenomenon is part of the author's style, or at least would have been found allowable by the author. Like other guidelines, this one cannot be invoked without regard for individual cases. Two passages in the *Metamorphoses* that contain the same repetition will illustrate the point.

Juno takes away Callisto's ability to speak (*Met.* 2.482–3):

> neue preces animos et uerba precantia flectant,
> posse loqui eripitur

> 482 preces ... precantia *uix ferendum*   preces] querela
> *Watt 1995*   precantia (*cf. 14.365*)] rogantia *Schepper* : potentia
> *Burman* : querentia *Shackleton Bailey 1981*   neue truces a.
> per u. precantia flectat *Heinsius*

So that her [Callisto's] prayers and prayerful words might not sway her [Juno's] mind,
her power of speech is snatched away.

Circe formulates magical incantations to capture the love of Picus (*Met.* 14.365–6):

> concipit illa preces et uerba precantia dicit
> ignotosque deos ignoto carmine adorat

> precantia] uenefica *N²³ U P*: potentia *Slater* (*cf. 2.482*)

She utters prayers and speaks prayerful words,
and worships unknown gods with unknown incantations.

Although both passages contain the repetition *preces* and *uerba precantia* in the same line, I think the first justifies a higher degree of suspicion than the second; for that reason my apparatus note on 2.482 contains the editorializing comment 'uix ferendum' ('hardly to be tolerated'), absent in the note on 14.365.[57] The framing verbs *concipit* and *dicit* in the latter passage soften the effect of the repetition, and the clearly emphatic repetition in the following line (*ignotosque deos ignoto carmine*) makes it seem possible that the earlier repetition also has rhetorical point, perhaps evoking the style of Circe's incantations.[58]

---

[57] There is a subtle distinction between including a comment such as 'uix ferendum' in the apparatus and placing an obelus in the text; the former seemed preferable both for reasons of prudence and because the locus of corruption, if corruption exists, is not easily pinpointed.

[58] For Kenney (2002), 64 n. 228, however, the repetition in 14.365 seemed 'difficult to swallow'. On other problematic examples of repetition in Ovid, see Kenney (1972), 41.

Another passage of the *Metamorphoses* provides a good test of a critic's tolerance for repetition. Perseus comes upon the bodies of his men, killed by the serpent's poisonous breath (*Met.* 3.55–9):

> ut nemus intrauit letataque corpora uidit
> uictoremque super spatiosi corporis hostem
> tristia sanguinea lambentem uulnera lingua,
> 'aut ultor uestrae, fidissima corpora, mortis,
> aut comes' inquit 'ero'.

> 56 corporis] tergoris *Heinsius*: gutturis *Slater*
> 57 uulnera] corpora *BFG*   (*uersum om. H*)   58 corpora] pectora *Heinsius*

When he entered the grove and saw their dead bodies,
and above them the victorious enemy with its huge body
licking their wounds with its bloody tongue, 'most loyal bodies',
he said, 'I shall be either your avenger or your companion'.

All manuscripts give forms of *corpus* in the same position in three out of four lines, and some manuscripts in all four lines. It is hard to believe that Ovid would have used the same word so often in such close proximity and to no obvious rhetorical effect, but it is difficult to decide which of the instances to alter, and with what to replace them. Heinsius, displaying his usual aversion to repetition, conjectured *tergoris* ('back') for *corporis* in 56 and *pectora* ('hearts') for *corpora* in 58, producing a succession of non-repeating terms (*corpora/tergoris/uulnera/pectora*). I have followed him in the second case (partly because *fidissima pectora* ('most loyal hearts') can be paralleled elsewhere in the *Metamorphoses* (9.248–9 *pectora ... fida*), but not in the first; another attempt to replace *corporis*, Slater's *gutturis* ('gullet'), would be appropriate if the serpent were eating its victims, but that is not the case. I have allowed the repetition *corpora – corporis* in 55–6 to stand, in part because the use of the same word for both the victims and their slayer might carry some rhetorical weight.

We can never be sure that conjecture will bring us closer to the original, but not attempting to correct the texts we can reconstruct from existing manuscripts will ensure that we get no closer. As in many endeavours of life, there is no guarantee of success, but lack of trying does guarantee lack of success.[59] In a similar way, Don Fowler speaks of interpretation as the desire

---

In *Ars* 1.709–10 *uerba precantia* in the hexameter is followed by *preces* in the following pentameter.

[59] 'The vast majority of attempts to produce a "better" text are destined to win only temporary approval and are quickly forgotten. All the same, there is no alternative to taking

for a journey in search of a past that is irretrievably lost: 'the desire for that journey [as] simultaneously hopeless and necessary: hopeless, because the belief that there can be anything between desire and memory that we can talk about in language is just another example of our deluded pursuit of the lost presence of the imaginary, necessary because without desire there can be no beginning at all, no setting out on the journey'.[60]

the risk and *trying*, at least, to reach as accurate a view as possible of what ancient authors wrote' (Beard and Henderson (1995), 57).

[60] Fowler (2000), 217.

5

Establishing the text 3: interpolation, collaboration, and intertextuality

'Forgery' is no doubt a convenient term. Yet it should now be asked how far it is useful or correct. The word exudes an odour of personal guilt and criminal handiwork; the intent is to defraud or at the least to deceive; and notions of legal penalty or redress may not be far distant ... All in all, 'imposture' will often prove a more helpful designation than 'forgery' ... A large number of literary impostures in any age have been perpetrated without any serious purpose or hope of deceiving the reader ... Most important, a deed of deception may actually be intended to be seen through sooner or later.

(Syme (1983), 8)

The attempt to locate and remove interpolations – non-authorial matter that has made its way into a manuscript tradition – is essentially a subdivision of conjecture. To bracket as interpolated words that are transmitted in all manuscripts is on a par with printing a reading that is the product of editorial conjecture in place of the reading(s) of all manuscripts. For several reasons, though, the pursuit of interpolation has long been an especially contentious area of critical practice. For one thing, it involves a drastic intervention on the critic's part (especially if the alleged interpolation consists of whole lines of text), thereby raising in an acute form the tension between respecting the transmitted text and subjecting it to careful scrutiny. Even critics who accept the need for conjecture sometimes baulk at efforts to diagnose interpolation, all the more so when the text in question enjoys a privileged place in the canon. If, as I suggested in an earlier chapter, critical choices are justified to the degree that they can be made convincing, the decision to excise material transmitted in all manuscripts creates a particularly heavy burden of persuasion for a critic.

Another reason why the study of interpolation has been a site of dispute is that it has often proven difficult to practice in moderation, and its excesses have fuelled resistance to the enterprise as a whole. Quickness to suspect interpolation was a distinctive feature of the hyperscepticism that animated much textual criticism in the second half of the nineteenth century – the age of August Nauck's Euripides (see p. 34) – and an equally extreme aversion to interpolation was typical of the conservative reaction that followed. That pendulum swing may help to account for a curious aspect of twentieth-century critical practice. All the great critics of the heroic age – Scaliger, Heinsius, Bentley – were skilled interpolation-hunters (to use the slightly pejorative term often employed by opponents), but for them the diagnosing of interpolations was just one tool among several with which they went about the process of emendation. In the twentieth century, however, most of the outstanding practitioners of conjectural criticism were much less inclined to invoke interpolation – I am thinking primarily of Shackleton Bailey, but the statement applies almost as well to Housman[1] – while some of the most energetic hunters of interpolation were not nearly as distinguished as conjectural critics: the names of Günther Jachmann and Eduard Fraenkel come to mind, arguably also Fraenkel's mentor Friedrich Leo. Another factor at work may be a certain snobbery on the part of conjectural critics, a feeling that spotting interpolations is a poor second to producing original conjectures.[2]

A brief look at the modern editing of Ovid's *Metamorphoses* will demonstrate the widely divergent approaches taken with respect to interpolation. In Rudolf Merkel's 1875 Teubner text, more than 250 unanimously transmitted verses were athetized. In the succeeding Teubner edition by Rudolf Ehwald (1915), all but one of those verses were freed from suspicion, the lone exception being 6.294, and that single verse is also the only one bracketed in the succeeding Teubner edition, by W. S. Anderson (1977, 1981). In my OCT text, I have attempted to restore interpolation to the editor's armoury, bracketing a little more than 100 verses. It will be some time before the verdict of the scholarly community on my edition will have been rendered in full. (E. Talbot Donaldson once quipped that if Methuselah had taken up editing as a young man, he might have lived to see how his work had been received.[3]) But first indications are that my practice

---

[1] In his edition of Manilius, Housman accepted a number of Bentley's deletions and proposed several of his own, but he more frequently transposed verses or added lines to fill alleged lacunae.

[2] In his earliest published paper, Housman referred to the bracketing of a problematic stanza in Horace (*Odes* 3.11.17–20) as a 'coward's remedy' (1882), 190.

[3] Donaldson (1970), 14.

is being assessed very differently by critics of differing outlooks. The late Georg Luck, a vigorous proponent of conjectural criticism, rejected every one of my proposed bracketings and suggested that my pursuit of interpolation may have interfered with 'the business of editing' (a revealingly question-begging formulation).[4] Others have reacted more favourably. In the multi-volume text with commentary currently being published by the Fondazione Lorenzo Valla, the editor of Books 1–3, Alessandro Barchiesi, has agreed with my deletions in four out of fifteen passages, and the editor of Books 4–6, Gian Piero Rosati, has accepted three of the six atheteses I proposed in those books. E. J. Kenney adopts my bracketing in twenty-one of twenty-six passages in Books 7–9, and J. D. Reed does so in six of ten places in Books 10–12. Finally, Paolo Fedeli, in a probing review, has expressed agreement with roughly a quarter of my proposed deletions.[5] A conjectural critic who saw even a quarter of her proposals accepted by other scholars would be mightily pleased. The discussion will continue, but I am glad to have persuaded at least some of my colleagues that interpolation is a genuine phenomenon in this text.

Yet another cause of opposition to interpolation study is the rhetoric its practitioners have often employed, a language of falsification and forgery in which the critic 'unmasks' inauthentic accretions to the text. Even Heinsius, who was generally restrained in his rhetoric, used such loaded terms when dealing with interpolation, for example, his reference to a 'sciolus nescioquis' ('some smart alec') as the putative author of a verse he suspected.[6] At its most extreme, the view of interpolators that this language conjures up is one of a motiveless urge to defraud or to infiltrate the original text; even less highly charged terms such as 'Bearbeiter' (reviser, redactor) imply a process of reworking that is hard to relate to any believable set of historical circumstances, except in the case of theatrical texts, where revision for later performances does provide such a context. It is not surprising that critical operations that seem to presuppose such an unlikely form of behaviour have often been found unpersuasive.

To replace such loaded terminology, I have proposed a typology of interpolations that distinguishes three main categories: emendation, annotation, and collaboration. The first two are means of dealing with defects or obscurities in a text, whether real or imagined, and the reader who employs interpolation to that end may be said to perform the function of an editor or

[4] Luck (2005b), 271. [5] Fedeli (2007), 609.

[6] Note on 15.502; in his note on 15.570, Heinsius similarly refers to a 'clever trifler' ('argutus nugator'). See Tarrant (1999), 292.

commentator. The third category is an imaginative response to a text that enhances or amplifies it simply because it allows for further elaboration. The article in which I proposed that category was entitled 'The Reader as Author', and although I did not make the connection at the time, it would be possible to regard collaborative interpolation as a particularly active form of reader response.[7] I would now modify that typology to create a closer connection between interpolations intended to fill a gap in the text and collaborative interpolation; the latter can be understood as almost a subtype of the former, except that the perceived lacuna that is being filled is not syntactical but thematic: the text seems not to have exhausted the possibilities it raises, and so can appear as incomplete.

The first benefit of this terminology – and of the concept of collaborative interpolation in particular – is that it removes interpolation from the realm of forgery or impersonation to which it has often been assigned and seeks to understand it as a form of emulation.[8] The second advantage is that it is now possible to situate many interpolations in an ancient cultural setting, as products of a society that prized and taught imitation of admired models of expression, and one in which some degree of skill in verse composition was a much more common attainment than it has become in modern western societies. Looking at interpolation in that light may also help to explain why it is found much more often in poetry than in prose, even prose that might seem to lend itself to elaboration, such as Ciceronian oratory. Roman practices of rhetorical education gave much more scope to the emulation of prose than to verse; apart from occasional public poetry competitions, verse *aemulatio* was more likely to be an individual and private activity, and so one indulged in primarily by readers. That way of contextualizing interpolation may get some support from the fact that some of the favourite sites for collaborative interpolations in poetry are related to themes that

---

[7] See Tarrant (1987) and (1989). Canfora's (2002) image of the scribe as author is similar to my 'reader as author'. Canfora also comments (16–17) on the inadequacy of normal terminology in this area: 'we usually say that <the scribe> "interpolates", but in so doing we trivialize and cheapen the original intervention of the copyist, a delicate and disturbing occurrence'. A. E. Housman practised a mischievous form of collaborative interpolation in response to fatuous or sentimental poetry, entering sarcastic or deflating supplements in the margins of his books; see Burnett (1998).

[8] Gnilka (2000), 460 strenuously objected to the concept of collaborative interpolation, arguing that an interpolator is still a 'Fälscher', even if there was no intent to deceive. The attack has been renewed in a stronger form by Gnilka's student Markus Mülke (2008), (2010); on the former, see Zetzel (2010).

were popular in declamatory rhetoric, for example, elaborate *descriptiones locorum* or storms at sea.[9]

Having suggested an answer to the question 'who would make such interpolations?', we can now address the question 'how did they become embedded in the texts as transmitted in medieval copies?'

As we have seen, the transmission of classical Latin literature in the centuries from the end of Antiquity to the Carolingian revival was not an orderly or systematic process.[10] No coordinated attempt to pass on the major achievements of that literature would have countenanced the loss of the two greatest tragedies written in Latin, Ovid's *Medea* and Varius' *Thyestes*, or of most of Livy's history, or of large parts of Tacitus' *Annals* and *Histories*. For those authors fortunate enough to survive, the character of the manuscripts that preserved their works was in many cases similarly random and haphazard. (The major exception would be school authors such as Virgil and Terence, where the commentary tradition guaranteed some degree of stability.) Most medieval traditions of Latin classical texts had as their point of origin private copies, which must have varied widely in the care with which they were written and in the degree to which they had been annotated and, potentially, interpolated. In Antiquity, the categories of reader and critic were not distinct: much emendation was carried out by owners of books as part of the reading process.[11] It is a nice paradox that some ancient readers were both emenders and interpolators; furthermore, in cases where an interpolation was produced to fill a real or apprehended gap in a text, the two processes coalesced into one. James Zetzel has taken this line of argument a step further, suggesting that ancient readers were not much concerned to maintain the purity of an 'authorial' text and may therefore not have felt it necessary to distinguish between the text as transmitted and their individual refashioning of that text.[12] I would not go so far, but to the extent that Zetzel is right, the presence of interpolations in our medieval traditions becomes easier to explain.

Even if that set of cultural and historical hypotheses seems plausible in theory, is there any evidence that ancient and medieval readers engaged in the sort of interpolation I have described? Evidence of such activity is in fact not difficult to find.

---

[9] For the idea that interpolations are more frequently found in certain contexts than in others, see, e.g., Finglass (2006) on interpolations in curses in Greek tragedy.

[10] See p. 7.

[11] The late antique *subscriptiones* provide tangible evidence of that activity.

[12] See Zetzel (2005), 144–61, esp. 153–7.

Some interpolations can be confidently regarded as ancient, most obviously if they appear in an ancient source (whether a manuscript or a quotation). One of the supplements to incomplete lines in the *Aeneid*, for example, was known to Seneca, who in *Epist.* 94.28 cites the phrase *audentis fortuna iuuat* ('fortune helps the daring') from *Aen.* 10.284 with the lame conclusion *piger ipse sibi obstat* ('the lazy man gets in his own way').[13] Other interpolations in the *Aeneid* introduce lines from elsewhere in the poem. In *Aen.* 4.125–7, Juno explains to Venus the plan by which she will arrange for Dido and Aeneas to take refuge from the storm in a cave: *adero et, tua si mihi certa uoluntas,* | *conubio iungam stabili propriamque dicabo.* | *hic hymenaeus erit* ('I will be present and, if I can be sure of your agreement, I will join <her to him> in a lasting marriage and consecrate her <as his>; this will be their wedding'). Line 126 is identical to 1.73, in a speech of Juno to Aeolus promising him a beautiful nymph as his bride if he assists her. In its earlier appearance, the line is perfectly apt, but in Book 4 'it does not fit the context easily: "her to him" has to be supplied with *iungam*, and the sense of *propriam* similarly completed, since Juno is not here speaking to the person who is to receive the bride'.[14] Several sceptical critics proposed bracketing the line (Peerlkamp, Ribbeck, Mackail), and Conte has now done so.[15] Its removal gives the end of Juno's speech additional point: 'this will be their marriage' is phrased so as to reassure Venus while hinting at Juno's true purpose (i.e., a mere pseudo-wedding). In a text like the *Aeneid* for which we have an editorial rather than an authorial version, it may not always be possible to distinguish between interpolations and traces of incomplete revision by the author. In my commentary I have suggested that *Aen.* 12.882–4 belongs to one of those categories.[16]

Passages plausibly identified as interpolations that appear in an entire manuscript tradition are almost certainly ancient in origin. In addition, some lines suspected as interpolations by modern critics have explicit ancient attestation: Seneca *Medea* 666, deleted by Peiper and Zwierlein, is in the text of a Michigan papyrus; Juvenal 9.5, deleted by Guyet and Clausen, is twice quoted by Servius, in his notes on *Georgics* 3.360 and

---

[13] It is noteworthy that this supplement has left no trace in the Virgilian manuscript tradition.

[14] Austin (1955), *ad loc.*

[15] For discussion, see Conte (2013), 43–4.

[16] By far the largest possible interpolation in the *Aeneid* is the so-called 'Helen Episode' (= *Aen.* 2.567–88), a passage known to Servius and therefore indubitably ancient. Its status is still debated; for the case against Virgilian authorship see Horsfall (2006–7). If the lines are interpolated, they probably represent an attempt to fill a lacuna in Virgil's narrative. For a possible interpolation in the *Eclogues* (4.23), see Ottaviano (2013).

Aeneid 7.115; Ovid *Met.* 8.87, missing in some manuscripts and deleted by Heinsius, is cited by the grammarian Priscian. Other interpolations can be securely classed as ancient on internal grounds, such as the eight lines that in some manuscripts precede the start of Horace's *Satires* 1.10; the writer is familiar with scholarly work on the text of Lucilius and mentions a 'Cato' who is almost certainly Valerius Cato, an influential neoteric poet-critic; such information is not likely to have been available to a post-classical interpolator.

Finally, interpolations that demonstrate command of a difficult metrical form are more likely to be ancient than medieval. Two cases in point are Horace's *Odes* and the works of Prudentius, in both of which entire stanzas of verse in lyric metres have been suspected as interpolations.[17]

A plausible example of a medieval interpolation comes from Ovid's account of the fight between the Lapiths and the Centaurs in *Metamorphoses* 12:

> Ante oculos stat et ille meos, qui sena leonum
> uinxerat inter se conexis uellera nodis,   430
> Phaeocomes, hominemque simul protectus equumque;
> caudice qui misso, quem uix iuga bina moverent,
> Tectaphon Oleniden a summo vertice fregit;
> [fracta uolubilitas capitis latissima, perque os
> perque cauas nares oculosque auresque cerebrum   435
> molle fluit, ueluti concretum uimine querno
> lac solet utue liquor rari sub pondere cribri
> manat et exprimitur per densa foramina spissus.]
> ast ego, dum parat hic armis nudare iacentem
> (scit tuus hoc genitor), gladium spoliantis in ima   440
> ilia demisi.

He too stands before my eyes [Nestor is recalling the event to Achilles], who had tied
the skins of six lions together with knotted cords,
Phaeocomes, protected both as man and as horse.
He hurled a tree trunk that two teams of oxen could scarcely budge
and crushed the head of Tectaphon, son of Olenus.
[The broad crown of his head was crushed, and through his mouth

---

[17] In Horace the passages in question are *Odes* 2.16.21–4, 3.11.17–20, 3.18.9–16 (on which see Cucchiarelli (2012)), and 4.8.15–19, 28, 33. Interpolation in Prudentius is the focus of many of the studies in Gnilka (2000).

and his hollow nostrils and his eyes and ears the soft brain
flowed out, as clotted milk tends to do through oaken wickerwork,
or as a thick liquid seeps through beneath the weight of a
widely-spaced sieve
as it is forced out through the closely-packed openings.]
But I, as he made ready to strip the corpse of its armour
(your father knows this), thrust my sword into the despoiler's guts.

Lines 434–8 are missing in all the oldest manuscripts but have been added by later hands in three of them; critics and editors since Bothe in 1818 have been almost unanimous in regarding them as interpolated, and even one twelfth-century scribe confidently stated *isti uersus non sunt autoris* (Florence Strozzi 121).[18] They contain several expressions found in Ovid or in other classical authors (e.g., 435 *cauas nares* – *Ars* 1.520; 436 *uimine querno* – Virg. *Aen.* 11.65; 437 *liquor rari ... cribri* – *Fasti* 4.770 *dent ... uiam liquido uimina rara sero*; 438 *per densa foramina* – *F.* 6.698 *per rara f.*), but the overall impression they give is of a post-classical style (in particular *uolubilitas capitis latissima* = 'the broad roundness of the head' or, more charitably, 'the broad dome of the skull'). They are probably the work of a medieval reader who felt that the description of Tectaphos' death was insufficiently gory and who set about filling the gap in a strikingly macabre fashion.

Medieval interpolation on a larger scale is exemplified by the metamorphosis story comprising forty-four hexameters entered in the margin of a fourteenth-century Vatican manuscript (Patetta 314), in which a bishop or abbot who has intercourse with an abbess and all of her nuns is punished by being turned into a cock.[19] The author gleefully employs the style and motifs of Ovidian metamorphosis to provide an ironically grand setting for a tale of clerical hypocrisy.

A substantial number of medieval and Renaissance interpolations in the manuscripts of Propertius were documented by James Butrica.[20] In addition to collaborative interpolations, Butrica noted several places where lines from other authors had been entered as marginal parallels; so, for example, Ovid *Ars* 2.277–8 *aurea sunt uere nunc saecula; plurimus auro* | *uenit honos, auro*

---

[18] The lines do figure, however, with no hint of suspicion attaching to them, in several modern English translations, including those by Rolfe Humphries, A. D. Melville, Allen Mandelbaum, Charles Martin, and Stanley Lombardo.

[19] Published by Anderson (1975) with refinements by Lebek (1978).

[20] Butrica (1997) 197–206.

conciliatur amor ('now the age is truly one of gold; from gold come the highest honours, love is procured with gold') found their way into several manuscripts of Propertius 3.13 and even into some early printed editions. (The intrusion of parallel passages into a text is easily noticed when the parallel comes from elsewhere in the same author or from another extant author; when the parallel is from a source now lost, it will either appear to be a gratuitous interpolation or will be mistaken for a portion of text that has wandered from its original position.) On medieval readers' ability to generate interpolations, Butrica made the important point that 'even in the twelfth century any reader educated enough and classically oriented enough to be reading Propertius would have been capable of composing elegiac couplets'.[21]

Before discussing other examples, I would note that we would be more aware of interpolation as a recurring phenomenon if editors provided fuller reports of manuscripts. In the case of the *Metamorphoses*, the generous apparatus of Hugo Magnus reveals the presence of several interpolated lines not mentioned by other editors; the lines are not found in the oldest witnesses and are therefore almost certainly late additions, and editors constructing an apparatus of limited scope are therefore justified in ignoring them, but if we wish better to understand the processes that lead to such interpolations, it is essential to see what the manuscripts (especially the manuscripts of the twelfth and thirteenth centuries) contain. My apparatus is far more selective than Magnus's, but because of my interest in interpolation I chose to cite a number of instances: for example, two lines inserted after 15.716 in at least one twelfth-century manuscript and several thirteenth-century manuscripts, *illis litoribus dantem post temporis urbi | seruantemque pie caietam nomina famae* ('Caieta, who in later time would give her name to a city on those shores and preserve her name of noted devotion'), an expansion of Ovid's allusive reference to Caieta, the nurse of Aeneas (*quam tumulauit alumnus* 'she who was buried by her nursling'), itself based on the opening lines of *Aeneid* 7. Another two-line insertion found after 15.744 in several noteworthy witnesses, *Bacchus et Alcides, Caesar per gesta deorum | nomina habent iuncta, sed sua facta magis* ('Bacchus, Hercules, and Caesar on account of their deeds have their names joined to those of the gods; but his achievements more so' [?]) is remarkable for being an elegiac couplet; it has some connection with *Am.* 3.8.51–2, rhetorically addressed to

---

[21] Butrica (1997), 199. Some of the interpolations that Butrica alleged in the archetypal text of Propertius do not persuade me, e.g., his bracketing of 2.34.67–84 – another case of interpolation-study falling victim to hyper-scepticism – but that does not invalidate his evidence of interpolations in later manuscripts.

human nature: *qua licet, adfectas caelum quoque: templa Quirinus,* | *Liber et Alcides et modo Caesar habent* ('as much as you can, you aim for heaven as well; Quirinus, Bacchus, Hercules, and more recently Caesar have temples'), a couplet that is itself regarded as an interpolation by several modern editors.

Two texts for which we possess more than usually full accounts of the manuscripts are a Latin translation of the *Iliad*, the so-called *Ilias Latina* (probably of Neronian date, possibly the work of one Baebius Italicus), and Claudian's *De raptu Proserpinae*.[22] They provide clear-cut examples that illustrate several ways in which interpolations arise; it is probably not a coincidence that both poems were popular in the Middle Ages as texts for teaching grammar and rhetoric. I will add a few more controversial proposals from better-known authors.

Ceres, fearing that her daughter may be taken from her, entrusts her to Sicily (*DRP* 1.137–42):

> despexit utrumque
> flaua Ceres raptusque timens (heu caeca futuri!)
> [commendat Siculis furtim sua pignora terris
> infidis Laribus natam commisit alendam],   140
> aethera deseruit Siculasque relegat in oras
> ingenio confisa loci.

> Golden-haired Ceres scorned both \<prospective suitors>
> and, fearing an abduction (how blind to the future!),
> [she entrusts her offspring to the land of Sicily]
> [she handed her child to an unfaithful house to be raised]
> she left the sky and removed \<her daughter> to Sicilian shores,
> trusting in the nature of the place.

Each of the lines 139–140–141 expresses a similar idea, and all three cannot stand in the text. Before Hall, most editors had accepted 139 as genuine and treated 140 and 141 as interpolated, but Hall observes that the evidence of the manuscripts closely links 141 with the lines that follow, that is, 142–214, a section of text omitted in one branch of the tradition: all the manuscripts that contain 141 also have the remainder of the passage, while in all the manuscripts that lack 142–214, 141 is also missing. On the other hand, each of 139 and 140 is found both in manuscripts that contain 142–214 and in

---

[22] For the *Ilias Latina*, I use the edition by Scaffai (1997), for the *De raptu* that of Hall (1969).

manuscripts that omit them, and furthermore they are found in different places, sometimes as marginal additions. One might add that the wording of 141 is less obvious than that of 139 and 140, since it requires *filiam* or *natam* to be understood as the object of *relegat*. Hall concludes: 'It must seem very likely that <139 and 140> are spurious intruders concocted after the loss of 141ff. to complete the sentence begun in 137 and subsequently diffused by contamination throughout a large part of the tradition'. It is remarkable that Hall uses such sinister language ('spurious intruders', 'concocted'), since according to his own argument the lines were an attempt to fill a genuine lacuna. If a modern scholar were to fill a lacuna with a line of her own composition, it would be called a conjecture.

Hector urges Paris and Menelaus to fight in single combat (*IL* 269–70):

> Vos, foedere iuncto,
> aduersas conferte manus, decernite ferro.

> Do you, joining in an agreement,
> come together in combat, decide with the sword.

> *post* 270 uestram nunc elenam sumat quis rectius ipsam *add. E³ mg.*, quis uestrum melius sit tanta coniuge dignus *L² mg.*

This is a clear example of an interpolation intended to fill an apparent, not a real, syntactical lacuna. Hector's speech ends with *decernite ferro*, where *decernite* is used in an absolute sense, 'settle (the dispute/the war)'. Readers or copyists who did not recognize the construction felt that a complement was required, and produced at least two forms of an indirect question, *uestram nunc Helenam sumat quis rectius ipsam* ('which of you with greater right is now to have Helen') and *quis uestrum melius sit tanta coniuge dignus* ('which of you is more worthy of such a wife').

The duel between Hector and Patroclus (*IL* 825–8):

> Tunc prior intorquet collectis uiribus hastam
> Dardanides, quam prolapsam celeri excipit ictu
> Patroclus redditque uices et, mutua dona,
> obicit et saxum ingenti cum pondere missum,   827a
> quod clipeo excussum uiridi tellure resedit.

> Then Hector, gathering his strength, cast his spear
> first; Patroclus swiftly caught it as it fell
> and, returning the favour with a gift in exchange,
> he also hurls a stone with all its huge mass,

which struck the shield and came to rest on the green earth.

> 827a Habent E³ mg. MNch¹ mg. nec non multi recc., ceteri omittunt nulla
> lacuna signata.
> Varia suppl. W³ mg. atque ferox iaculum toto cum robore mittit, nec non E³c
> ante 827a uiribus extortis (et totis c) telum contorsit in hostem

Line 827a is missing in a number of manuscripts, and many editors have treated it as an interpolation devised to fill a lacuna, completing the sense of the preceding verses while providing an antecedent for the otherwise unexplained neuter forms in line 828 (*quod ... excussum*). Scaffai, however, believes it is genuine, and that Patroclus both throws Hector's spear back at him and also hurls a massive rock at him. Whatever the truth may be, manuscripts that lack 827a contain at least two versions of a similar attempt at completion: *atque ferox iaculum toto cum robore mittit* ('and he fiercely throws his spear with all his might') and *uiribus extortis telum contorsit in hostem* ('gathering his strength [?] he cast his weapon at the enemy'), each of which introduces a neuter synonym for *hasta* (*iaculum* and *telum*). The second line is modelled on *Aeneid* 12.266 *aduersos telum contorsit in hostis* ('he cast his weapon against the enemy'); since the author of the *Ilias Latina* so often drew inspiration from the *Aeneid*, it is only fitting that interpolators of the poem should do likewise. The second supplement is found in the margin of at least one manuscript that also contains line 827a, showing how easily interpolations can migrate from one manuscript to another.

From the two foregoing passages it is possible to draw a more general conclusion, that when a text either is or appears to be incomplete in sense or syntax, more than one attempt at filling the gap will be found.[23] The various supplements could have an independent origin, but in some cases they may be the result of a sort of competition among readers and copyists.

The notorious sinners in the Underworld receive a temporary suspension of their torments (*DRP* 2.335–42):

> non rota suspensum praeceps Ixiona torquet,
> non aqua Tantaleis subducitur inuida labris;
> [soluitur Ixion, inuenit Tantalus undas]
> et Tityos tandem spatiosos erigit artus
> squalentisque nouem detexit iugera campi
> (tantus erat!) laterisque piger sulcator opaci

---

[23] In *Met.* 11.57 the replacement of *os petit* by *obstitit* in all early manuscripts left the line syntactically incomplete, prompting at least four distinct supplements. See Tarrant (1987), 288.

inuitus trahitur lasso de pectore uultur
abreptasque dolet iam non sibi crescere fibras.

The swift wheel does not whirl Ixion in mid-air,
the spiteful water is not withdrawn from Tantalus' lips;
[Ixion is released, Tantalus found the waters]
and Tityos at last lifts his sprawling limbs
uncovering nine acres of the filthy plain
(so large was he!), while the slow furrower of his innards,
the vulture, is unwillingly dragged from his weary breast
and grieves the loss of the flesh that grows for it no more.

Hall allows that line 337 might be genuine, an author's alternative version to
the previous two lines, but the plain style of the line jars with the ornate language of the surrounding passage as a whole. The artless mixture of tenses
(*soluitur, inuenit*) also points to an interpolator. One might suspect that the
line originated as a gloss, but the torments of Ixion and Tantalus were too
well known to ancient and medieval readers to require explanation, and the
line is more a paraphrase of the previous two than an explanation. Another
possibility is that the line is the product of an exercise in rhetoric in which
an elaborate statement is to be reworded in simpler terms.

The fortunes of war alternate between Greeks and Trojans (*IL* 789–95):

> inde cadit Priameia pubes
> [acrius insurgunt Troes ad Achaica bella],   790
> pulsa metu uallumque et muros aggere saeptos
> transiliunt, alii fossas uoluuntur in ipsas.
> Aduolat interea Danaum metus impiger Hector;
> confugiunt iterum ad classes Agamemnonis alae
> atque inde aduersis propellunt uiribus hostem.   795

> then the Trojan youth fall back
> [the Trojans rush forward more fiercely against the Greeks]
> stricken by fear: they leap over the rampart and the fortified walls,
> while others are swept right into the moats.
> Meanwhile tireless Hector, feared by the Greeks, comes running;
> Agamemnon's troops flee once again to the ships,
> and from there drive back the enemy with all their strength.

> *790 secl. Courtney, post 794 transp. Vollmer.*
> *Post 790 [791] exhib. E³mg. h¹ mg. Instaurantque manus.*
> cedit pelopeia pubes. *In text. receperunt edd. ante Baehrens*

Line 790 is clearly out of place in its transmitted position: it interrupts the syntax that runs continuously from 789 to 791 (*inde cadit Priameia pubes | pulsa metu*, etc.), and also anticipates the revival of the Trojans' spirits on Hector's return, described in line 794. Vollmer accordingly placed it after 794. But Courtney pointed out that the line also contains an internal flaw, the spondaic scansion of *Troes*; he plausibly concluded that it is an interpolation: 'no doubt the interpolator, offended by the brevity of the narration in 794–5, placed it in the margin intending it for the position where Vollmer put it'.[24] The passage is also instructive for another reason: in an unsuccessful effort to make 790 fit its transmitted position, some readers or copyists added a verse, *instaurantque manus; cedit Pelopeia pubes* (or *iuuentus*) ('and they renew the battle; the Greek youth give ground').

At this point, I would venture two more general conclusions. First, once an interpolation has entered a text it has the capacity to generate further interpolations; in fact, further interpolations are likely, since the text as initially interpolated will often be or seem to be incoherent, thereby prompting new efforts to supplement or reorder it. Second, when a verse or set of verses appears to be misplaced, editors ought to consider the possibility of interpolation alongside that of transposition, especially when transposition does not produce a satisfactory result. One author for whom that observation has particular relevance is Propertius, and it is good to see that Stephen Heyworth in his OCT text is more willing than many of his predecessors to bracket lines that do not fit their transmitted position rather than transposing them.

Another possible instance of successive interpolations, this one more controversial.

Juvenal *Sat.* 10.354–66:

Vt tamen et poscas aliquid uoueasque sacellis
exta et candiduli diuina thymatula porci,   355
orandum est ut sit mens sana in corpore sano.
fortem posce animum mortis terrore carentem,
qui spatium uitae extremum inter munera ponat
naturae, qui ferre queat quoscumque labores,
nesciat irasci, cupiat nihil et potiores   360
Herculis aerumnas credat saeuosque labores
et uenere et cenis et pluma Sardanapalli.
monstro quod ipse tibi possis dare; semita certe

[24] Courtney (1968), 22–3.

tranquillae per uirtutem patet unica uitae.
nullum numen habes, si sit prudentia: nos te,   365
nos facimus, Fortuna, deam caeloque locamus.

Still, that you may have something to ask for, some reason to offer
the holy sausages and innards of a little white pig in a chapel –
you ought to pray for a healthy mind in a healthy body.
Ask for a valiant heart which has banished the fear of death,
which looks upon length of days as one of the least of nature's
gifts; which is able to suffer every kind of hardship,
is proof against anger, craves for nothing, and reckons the trials
and gruelling labours of Hercules as more desirable blessings
than the amorous ease and the banquets and cushions of Sardanapallus.
The things that I recommend you can grant to yourself; it is certain
that the tranquil life can only be reached by the path of goodness.
Lady Luck, if the truth were known, you possess no power;
it is we who make you a goddess and give you a place in heaven.

(Trans. Niall Rudd)

More than forty years ago, Michael Reeve argued that the most famous
line in this famous passage, *orandum est ut sit mens sana in corpore sano*,
was an interpolation.[25] I am fully persuaded by Reeve's arguments, but
I believe that the passage may contain still more interpolations. The final
two lines, which largely coincide with two lines of the fourteenth satire,
were bracketed by Guyet and Leo; the mention of Fortuna has no relevance
in this context, and the second-person address (*nullum numen habes*) is
awkward coming immediately following a different use of the second person in the previous lines (*ipsi tibi possis dare*). But those two lines themselves (363–4) strike me as at least worthy of suspicion. Since the point
of departure for this passage, as for the satire as a whole, is the desire to
find a suitable object for prayers to the gods (*ut poscas aliquid*, etc.), it
seems contradictory to conclude by saying that a strong mind is a boon
one can confer on oneself; in addition, the promise of a tranquil existence
(364 *tranquillae ... uitae*) clashes with the endurance of hardships elabo-
rated in 359 and 360–2; finally, the bland language of the lines (e.g., the
entirely superfluous *certe*) is an anticlimax after the rhetorical crescendo
that has been building over the six previous lines, to which the sonorous
proper name *Sardanapalli* provides a suitably strong closure. Juvenal likes

[25] Reeve (1970).

99

to conclude a section with a proper name, either a resonant one for cli-
mactic effect (as I argue is the case here) or an unprepossessing one for a
deliberate anticlimax (cf., e.g., 1.80 *Cluvienus*, 2.108–9 *Cleopatra*, etc.,
2.170 *Artaxata*, 8.38 *Creticus aut Camerinus*, 10.14 *Britannica maior*,
10.322 *Oppia siue Catulla*, 15.46 *Canopo*). I suspect that a first interpolation – perhaps the *mens sana* line – inspired further additions to an already
well-known passage.[26]

A recurring feature of poetic interpolations is the use of language found
elsewhere in the same author, often in the same work. This method of composition could be seen as an aspect of successful impersonation (to pass
oneself off as Ovid, one needs to write like Ovid), but it might also be a way
for the interpolator to demonstrate an ability to reuse the author's language
in a new context. Seen in that light, the parallels become not mere borrow-
ings, but intertextual allusions meant to be noticed and appreciated by an
alert reader.

Metamorphoses 11.592–602 (the cave of Sleep):

Est prope Cimmerios longo spelunca recessu,
mons cauus, ignaui domus et penetralia Somni,
quo numquam radiis oriens mediusue cadensue
Phoebus adire potest; nebulae caligine mixtae   595
exhalantur humo dubiaeque crepuscula lucis.
non uigil ales ibi cristati cantibus oris
euocat Auroram, nec uoce silentia rumpunt
sollicitiue canes canibusue sagacior anser;
non fera, non pecudes, non moti flamine rami   600
humanaeue sonum reddunt conuicia linguae;
muta quies habitat.

Near the land of the Cimmerians is a cave with a deep recess,
a hollow mountain, the home and inner sanctum of indolent Sleep,
where Phoebus can never enter with his rays, not rising nor at mid-day
nor setting; clouds mingling with mist breathe forth
from the ground, along with the murky light of dusk.
No wakeful bird there summons the Dawn with the crowing
of its crested head, nor do fretful watchdogs break the silence

---

[26] Michael Reeve was not persuaded by this deletion when I first floated it, and he may not
feel any better disposed to it now. Indeed he and my readers may be led to conclude that
Housman's phrase about Sin when she gave birth to Death (see p. 32) can apply as much
to sceptics as to conservatives.

with their cries, nor the goose, more alert even than dogs;
no wild beast, no flocks, no branches moved by the breeze
nor the angry words of human tongues give back a sound;
mute silence dwells there.

Several features of lines 600–1 generate strong suspicion: (a) after 598–9, which name three animals almost synonymous with their noisemaking habits (rooster, dog, and, in emphatic final position, goose), the vagueness of *fera* and *pecudes* is blatantly anticlimactic; (b) given the stress in 592–6 on the other-worldly remoteness and perpetual darkness of the place, the notion that the silence might be broken by the sound of people arguing (601 *humanae ... conuicia linguae*) borders on the ludicrous; (c) both lines are made up almost entirely of elements used – and, I would argue, used more appropriately – elsewhere in the poem: cf. 3.408–10 [*fons*] *quem neque pastores neque pastae monte capellae | contigerant aliudue pecus, quem nulla uolucris | nec fera turbarat nec lapsus ab arbore ramus* ('a spring which neither shepherd nor mountain-grazing goats had touched nor any other flock, which no bird had disturbed and no branch falling from a tree'); 3.498 *haec* [sc. Echo]*quoque reddebat sonitum plangoris eundem* ('she too gave back the same sound of the blows'); 7.629–30 *intremuit ramisque sonum sine flamine motis | alta dedit quercus* ('the tall oak trembled and, as its branches moved without a breeze, it gave forth a sound');[27] 13.306–7 *neue in me stolidae conuicia fundere linguae | admiremur eum* ('do not marvel that he pours out against me the angry words of his doltish tongue').

Most collaborative interpolations aim to amplify a textual moment by prolonging it, but a few can be termed anticipatory: they retroject an element from a later point in a narrative (of which the interpolator naturally has knowledge) into a context where it is premature. Ovid's episode of Pygmalion in *Metamorphoses* 10 furnishes what I regard as a likely example.

> saepe manus operi temptantes admouet, an sit
> corpus an illud ebur, nec adhuc ebur esse fatetur. 255
> oscula dat reddique putat loquiturque tenetque 256
> et credit tactis digitos insidere membris
> et metuit, pressos ueniat ne liuor in artus.
> et modo blanditias adhibet, modo grata puellis
> munera fert illi ... 260

---

[27] There is a subtle but perceptible difference between *sonum dare*, 'to give forth a sound', and *sonum reddere*, 'to give back a sound', i.e., to echo a sound. The lines in question use *sonum reddere* as if it were synonymous with *sonum dare*.

Often he reaches out to the work with his hands, testing
if it is ivory or flesh, and does not yet admit it is ivory.
He kisses it and thinks his kisses are returned, talks to it, holds it
and believes his fingers are sinking into the limbs he touches
and fears that a bruise might appear in the places he has pressed.
And sometimes he offers it flattery, sometimes he brings it gifts
pleasing to girls ...

Thus the manuscripts and all editions prior to mine (omitting minor differences in punctuation). In the lines on either side of 256 the focus is on Pygmalion's touching the statue, and indeed those lines work best as parts of a connected thought: 'he is not yet willing to admit that the maiden is made of ivory rather than flesh, but instead believes that his fingers are sinking into her limbs' and so forth (for the contrast between the halves to register, we would need to make the slight change of *et* to *sed* in 257). Into that carefully constructed sequence line 256 inserts a jumble of unrelated actions, which interrupt both the immediate thought and the step-by-step progress of Pygmalion's infatuation in the first part of the episode (250–69). Specifically, the reference to kisses (*oscula dat reddique putat* 'he kisses it and thinks his kisses are returned') appears premature when compared to the later passage in which Pygmalion kisses the statue (281): there, even though the statue appears to grow warm (*uisa tepere est*), and even though further testing confirms that the ivory is softening in response to his touch, Pygmalion still cannot quite believe his good fortune (287). The culmination of the story is marked by a kiss in which he finally (*tandem*) presses a real face to his own (291–2 *oraque tandem | ore suo non falsa premit*). I find it highly unlikely that at an early stage in his courtship of the statue the timid lover that Ovid presents would confidently think that his kisses were being returned. Pygmalion's actions as described in 256 are at the same time too matter-of-fact and too forward.

A final advantage of employing a rhetoric of collaboration is that it allows us to see a connection between interpolation on the small scale and interpolation on a larger scale, the creation of entire works that purport to be by a given author.

The discussion of works of questionable authenticity, like that of alleged interpolations, has long been hampered by the use of an inappropriate language of forgery and falsification. It is more accurate to see such works as large-scale allusions to the authors whom they purport to impersonate. Eduard Fraenkel's classic analysis of the pseudo-Virgilian *Culex* showed what such an approach can achieve, convincingly interpreting the *Culex* as filling an apparent gap in Virgil's poetic career by supplying a specimen of the juvenilia that any great poet would be expected to produce before writing the first of his mature poems.[28]

Some of the disputed letters in the *Epistulae heroidum* attributed to Ovid might profitably be interpreted as examples of collaborative interpolation, specifically as additions that extend a series by incorporating material from the author in question, with the aim of supplying Ovidian versions of letters from heroines that Ovid had not included. In *Heroides* 12 (Medea to Jason), the link to Ovid is direct: Ovid narrated Medea's meeting with Jason in Colchis in *Metamorphoses* 7 and almost certainly treated the story of her murder of their children in his tragedy *Medea*; probably for that reason, the *Metamorphoses* narrative passes over the infanticide in a mere four lines (7.394–7). The writer of *Heroides* 12 saw an opportunity to join the two phases of Medea's career that Ovid had dealt with separately. Echoes of the *Metamorphoses* and the tragedy are intended to be noticed and understood as means to that end.[29]

On the *Epistula Sapphus*, I have not altered my opinion that it is a post-Ovidian work, but I do regret some of what I previously wrote about the poem.[30] In particular, my low opinion of the poem's quality now strikes me as misguided, and I would take a different view of the many echoes of Ovid that it contains, seeing them not as signs of ineptitude or lack of imagination but as deliberate markers: the presence of echoes from the exile poetry as well as from the *Ars* and *Amores* is part of the design by which the Sappho of this poem becomes a fully Ovidian character.

To cite only the first instance, the opening lines of the *ES*

> Ecquid, ut adspecta est studiosae littera dextrae,
>   protinus est oculis cognita nostra tuis?
> an, nisi legisses auctoris nomina Sapphus,
>   hoc breue nescires unde ueniret opus?

> When the script of this eager hand was viewed,
>   did your eyes recognize it right away as mine?
> Or, if you hadn't read the author's name, Sappho,
>   would you not know the source of this brief work?

---

[28] Fraenkel (1952). Peirano (2012) fruitfully applies a similar approach to several other poetic impersonations of the first centuries BCE and CE.

[29] The point is controversial: Hinds (1993), among others, supports Ovidian authorship.

[30] Tarrant (1981). For a defence of Ovid's authorship, see Rosati (1996).

bear an unmistakable resemblance to the opening of Ovid's *Epistulae ex Ponto* 2.10:

> Ecquid ab impressae cognoscis imagine cerae
>   haec tibi Nasonem scribere uerba, Macer,
> auctorisque sui si non est anulus index,
>   cognitane est nostra littera facta manu?

> Do you recognize from the image impressed on the seal
>   that Naso is writing these words to you, Macer,
> and, if the ring does not reveal the author's identity,
>   was the script recognized as the work of my hand?

If the *ES* is drawing on the Ovidian text, opening the poem in this way advertises the author's strategy of creating a *Sappho Ouidiana* by having her speak in Ovid's own words. The initial question – 'do you recognize whose writing this is?' – is addressed as much to the reader as to the neglectful Phaon.

The *ES* and other non-Ovidian *Heroides* can therefore be regarded as creative supplements[31] to the corpus of *Heroides*, a sympathetic extension of Ovid's work that functions on the large scale in a similar way to the smaller collaborative interpolations we have examined.

At this point we are close to the borderline between textual and literary criticism. A particularly problematic case of how those perspectives are to be combined is Propertius, the subject of the next chapter.

---

[31] I have adopted this felicitous term from Peirano (2012), 10.

6

Textual criticism and literary criticism: the case of Propertius

Young Housman: <Propertius is> difficult – tangled-up thoughts, or, anyway, tangled-up Latin … if you can believe the manuscripts – which you can't because they all come from the same one, and that was about as far removed from Propertius as we are from Alfred burning the cakes!

(Tom Stoppard, *The Invention of Love*)

Enter 'Vegetius' on Amazon Books, and one of the items that appears is *Epitoma rei militaris* (Oxford Classical Texts) by Vegetius and M. D. Reeve. Treating an editor as a co-author is an amusingly literal version of a simple fact: editors do create the authors they edit, in that the text of author X in editor Y's edition is made up of the sum total of editor Y's textual decisions. In most cases the variation between the authors created by different editors does not fundamentally affect the impression given of the text: Cicero will look Ciceronian whatever edition of his work is used, and while my text of the *Metamorphoses* differs from W. S. Anderson's in more than 600 places, the two texts are recognizable as versions of the same poem. But there are instances where the overall impression of an author can be shifted by differing editorial decisions. Most such cases turn on the issue of anomaly versus analogy, that is, the extent to which departures from standard usage in the transmitted text of an author reflect genuine idiosyncrasies of style as opposed to scribal deformations. Tacitus (especially the *Annals*) is one example, Valerius Flaccus another; but nowhere is the question posed so starkly as in the case of Propertius. Here contrasting views of what kind of poet he was, and corresponding differences in dealing with his text as transmitted, have in recent years produced a divergence so great that J. S. Phillimore's often-cited phrase *Quot editores tot Propertii* ('as many Propertiuses as there are editors'), originally a warning of the anarchy that would ensue if editors transposed large numbers of couplets, now seems like a fairly accurate description of the present situation.

Disputes about the text of Propertius involve many of the issues discussed in earlier chapters, for example, recension (specifically, disagreement over the shape of the stemma), the proper scope of conjecture, weighing of an author's habits of expression as they can be elicited from a controversial transmission, the place to be given to interpolation. But because Propertius is agreed to be a major poet, even a great one, the disputes surrounding so many of his lines can also show how textual and literary considerations interact. That topic will be the focus of this chapter, after a brief review of Propertius' recent editorial history.

For a few decades in the mid to late twentieth century, the text of Propertius seemed to have attained a degree of stability after a period marked by extremes of conservatism and scepticism. The most widely used text from that period is the OCT of E. A. Barber (1953, revised 1960). In producing his 1960 revision, Barber was influenced by the work of Shackleton Bailey, especially his *Propertiana* of 1956, a textual commentary on all of Propertius that contributed a number of brilliant conjectures but was characterized overall by restraint: confronted with an unreliable manuscript tradition and an author believed to cultivate an idiosyncratic style, Shackleton Bailey often concluded that the transmitted text might well be corrupt but that no attempt to correct it commanded assent. He was also dismissive of hypotheses that postulated widespread relocation of couplets or that bracketed large numbers of couplets as interpolations. Barber's editorial policies followed similar lines: while accepting numerous conjectures and a smaller number of transpositions and deletions, he confined many plausible suggestions to the apparatus, producing what might be described as a moderately conservative text. The other noteworthy edition from this period, Paolo Fedeli's Teubner of 1984, is markedly more conservative than Barber's without displaying the extreme resistance to conjecture manifested by some editions of a century earlier.[1]

In the same years, however, a powerful assault on the editorial vulgate began to be mounted. The opening salvo was fired in 1966 by George Goold

---

[1] At that time, Fedeli described his editorial position as 'accortamente conservatrice', or 'sensibly/shrewdly conservative': Fedeli (1986), 108. Since then, his views have evolved significantly: 'over the years I have often changed my confidently conservative attitude and have accorded ever greater space to doubt and lack of trust in the manuscript tradition' (2013), 514. He describes his current position as 'a healthier and more realistic scepticism' (2014), 281.

in a long article entitled *'Noctes Propertianae'*. Goold set out to show that 'our current texts and commentaries are shot through and through with error and misunderstanding'[2] and called for an edition that would embody all the true conjectures that had been made in the text of Propertius – a figure he estimated at some 2,000. Nine years later, Margaret Hubbard adduced a new argument to justify suspicion of the transmitted text. Challenging the conventional view of Propertius as 'a poet of tormented obscurity', Hubbard noted that the judgements of his work found in ancient sources suggested instead 'a poet of finish, grace, and charm'. With remorseless logic, she concluded that 'as <the manuscript tradition> presents us with a difficult poet whose words can sometimes hardly be forced into sense, its text is not the one known to the ancient world'.[3] The consensus view of the text also came under attack from Stephen Heyworth in a review of Fedeli's edition; Heyworth noted that Fedeli 'rarely chooses readings from outside the circle prescribed by the modern vulgate. The text consequently contains much that Propertius did not write'.[4]

In the last two decades, the sceptical onslaught has only intensified. In 1990 Goold published a revision of H. E. Butler's Loeb edition that, although not as radical as might have been expected from his 1966 statements, still marked a major departure from the vulgate. The late James Butrica developed Hubbard's arguments into a manifesto calling on editors to do whatever was needed to restore Propertius to his ancient description as a poet of grace and elegance.[5] Hans-Christian Günther's 1997 monograph *Quaestiones Propertianae* renewed the arguments for transposition and interpolation as major factors in the formation of the paradosis. In 2007 Stephen Heyworth published a new OCT edition and a large companion volume of textual notes entitled *Cynthia*. Heyworth's text represents a fundamentally new recension of the kind called for by Goold; from almost the first line of the text to the last, Heyworth asserts his willingness to depart from the editorial vulgate. The companion volume is without doubt the most significant contribution to the study of Propertius' text since Shackleton Bailey's *Propertiana*, with which *Cynthia* implicitly asks to be compared and to which it often explicitly responds. Heyworth, however, does not represent the highwater mark of contemporary scepticism: that distinction goes to the late Giancarlo Giardina

---

[2] Goold (1966), 59.

[3] Hubbard (1975), 2–3, citing Quint. *Inst.* 10.1.93 and Pliny *Epist.* 9.22.2.

[4] Heyworth (1985), 283. The fierce tone of Heyworth's criticisms elicited from Fedeli (1986), 239 an accusation of 'philological terrorism'.

[5] Butrica (1997).

(1939–2014), who produced two editions in the Urbino series *Testi e commenti/Texts and Commentaries* (2005 and 2010). Giardina's propensity to conjecture makes Heyworth look timid by comparison: his 2010 edition places nearly a thousand of his own suggestions in the text and mentions hundreds more in the apparatus. To describe his editions as the work of 'Propertius and Giancarlo Giardina' would be no exaggeration.[6]

The sceptics now hold the field.[7] Although they are united in their readiness to emend the transmitted text, they divide on two fundamental issues, the character of Propertius' poetry and the reasons for the deplorable state in which they believe it has been preserved.

On the first point, Butrica occupies the most radical position, holding that 'editors have good reason to be less tolerant of even slight awkwardness in the transmitted text'.[8] Giardina has aligned himself with Butrica, and his editions show how that position might play out in practice. (That is not to say that Butrica would have approved of Giardina's choices.)

Goold, on the other hand, describes Propertius as 'an allusive and even cryptic author ... given to novel and recondite ways of expressing himself',[9] and in a number of places Heyworth shows that he too regards Propertius as prone to daring and elliptical writing: for example, 2.1.28 *Siculae classica bella fugae* ('an odd phrase' 107); 2.7.11 'the expression *canere somnos* is a striking extension of usage' (142); 2.29.11 *in medium propellere* ('seems comprehensible, if elliptical' 239); 2.34.41–60 'the sequence 47 ff. is not easy, but hardly exceeds the limits of what Propertius demands from his readers' (272); 4.7.81 on *pomifer Anio* and *ramosis aruis*: 'the epithets are deliberately paradoxical but evocative' (472); 4.8.23 'linguistically bold' (478).[10]

---

[6] See further Tarrant (2015).

[7] The only recent exception to the sceptical tendency is the Budé edition (2005) of Simone Viarre, an estimable literary scholar who was not equal to the demands of producing a critical edition. Her text is essentially the vulgate with some alterations inspired by Goold's Loeb. The apparatus records only conjectures adopted in the text, a policy that in a highly disputed text such as this gives a misleading impression of certainty. Space is wasted on trivial manuscript variants and lists of editors who have accepted a given conjecture or editorial decision. Scholars' names are not infrequently garbled. It is pleasing to imagine how the shade of A. E. Housman might receive the news that he had delivered a paper entitled 'L'Élégie romaine: enracinement, thèmes, diffusion' at a conference held at Mulhouse in 1979. Reviews of Viarre's edition show that the divide between British and continental scholarship (see pp. 25–6) is as wide as ever: contrast Deremetz (2006) and Hall (2007).

[8] Butrica (1997), 183.   [9] Goold (1990), 30 and 19 respectively.

[10] All citations from Heyworth (2007b).

The second issue is whether the corruption allegedly present in the transmitted text can be accounted for by the usual processes of transmission or
whether the intervention of a reviser is required. On that question Heyworth
and Giardina do not take an explicit stand. Butrica inclines to the first
view: he writes that 'the text of Propertius has been affected by the ordinary
vicissitudes of copying (though now and again it seems to have gone through
the hands of someone more prone to error than most)' and 'it may well be
that one or two stages in the ancestry of our archetype were entrusted to the
sort of scribe who is inclined to omit and dislocate'.[11] Butrica also believed
that interpolation had been at work at more than one stage, extending to the
inclusion of entire poems by other authors in the latter part of Book 2, but he
regarded the passages in question as either intruded parallels or collaborative
interpolations (in my sense, cf. pp. 87–8), and was at pains to stress that he
saw nothing sinister or diabolical in the process.[12]

'Sinister' and 'diabolical' are just the terms to describe the figure invoked in
Goold's 1966 article, a 'Propertiast' and 'a pseudo editor whose crazy notions
have driven him to ruthless rewording'.[13] By the time of his Loeb edition, the
temperature of Goold's rhetoric had lowered somewhat: there he spoke of a
'medieval corrector', 'one energetic figure whose bold dedication and endeavours have proved not a salvation but a disaster for Propertius'.[14] But even if
we accept the premise of an unscrupulous reviser, it is hard to see why in so
many places that character would have replaced perfectly clear expressions
with crabbed and obscure equivalents, an assumption that underlies many of
the conjectures introduced or adopted by Goold, Heyworth, and Giardina.

The examples of rewriting discussed most fully by Goold do not in
fact involve substituting difficult expressions for straightforward ones, and
indeed Goold himself described the aims of his medieval corrector in precisely opposite terms: 'to smooth the path of understanding by attempting to
clarify what was obscure and also to correct the manifold errors with which
the text abounded'.[15]

As an instance he cited 3.11.5, of which he thought the original text
read *uentorum melius praesagit nauita morem* ('the sailor best predicts the
temper of the winds') but which is transmitted as *uenturam m. p. n. mortem* ('the sailor best predicts <his> coming death'; *uentorum* was conjectured by Postgate, *morem* by Barber). Goold suggested that *morem* was
accidentally miscopied as *mortem*, and that the corrector, realizing that

---

[11] Butrica (1997), 208 and 196 respectively.

[12] Butrica (1997), 199.   [13] Goold (1966), 87.

[14] Goold (1990), 20.   [15] Goold (1990), 19–20.

uentorum ... mortem made no sense, altered *uentorum* to *uenturam*. Granting for the sake of argument that this reconstruction is true – Heyworth keeps the paradosis but brackets 5–6 as an interpolation – it should be noted that the alleged result of the corrector's intervention yields a more banal and obvious sense than the putative original.

The same goes for another of Goold's exhibits, 3.7.25, where he argued that Propertius' *reddite corpus, aquae!* ('give back his body, you waters!') was altered to *reddite corpus humo* by an interpolator who thought that *aquae* was dative rather than vocative and who therefore replaced 'restore his body to the water' (absurd with reference to the drowned Paetus) with the apparently more appropriate 'restore his body to the earth'.[16] As Goold notes, the alleged interpolator's action is perfectly rational and intelligible given his misconception of the syntax, and here too the product of the rewriting is more straightforward than the conjecturally restored original.

Many of the corruptions postulated by the sceptics presuppose a very different type of rewriting, however, and one much less easily explained. For example, 1.16.2 speaks of a house famed for 'Tarpeian chastity' (*Tarpeiae ... pudicitiae*). If the reference is to the Vestal Virgin Tarpeia, who attempted to betray Rome to the Sabines out of love for their king, the phrase looks blatantly oxymoronic; as Goold delightfully observed, 'this is like describing a monastery as famous for the loyal discipleship of Judas Iscariot'.[17] But for that very reason it does not seem like the sort of alteration a scribe, or even a wilful interpolator, would make to a perfectly intelligible expression such as 'patrician chastity' (*patriciae ... pudicitiae*, conjectured by Phillimore and printed by Goold and Heyworth). Other instances of mystifying or perverse alterations: in 1.18.27 a reference to mountains (*dumosi/cliuosi/continui montes*) became the enigmatic *diuini fontes* ('divine springs'); in 2.15.48 *proelia* ('battles'), which neatly compares the lovers' struggles to the real warfare of Actium, was replaced by *pocula* ('wine cups'), unbalancing the parallel between bedroom and battlefield; in 2.25.1 a straightforward *Cynthia* became the adjective *unica*, arguably pleonastic with *pulcherrima* in the same line.[18] Accounting for what the sceptics believe has happened in these and similar places would call for the intervention of an even weirder creature than Goold's cloven-hooved booby.[19]

---

[16] Goold (1988), 37. *Aquae* was conjectured by Damsté.

[17] Goold (1988), 33.

[18] For some other examples, see Tarrant (2006), 49–55.

[19] 'Not this once only, but hundreds of times shall we detect the cloven hoof of this booby in the text of our poet' ((1966), 61).

Conservatives and sceptics agree on the necessary interconnection of textual and literary criticism. Here is Fedeli: 'from one point of view the activity of *recensio* ... implies a continuous reflection on the right way of understanding the Propertian text, while from another the task of anyone who wishes to understand, explain and comment can never be entirely separated from a full awareness of the limits of <the> Propertian manuscript tradition'.[20] Goold wrote that 'without a good text of Propertius no authentic appreciation of him is possible',[21] and Butrica called a reliable text the only sound basis for assessing Propertius' achievement as a poet.[22] Beneath such generalities, though, lies deep disagreement between conservatives and moderates on one side and sceptics on the other about what constitutes both a good text and a proper appreciation of Propertius as a poet.

Although I cannot hope to resolve those issues, I believe that progress can be made. I will first attempt to refute the hypothesis, enunciated by Butrica and put into practice by Giardina, that any departure from a graceful and elegant style is the result of corruption. I will then try to show that the degree of difficulty in Propertius' writing is greater than is allowed by Goold and Heyworth. Underlying many of my specific arguments is a more general conception of the place of difficulty in Propertius: not simply as a stylistic mannerism or an unfortunate habit, but as a positive source of expressive power. I realize that similar arguments have in the past been invoked to defend manuscript readings that I regard as indefensible. I hope to employ such literary considerations with tact, but readers must be the judge. I will limit the discussion to verbal criticism, leaving aside interpolation and transposition, both of which are also significant issues in the editing of Propertius.[23]

I begin with some places where even the most sceptical editors accept difficult readings; here Giardina's approach is useful in establishing an irreducible minimum of such readings. I have arranged the passages in a rough typology, but the categories are not hard and fast, and some passages exhibit more than one of the features mentioned.

Striking collocations of words, in particular those that couple terms belonging to different spheres (e.g., the physical and the abstract).
A relatively mild example is *una ratis fati* ('one boat of death' 2.28.39); as Camps *ad loc.* observes, *ratis fati* brings to mind Charon's boat but is not identical with it.

---

[20] Fedeli (2006), 3 (my insertion).
[21] Goold (1966), 58.   [22] Butrica (1997), 208.
[23] For brief remarks on transposition see pp. 79–80.

1.15.20 *ut semel Haemonio tabuit hospitio* 'once she had melted <with desire> for her Thessalian guest' (*hospitio = hospite*).

3.10.22 *crocino nares murreus ungat onyx* 'let the jar of perfume anoint our nostrils with saffron': the idea of moisture is transferred from the liquid perfume to the scent itself ('striking, but justifiable', Shackleton Bailey (1956), 167).

4.4.83 *mons erat ascensu dubius festoque remissus* 'the hill was difficult to climb and left free for the festival': *mons ... remissus* is difficult in itself (the idea of relaxation is transferred from the people to the place) and also in conjunction with *ascensu dubius*; the main difficulty could be removed by Shackleton Bailey's conjecture *custosque* for *festoque*, but no editor has adopted it.[24]

Words used in unusual or unparalleled senses or with unusual syntax.

2.9.1–2 *fors et in hora | hoc ipso eiecto carior alter erit* 'but perhaps he will be discarded presently and another preferred' (Goold); '*in hora* is a remarkable expression variously rendered "in his hour", "one day", "dans une heure",' Shackleton Bailey (1956), 78.

2.13.42 *non nihil ad uerum conscia terra sapit*: the line, *ad uerum* in particular, has been variously interpreted ('man's dust has consciousness, and is not heedless of the truth' (Goold)); 'for truth the earth is conscious and does have some feeling' (Heyworth), but no emendation has found favour.

3.22.11 *propellas remige Phasin* instead of the normal *remis propellere nauem* (e.g.); Heyworth (2007b), 403 convincingly justifies the inversion as alluding to Apollonius Rhodius 2.1264–78.

Elusive expressions, where the individual words and their syntactical relations are not difficult but where the meaning is hard to pin down (perhaps because it was not meant to be precisely defined).

2.17.3 *horum ego sum uates* can mean either 'I am the singer of these <sorrows>' or 'I am the prophet of these <disasters>'. Less likely is 'I am the poet of these disappointed lovers' (Giardina).

3.5.8 *pectoris egit opus* (of Prometheus) appears to have remained untouched by conjecture, but translations suggest its oddity (Goold 'the making of man's reason', Heyworth 'he did his work on the intellect').

---

[24] Giardina accepts *dubio* (*recc.*) for *dubius*, but keeps *festoque*. Goold accepts Jacob's *mons erat ascensus, dapibus festoque remissus* ('now had the hill been scaled, unguarded through feasting and revelry'), which leaves *mons ... remissus* intact.

3.9.36 *sub exiguo flumine nostra mora est* 'our time is spent … beneath the banks of a tiny river' (Heyworth) is not an obvious expression. 'Nauigantem dici a Propertio potuisse morari sub exiguo flumine, non credo' ('I do not believe that Propertius could have said that one sailing was "lingering beneath a tiny river"' Madvig, cited by Shackleton Bailey (1956), 162).

3.24.5 *mixtam te uaria laudaui saepe figura*: 'I praised you as made up of many aspects' (Shackleton Bailey (1956), 213); 'the you I often praised was concocted from the appearance of various women' (Heyworth (2007b), 586); 'often I mixed all manner of beauties in praise of you' (Camps *ad loc.*, rendering so as to reflect the ambiguity he sees in the expression).

Compressed, ambiguous, or elliptical expressions.

1.6.28 *multi longinquo periere in amore libenter,│in quorum numero me quoque terra tegat* 'many have willingly perished in a long-lasting love; in their number may the earth cover me as well'. The pentameter combines two ideas that are not quite on the same level; a literal reading would suggest a graveyard of long-term lovers in which Propertius wishes to be buried.

1.11.5 *nostri cura subit memores adducere noctes?*: it is not clear whether *nostri* is to be understood with *memores* ('does any concern arise to bring on nights when you remember me?' (Goold) or with *cura* ('is it the case that any care for us creeps up on you, to bring nights of remembrance?' (Heyworth), or both (Giardina). If *adducere* is emended to *a! ducere* (Scaliger), the phrase remains difficult; in particular it then becomes ambiguous whether it is Propertius or Cynthia who is passing nights mindful of the other.

3.4.17 *tela fugacis equi*: 'a rather loose possessive genitive: "the arrows that are shot from horses in flight"' (Camps *ad loc.*).

3.11.55 *tanto tibi ciue*: 'when you had so great a citizen to protect you' (clarified somewhat by the reference to Augustus in 49).

3.18.21 *sed tamen huc* [*recc.*: hoc Ω] *omnes, huc primus et ultimus ordo* 'yet everyone goes this way, this way the highest and the lowest class' (Heyworth): whether one reads *hoc* or *huc*, and even if *sed tamen* is emended to (e.g.) *tendimus* (Heinsius), the expression is elliptical, since no reference to a place (such as the Underworld) precedes; rather it seems that the idea is developed from the mention of funeral pyres (*ignibus*) in the previous line.

Passages like those (and the list could easily be extended) show that the attempt to turn Propertius into a stylistic twin of Tibullus or Ovid by large-scale rewriting of the transmitted text is fundamentally misconceived. Even in Giardina's heavily normalized version, Propertius remains a writer fond of quirky expressions. That conclusion in turn casts some doubt on the sceptics' argument from external sources: it would seem that the references to Propertius by ancient readers are not specific enough to be of much help in constructing a text.[25]

As Heyworth and Goold acknowledge, the real question is where to draw the line between authentically Propertian difficulty and that produced by scribal error and/or interpolation. I will discuss a number of cases where one or more of the sceptics emend readings that resemble in character the passages discussed earlier and that therefore have some claim to be regarded as genuine. The transmitted readings in question are also arguably apt in literary terms (e.g., they are well suited to their context or are in some other way poetically effective).

Only Giardina emends:

1.6.7 *illa mihi totis argutat noctibus ignes* 'all night long she shrills her passion at me' (Goold): a verb of speaking (here used in a rare transitive form) governs a logically impossible object (*ignis* as a metaphorical synonym for, e.g., *amor*), in a combination like those in my first group of passages. (Giardina emends to *obtundit … aures*, 'she batters my ears'.)

4.4.20 *pictaque per flauas arma leuare iubas* 'uplifting his blazoned arms over his horse's golden mane' (Goold), on which Heyworth (2007b), 449 writes 'I know of no persuasive explanation or correction of these words'. Hartman's *lora* for *arma*, accepted by Giardina, only slightly reduces the difficulty; Goold's translation clarifies the picture by introducing the horse not mentioned in the Latin.

4.11.85 *seu tamen aduersum mutarit ianua lectum* 'if, however, the door changes the wedding-bed facing it', a line that seems before Giardina to have attracted almost no attempts at emendation,[26] and that receives no note in *Cynthia* or the OCT apparatus, is a fine specimen of Propertian compression. Shackleton Bailey (1956), 266 canvasses three

---

[25] There is, of course, another possible conclusion, namely, that the corruption in the manuscripts is so pervasive that even wholesale rewriting has not yet entirely eradicated it.

[26] Smyth (1970) records only Boot's *mutarint atria* for *mutarit ianua*, which would not affect the essential element of compression.

explanations: (a) the door is said to do what is actually done by others in its presence; (b) the reference is to the door opening to let the old bed out and the new bed in; and (c) (his preferred interpretation) the *lectus aduersus* depends for its name on the fact that it faced the door. So it is appropriate to say that the door gets a new Opposite Bed in place of an old one. Giardina (2005) rewrites the line as follows: *seu timida aduersum mutarit domina lectum* ('or if a timid mistress changes the facing bed'), which robs *aduersum* of its point.[27]

Heyworth and/or Goold emend:

2.32.47 *qui quaerit Tatios ueteres durosque Sabinos,* | *hic posuit nostra nuper in urbe pedem* 'anyone who expects to find ancient Tatiuses and austere Sabines has only just set foot in our city'. It seems overly rational to alter to *Tatium ueterem* (as Heyworth does, followed by Goold) on the grounds that there was only one Tatius; the literally nonsensical plural may be an indication that Propertius' moralizing tone is not to be taken seriously.

4.11.3 *cum semel infernas intrarunt funera leges* 'when once the corpse has entered the jurisdiction of the Underworld': a verb of motion is surprisingly combined with a non-local object (*leges*). Heinsius' *sedes* (adopted by Goold) is an easy change, but Heyworth 2007b, 503 points out well that *leges* introduces the juridical motif that pervades Cornelia's apologia.

4.11.38 *sub quorum titulis, Africa, tunsa iaces* 'under whose titles you, Africa, lie crushed'. 'The boldness of the image is very striking ... feet pound (Hor. *ars* 430), titles do not' (Heyworth (2007b), 511). Heyworth considered emending *titulis* to *plantis* (suggested to him by J. B. Hall), but did not do so in the OCT text. The phrase is an excellent example of Propertius' blurring of ideas; it probably also hints at a triumphal procession in which representations of conquered territories (or actual inhabitants of them) were displayed beneath the *tituli* that proclaimed Roman victories.

4.11.64 *condita sunt uestro lumina nostra sinu.* Heyworth accepts Scaliger's *uestra ... manu* because 'the eyes of the dead are shut by hand, not by embrace' (2007b), 512; but if *uestro ... sinu* is understood as abl. of place rather than means ('in your embrace were my eyelids closed',

---

[27] The same is true of his 2010 rewriting (*seu nimis aduersum mutarit improba lectum*), in which word order would suggest that *nimis* actually qualifies *aduersum*.

Goold), the expression aptly evokes the image of Cornelia dying in her sons' arms.

3.13.21 (in a description of suttee) *ardent uictrices et flammae pectora praebent* 'the victorious burn and offer their breasts to the flames'. '*ardent* makes for a rather awkward hysteron proteron: the chosen wives burn before they expose themselves to the flames' (Heyworth (2007b), 349); he emends *ardent* to *gaudent* (Stephanus) 'the winners rejoice', on the basis of other accounts of the practice, notably Cic. *Tusc.* 5.78 *quae est uictrix, ea laeta ... una cum uiro in rogum imponitur* ('the one who wins is happily placed on the pyre alongside her husband'). In Propertius' description, however, the paradoxical nature of the contest has already been stressed in the previous couplet (*certamen habent leti ... pudor est non licuisse mori* 'they compete for death ... not to be allowed to die is a disgrace'), after which *gaudent* would make no further point; *ardent uictrices* encapsulates the bizarre result of the competition.

1.1.33 *in me nostra Venus noctes exercet amaras.* Heyworth emends *in* to *nam*, making *me* the object of *excercet* and *noctes amaras* an acc. of duration ('Venus ... troubles me through the bitter nights'). The transmitted text is admittedly difficult: *in me* could mean 'in my case' (abl.) or 'against me' (acc.), and the sense of *excercet* is also ambiguous ('wears out' or 'wields'). Although Shackleton Bailey (1956), 7–8 was not himself persuaded by the numerous examples he cited of *exercere* = 'to ply against', it does not seem excessively hard to understand *noctes amaras* as the equivalent of an object such as *saeuitiam* or *iram*. 'Against me Venus wields bitter nights', that is, she forces me to endure them.

1.11.24–5 *omnia tu nostrae tempora laetitiae.* | *seu tristis ueniam seu contra laetus amicis.* 'The identification of an addressee with *tempora* is not one found elsewhere ... *laetitiae* anticipates *laetus* in verse 25, and there is a slight conflict between the two lines, in that 24 stresses Cynthia's responsibility for joy, while 25–6 see her as the cause of unhappiness and joy alike' (Heyworth (2007b), 56). The last two objections can be met by seeing 25–6 as the summation of Propertius' thought over the past 18 lines: 7–20 detail the reasons why Cynthia (or her imagined behaviour at Baiae) brings him unhappiness, while 21–4 affirm her central place in his life. Heyworth's preferred reading, Fontein's *omni tu nostrae tempore deliciae* ('you are at every moment my delight') would not remove the alleged conflict between 24 and 25–6. Parallels apart, the sense of 24 is clear and unexceptionable: 'you are my every moment of happiness' (Goold).[28]

4.7.19–20 *pectore mixto* | *fecerunt tepidas pallia nostra uias* 'breast to breast our cloaks warmed the road beneath us'. According to Heyworth, '*pallia* is not perhaps impossible … but parallels are not forthcoming' ((2007b), 465); Heyworth and Goold accept the old conjecture *proelia*. But in a poem so thick with *Realien*, a reference to clothing rather than the tired poeticism *proelia* seems more at home. Heyworth writes that 'the idea of warming the streets with blankets (or cloaks) is so bathetic in the context that it must be counted improbable'; I had assumed that the sense was that the heat of the lovers' bodies was so intense that it percolated through the cloaks on which they were lying and warmed the roadway.[29]

4.7.4 *murmur ad extremae nuper humata uiae*, 'recently buried near the noise of the edge of the road' (Heyworth). Heyworth rejects the usual interpretation ('near the edge of a noisy road') because 'the grammatical oddity goes unexplained', and accepts Housman's *tubae* for *uiae*.[30] But a reference to Cynthia's ignominious grave site seems much more apposite in the context of her complaint than mentioning a random detail of her funeral; also, while Propertius uses *extremus* of *rogus* (1.19.2) and *funus* (2.11.4), and while 'the last trumpet' has a familiar sound to modern ears, precise parallels for *extrema tuba* are, as Heyworth might say, not forthcoming (see also on 1.11.6 in the text that follows).

4.8.23 *serica nam taceo uulsi carpenta nepotis* | *atque armillatos colla Molossa canes* 'for I say nothing of the smooth-skinned spend-thrift's silk-hung trap and his Molossian dogs with bracelets around their necks' (Goold) [serica nam ς: siriginam Ω]. 'We may wonder (even in this linguistically bold context) whether *serica* … is an apt adjective for *carpenta*' (Heyworth (2007b), 478). Everything else in the couplet highlights the pampered indulgence of the young man, so a reference to a 'silken carriage' (however explained) is thematically apt. Heyworth

---

[28] I should admit that line 24 in its transmitted form is one of my favourite lines of Propertius, so I may be particularly resistant to seeing it altered.

[29] Giardina adopts *proelia* and alters *tepidas* (*trepidas* in some MSS) to *tremulas*. Vigorous lovemaking can make the bed shake, as in Catullus 6.10–11 *tremuli … quassa lecti* | *argutatio inambulatioque*, but to have it shake the streets takes hyperbole rather far.

[30] Heyworth writes that '*tubae* for *uiae* is very simple palaeographically (with b often written u, and ta preceding)' (2007b, 464); if he can cite an instance in a medieval manuscript of *tuba* written *tuua*, I will gladly treat him to lunch when we next meet.

accepts Bonazzi's *sed uaga iam*; *uaga* ('wandering') is either feeble or, if taken in a stronger sense (Heyworth translates 'erratic'), introduces a discordant detail. It is cause for concern, though, that Propertius nowhere else postpones *nam*; perhaps one could consider *serica iam taceo*, with *iam* in the sense 'at this time'.

1.11.6   *ecquis in extremo restat amore locus?*

> restat amore locus] r. a. calor *Giardina*: r. amor iecore *Housman, parum*
> *eleganter*: r. amare loco *Kraffert*: pectore r. amor *Heimreich*

As the apparatus shows, *restat amore locus* is a much-emended phrase. Heyworth prints *ecquis in extremo pectore restat amor* (Heimreich) 'is there any love left in the depths of your heart?'; *in extremo amore* in the sense 'in the farthest corner of your love' is undoubtedly challenging, but in a poem centred on spatial separation and its emotional consequences we should be reluctant to rule out a spatial conception of love. *Extremus* is an adjective of which Propertius is fond – it occurs almost as often in his work as in Ovid's much larger elegiac corpus – and which figures in other difficult expressions. For example, 1.17.23 *illa meum extremo clamasset puluere nomen* (where *extremo … puluere*, an abl. of place, means 'over my last ashes'),[31] 1.6.26 *hanc animam extremae reddere nequitiae*, where Heyworth reads *aeternae* (his own conjecture) in place of *extremae*, 4.7.4 *nuper ad extremae murmur humata uiae* (see earlier text). One or two atypical uses of the same adjective could be put down to chance or scribal error, but when a word occurs several times in distinctive ways a critic should be wary of emending them all away.

4.7.63–70   Andromedeque et Hypermestre sine fraude maritae
                  narrant historias, tempora nota, suas …
              sic mortis lacrimis uitae sanamus amores;   69
                  celo ego perfidiae crimina multa tuae.

              Andromeda and Hypermestra, wives without treachery,
                  tell their stories, those well-known events …
              So with the tears of death we heal the loves of life;
                  I conceal your many crimes of faithlessness.

> 64 historias … suas *Markland*: -ae … -ae codd.   tempora *Ayrmann*: pectora
> *codd.*: foedera *Heinsius*: uulnera *Fontein*   69 sanamus] sancimus
> *Rossberg*: solamur *Passerat*: memoramus *Paldamus*: renouamus *Giardina*

---

[31] Giardina reads *murmure* (Heinsius) for *puluere*.

Heyworth and Goold are among a number of editors who have accepted Rossberg's *sancimus* ('we confirm/ratify') for *sanamus*; the conjecture is highly plausible on palaeographic grounds (*ci* and *a* closely resemble each other in half-uncial and some early minuscule scripts), but it flattens out what is for me one of Propertius' most beautiful and touching lines. Much discussion has focused on the relevance of 69–70 to the lives of the mythological figures who have been previously mentioned, Andromeda and Hypermestra; the couplet is perhaps best understood as referring primarily to Cynthia herself, with the sense of *sanamus* clarified by the pentameter: 'so with the tears of death we make whole the loves of life (which were not whole because of your faithlessness)'. In the background is the typically Propertian connection between love and disease.[32]

I conclude that a number of the conjectures that Heyworth and/or Goold have adopted are probably normalizations of what should be accepted as genuine Propertian language.

It may be useful to mention a case that I regard as borderline, partly to locate the limits of my own tolerance for difficult expressions and partly to illustrate the larger point that in this text there is a grey area of some size in which the decision whether to retain or to alter the transmitted text is not easily made.

4.3.49–50   omnis amor magnus, sed aperto in coniuge maior;
              hanc Venus, ut uiuat, uentilat ipsa facem.

              every love is great, but it is greater in a manifest husband;
              Venus herself fans this flame to give it life.

              49 aperto in] rapto *Hoeufft*: adempto *nescioquis apud*
              Hoeufft: deserta in *Burman* (sed del.*)*

aperto in coniuge, if sound, is a distinctly unusual expression; logically Shackleton Bailey (1956), 232 is right to note that an *apertus coniunx* is the opposite of a *furtiuus uir* ('a secret lover'), but the combination remains verbally idiosyncratic. Furthermore, designating Lycotas as *coniunx* (i.e., a legitimate husband) makes *apertus* redundant. The most telling point for me, though, is aptness to the context: it seems more pertinent for Arethusa to stress her husband's absence than the legitimacy of their union. Hoeufft's

---

[32] The explanation of Shackleton Bailey (1956), 253, that after mentioning Andromeda and Hypermestra Propertius was reminded of Dido and other heroines whose loves had been unhappy, and was led by that recollection 'into language not strictly appropriate to the two names which he happens to have singled out', looks like special pleading.

rapto ('a husband taken away'), which Heyworth prints, gives an apt sense and is not far removed from the paradosis.

As an area for further study, I would suggest that difficult expressions in Propertius may not be limited to individual passages, but may also appear in connection with recurrent themes. For example, several striking expressions cluster around the idea of death and its after-effects; one might infer that the emotional intensity generated by the theme manifests itself in heightened pressure on language.

1.17.20 *illic si qua meum sepelissent fata dolorem | ultimus et posito staret amore lapis* 'if at home some fate had buried my sorrow and a gravestone stood where love lay': the non-personal nouns *dolor* and *amor* take the place of the lover's body.

1.17.23 *illa meum extremo clamasset puluere nomen*: see p. 118.

1.19.19 *quae tu uiua mea possis sentire fauilla*: Heyworth (2007b, 85) interprets *mea ... fauilla* as an instrumental abl. ('may you ... be able to recognize this ... from my embers'), which entails a substitution of *mea fauilla* for *me mortuo*; on other views the language is even more idiosyncratic; for example, Butler and Barber see either 'a bold abl. of circumstance = "when I am glowing ashes", or an abl. of place = "at my ashes"'.

2.14.15–16 *atque utinam non tam sero mihi nota fuisset | condicio: cineri nunc medicina datur* 'if only the rationale [Heyworth] had not been made known to me so late: as it is, medicine is being given to ashes': 'the absence of a genitive or defining clause with *condicio* is unusual' (Shackleton Bailey (1956), 91), and the combination *cineri* [= *mortuo*] *medicina datur* (*data est* Heyworth in the apparatus) is arresting.

3.6.24 *insultet morte mea*, if *morte mea* means, as Shackleton Bailey (1956), 149 prefers, 'dance on my dead body'.

Finally, it appears that in at least one elegy Propertius has used difficult expressions as an organizing device, to underscore the poem's structure and themes. The elegy is 4.8 and the relevant passages contain the word *mora* ('delay'). This poem accounts for three occurrences of *mora* out of twenty-one in all of Propertius' work; Book 2 has only two, and no other poem has more than one, so there is an initial likelihood that the word carries some thematic weight. That likelihood is increased by the placement of the word within the poem: it appears first in line 4, next in line 51 and for the third time in line 78; in other words, near the beginning and end and shortly after the midpoint. In its first and last appearances, *mora* forms part of an elliptical or otherwise challenging expression, while the middle instance has it in the stereotyped phrase *nec mora* ('without delay'). After a quick look at the two difficult cases I will try to draw out the significance of the word for the poem as a whole.

4.8.4 *hic ubi tam rarae non perit hora morae.* This is another example of a type discussed earlier, where the individual words are as plain as day but their combination produces something new and strange. Propertius seems to have combined idioms familiar from colloquial speech, for example, *perire* 'be wasted' and *rara mora* 'an exceptional <reason for> spending time'. So Heyworth: 'where an hour spent on such uncommon tourism is not wasted'. This seems more likely than Goold's 'an hour spent ... on so infrequent a visit'.[33]

4.8.78 *aut lectica tuae sudet aperta morae.* In its transmitted form, the line is unintelligible; *sudet* in particular seems to require some alteration. The slightest change is Gruter's *se det*, adopted by Goold, which yields the sense 'take care [*caue* from preceding line] that an open litter does not offer itself to your lingering gaze' (literally 'to your lingering'). Heyworth reads *nudet* (Koch) for *sudet* and *operta* (*recentiores*) for *aperta*, translating 'don't you linger and let a litter bare its secrets to you'. Giardina keeps *aperta* and accepts Palmier's *sidat*, creating an image of the litter sinking to the ground and allowing Propertius to look inside. Whatever one does with *sudet* and *aperta*, the elliptical phrase *tuae ... morae* (= *tibi moranti*) seems immune to doubt.

The uses of *mora* near the beginning and end of the poem parallel the actions of the main characters: Cynthia's prolonged absence in Lanuvium triggers Propertius' attempt to retaliate by dallying with the floozies Phyllis and Teia. In line 4 *mora* applies to someone, who in the scenario of the poem turns out to be Cynthia, passing time at Lanuvium; in line 78 *mora* applies directly to Propertius and describes dwelling on the attractions of another woman. The third occurrence of *mora* (51), in the negative form *nec mora*, comes at the moment when Cynthia throws open the doors of the place where Propertius and his companions are partying: her sudden reappearance puts an immediate end ('without delay') both to her absence and to his tryst.

It seems that difficult modes of expression in Propertius can function as an expressive device. Further exploration of that possibility might be one

---

[33] Giardina replaces *ubi tam* with *ibidem* and *rarae* with *paruae*.

way of progressing in our understanding of Propertius as a poet, as well as helping to resolve at least some of the problematic places in his text.

*****

> *Old Housman:* When I was a young man at Oxford my edition of Propertius was going to replace all its forerunners and require no successor.

> *Young Housman:* Wouldn't that be something! I have been thinking of it, too. You see, Propertius is so corrupt [that] it seems to me, even today, here is a poet on which the work has not been done. All those editors!, each with his own Propertius, right up to Baehrens hot from the press! – and still [there's] the feeling that between the natural chaos of his writing and the whole hit-or-miss of the manuscripts, nobody has got the text near right. Baehrens should make everyone obsolete – isn't that why one edits Propertius? It's certainly why I would edit Propertius!

> *(The Invention of Love)*

Old Housman's youthful notion of an edition that would require no successor is obviously a fantasy, and not only as regards Propertius; as we have seen, no edition of a classical text can be definitive. In the case of Propertius, it may not even be possible for an edition to win widespread acceptance.[34] But editions can render their predecessors obsolete, for a variety of reasons. One is improved information about the manuscript tradition, and in that respect Heyworth does set a standard that makes it unnecessary to return to previous editions. His apparatus also surpasses all its predecessors in its recording of conjectures. It is in the constitution of the text where the relationship of Heyworth's edition to others is hardest to define, and it will be some time before the classical community renders a final verdict on that aspect of his work.[35] One thing is clear: Heyworth's achievement is such that no return to a text like Barber's or Fedeli's seems possible, and the next editor of Propertius will need to emulate him by rethinking the problems of the text from the ground up. That enterprise will be at least as much a work

---

[34] In the lapidary judgement of La Penna (1982), 523, 'an edition of Propertius that could obtain widespread agreement is perhaps impossible'.

[35] Heyworth's edition has been welcomed with enthusiasm by a fellow-sceptic, H.-C. Günther (2008); the reaction of Richard Thomas (2009) was noticeably more guarded.

of literary criticism as of philology in the narrow sense of that term, since at this point a heightened awareness of Propertius' poetic aims and methods offers the best hope of defining more precisely the line that divides authorial eccentricity from scribal negligence.[36]

The foregoing discussion also raises a broader issue: what is the appropriate editorial approach to an idiosyncratic author preserved by a highly fallible manuscript tradition? A possible answer is that the editor, in the words of Housman about the *Culex*, should be slow to emend the text and slow to defend it,[37] and willing to employ the obelus when the text seems too deeply corrupt for any emendation to inspire confidence (which will be fairly often). In specific cases the editor may choose to render a judgement of *non liquet*, or to follow the example of Heinsius in some of his notes on the *Metamorphoses* and entertain more than one solution;[38] negative capability is not often listed as one of the virtues of an editor, but it may claim a place when dealing with an author like Propertius.

Leaving questions open or admitting that a case can be made for more than one answer runs counter to the conventions of the traditional critical edition, which compel an editor to print one reading and one only, relegating all alternatives to the apparatus. That and other limitations of our customary editorial practices will be discussed towards the end of the next chapter.

---

[36] A notable contribution is Riesenweber (2007) on Propertius' use of figurative language, which appeared at the same time as Heyworth's edition and so could not respond to it; for a judicious assessment, see Fedeli (2013).

[37] Housman (1902), 339.

[38] See earlier text pp. 46–7 (Chapter 2).

CHAPTER

7

Presenting the text: the critical edition and its discontents

Every scholarly edition has to be understood as an embodied argument about the textual transmission. It asks for engagement as an interpretation of the evidence by opening up for inspection the instabilities of composition and revision recorded in the textual apparatus. At the same time, it closes them down in the clear reading text. It *fixes* a text at the same time as its explanatory apparatus opens it out into the discourses of its day. Editions can and need to be read with and against the grain. (Eggert (2009), 177)

In his introduction to Friedrich Leo's *Kleine Schriften*, Eduard Fraenkel recalled one of his first encounters with the scholar who would become his mentor: 'soon after my arrival <in Göttingen> Leo invited me to lunch on a Sunday. After lunch, we went into his lovely garden and he inquired in a friendly way about my work. At the time, I had read most of Aristophanes and began to enthuse about him to Leo, going on at length about the magic of the poetry, the beauty of the choral songs, and heaven knows what else. Leo let me declaim without interruption, perhaps for ten minutes, with no hint of impatience or disapproval. When I had finished, he asked 'exactly what edition are you reading Aristophanes in?' I thought to myself 'was he even listening to me? What has that question got to do with what I was telling him?' After a moment's ill-tempered delay, I answered 'in the Teubner edition.' He replied 'oh, you read Aristophanes without a critical apparatus.' He said it absolutely calmly, with no harshness and no trace of mockery, just honestly amazed that a tolerably intelligent young man could do such a thing. I looked down at the grass and had a single over-whelming sensation: νῦν μοι χάνοι εὐρεῖα χθών ['now let the broad earth gape open for me'= *Iliad* 4.182, 8.150, with νῦν substituted for τότε].

124

Later it seemed to me as though in that moment I had grasped the meaning of proper philological study.[1]

Few teachers today would respond to a student's enthusiasm as Leo did, and even fewer students' embarrassment would take the form of a Homeric tag neatly adapted to fit the circumstances; nevertheless, the status of the critical edition, and of the critical apparatus in particular, as a badge of scholarly seriousness has not changed in the intervening years. A scholar today preparing an article or a monograph dealing with a classical text will normally base his or her references not on a Loeb edition – however good the Loeb text in question may be – but on a critical edition with an apparatus, even if the focus of the discussion is not textual.

The main purpose of a critical apparatus is to record the evidence on which the text printed by the editor rests. In editions constituted on eclectic grounds – as are almost all editions of classical texts – that function is particularly important, since the basis for the text as printed can vary from word to word, and without an apparatus a reader would have no way of knowing whether a given reading in the text is attested by all manuscripts, by only some manuscripts, or, in the case of a conjecture, by no manuscript at all. The apparatus is thus a constant reminder of the synthetic nature of classical editing. In addition, by making the editor's acts of judgement visible, the apparatus renders them liable to the reader's evaluation.

The format now standard for critical editions of classical texts, in which the apparatus of variants is placed below the text, evolved in the course of the eighteenth century from earlier modes of presentation in which information about manuscript readings was usually embedded within a larger commentary surrounding the text on three or four sides – a format ultimately deriving from thirteenth-century manuscripts of texts with commentaries. The practice of denoting manuscripts by single-letter abbreviations or *sigla* also developed over several centuries, and not until the first half of the nineteenth century did it entirely supersede the practice of referring to manuscripts by Latin names such as *codex Mediceus* or *liber Palatinus vetustissimus*.[2] Some years ago, I came across an intriguing medieval antecedent of a text with *apparatus criticus*: Florence Laurentianus 37.1, a late

---

[1] Fraenkel (1960), xl–xli, my translation. The Teubner edition of Aristophanes referred to is that of Theodor Bergk (second edition 1857, reprinted many times in the following decades), which does indeed lack a critical apparatus.

[2] Fuller discussion in Kenney (1974), 152–7; he observes that, as long as classical scholarship was regarded as part of *bonae literae*, 'good literary manners would inculcate a distaste for the curt, the technical, the algebraical'.

fourteenth-century manuscript of Seneca's tragedies that records variants at the foot of each page.[3] Like other discoveries in this field, the essential concept of the apparatus appears to have been grasped centuries before it became standard practice.

One might think that, in contrast to establishing the text of a classical author, the construction of an *apparatus criticus* would be relatively free of controversy. That is far from being the case, as the contradictory assessments of Badalì's apparatus to Lucan cited earlier suffice to show.[4] In fact, much of what I have argued about the text – for example, that there can be no definitive form, and that subjectivity plays a determining role – is also true of the apparatus. A dictum of E. J. Kenney states that 'the apparatus to a critical edition should be as judiciously constructed as the text itself';[5] that pronouncement only makes sense if the apparatus is the result of editorial judgement and not simply the application of a set of rules.

Although an apparatus is as essential to a critical edition as the text itself, it is constructed on principles distinct from those that govern the establishment of the text. It is not difficult to imagine an edition containing a well-constructed apparatus but a highly questionable or flawed text, and – although I find this harder to conceive – the reverse is also apparently possible. Michael Winterbottom, reviewing an edition of three lives by St Jerome in the *Sources chrétiennnes* series, declared the apparatuses 'disaster zones', then went on to say that 'the texts … read quite happily'.[6] That disparity suggests that the ability to construct an apparatus may be even rarer today than the skills required to produce an acceptable text.

The basic questions raised by an *apparatus criticus* are, what evidence to include, and how best to report it?

On the first point, there is no reason for all apparatuses to pursue the same goal. Antonio La Penna has sensibly argued for the legitimacy of several types of critical edition, from one type with a severely pared-down apparatus giving only what is essential for the constitution of the text (like the apparatus of Eduard Norden's edition of *Aeneid* 6) to another with a very expansive apparatus, intended for the use of scholars, such as that found in some recent Teubner editions, with bibliography and citations of parallel passages; he also recognized a place for editions that present a slender apparatus but collect

---

[3] Tarrant (1976), 41, MacGregor (1985), 1153. The manuscript is also of interest as the only known witness for part of the commentary on *Hercules furens* by the Paduan pre-humanist Albertino Mussato (d.1329); see MacGregor (1980).

[4] See pp. 25–6 (Chapter 1).

[5] Kenney (2004), 369.   [6] Winterbottom (2008), 373.

in an appendix interesting readings from the *recentiores* or conjectures that do not wholly convince but seem worth considering.[7] All the types mentioned by La Penna are well represented among current critical editions of Latin classical authors, but the state of peaceful coexistence among them that he envisaged has not yet been attained.

For all their diversity, however, the apparatuses of most classical editions are alike in one respect that sets them apart from the apparatus to a textual edition of many printed texts. Modern textual editing has espoused an ideal of completeness to which classical editors hardly ever aspire. Given sufficient editorial time and a well-subsidized publisher, it is possible to produce for many modern texts editions with a truly comprehensive apparatus of variants, that is, a full account of all versions that have or could have any direct connection with the author. What that means in practice may be seen from the ongoing *Variorum Edition of the Poetry of John Donne*, begun in 1981, of which four volumes have so far appeared. The text of Donne's first Elegy, *The Bracelet*, occupies 114 lines, or three printed pages in the edition; it is followed by a textual apparatus of twenty-three pages listing every variant reading of the sixty-three manuscript copies and eight seventeenth-century print sources in which the poem appears, in whole or in part. Even this apparatus, however, is not comprehensive by the most inclusive standards of modern textual editing, since it does not register differences in incidentals such as spelling and capitalization; that is only done for variants between the single copy chosen as base text and the printed text, where such differences as 'which' for 'w^{ch}' and 'For' for 'for' are listed as 'emendations'.[8]

Such exhaustive recording of variants is almost non-existent in classical editing; the only exceptions I know of are editions of short texts that survive in only a few witnesses. For example, J. A. Richmond's edition of the 134-line *Halieutica* attributed to Ovid contains a full report of what Richmond regarded as the only manuscript with independent authority, Vienna lat. 277; Richmond's apparatus, even though it reports just one manuscript, is voluminous enough to be printed alongside the text rather than beneath it.[9] Ignazio Cazzaniga's edition of the 93-line *Peruigilium Veneris* gives substantially complete reports of the three independent manuscript witnesses, as well as of two probably derivative sources.[10]

No edition so far published, however, of a classical text preserved in a sizeable number of manuscripts includes more than a limited selection of

---

[7] La Penna (1982), 517. A recent example of an edition with an appendix of that kind is Tobias Reinhardt's 2003 edition of Cicero's *Topica*.

[8] Stringer (2000), 20–1.   [9] Richmond (1962).   [10] Cazzaniga (1959).

variants. Some degree of selectivity can be justified by the wide separation in time between the original text and the bulk of the surviving manuscript copies; even if late manuscripts cannot be eliminated as derivative on stemmatic grounds, an argument can be made that the likelihood of their having preserved authentic readings is too small to warrant full citation of their readings. At least as powerful a factor, however, has been the practical difficulty of compiling and presenting a comprehensive apparatus.

A textual point in the *Metamorphoses* can illustrate what would be involved. In the opening lines of Book 6, Ovid describes the humble background of Arachne, the daughter of Idmon, a dyer of cloth, and the inhabitant of a small town in Lydia: *orta domo parua paruis habitabat Hypaepis* ('born in a small house, she dwelt in small Hypaepa', 6.13). Medieval copyists were often puzzled by unfamiliar proper names, and Hypaepa is about as recherché as they come; its only other appearances in Latin literature are in texts that had almost no circulation in the Middle Ages, Petronius' *Satyricon* (133.3) and Tacitus' *Annales* 1–6 (4.55.2). Not surprisingly, Ovid's scribes transformed *Hypaepi*s into a variety of forms, among them *hipelis, hipeis,* and *hipeplis*. (The name of Arachne's father Idmon was similarly transmogrified, appearing as *edmon, hydmon, ethmon, ithmon, hismon, hysmon, ismon, igmon, imon,* and *amon.*) In the orthographical appendix to my edition, where I recorded significant variations of proper names, the situation is summarized as follows: (h)(y/i)p(a)epis *(cf. Petr. Sat. 133)* U^{4c} φ: -eplis *uel* -elis *uel* -eis Ω; from this a reader could with some effort gather that the essentially correct form is found in a late correcting hand in manuscript U and in at least three twelfth-century manuscripts (the meaning of the collective *siglum* φ), but that reader would receive no information on the manuscript evidence for other forms of the name; also omitted are manuscripts later than the twelfth century that have some version of the correct form and variants attested by only one late manuscript. A full account of the witnesses known to me or reported by earlier editors would look like this (*sigla* are as in my edition; *recentiores* that have not yet been given *sigla* are cited by the number of their entry in Franco Munari's catalogue of *Metamorphoses* manuscripts):

(h)(y/i)p(a)epis U^{4c} (hip*epis*) F^{2c} (-ebis) W^c *acde²ᵛfh^ck* (bip-) l_4^c $l_6^{ac?}$ *o* p_2 $r^{1c}svw$ *36 80 238 338 349^c 368 59 75 87 341* c*Freiburgensis* c*Vratislauensis (teste Magno)*: -elis *UrbEMZ* b^1 c*Bersmanni* (iph-) *55*: -eis $BF^{ac}GL$ $b^vegl_2l_3l_4^{ac}z$ *63 149 349^{ac} 34^{ac} 346* (hyph-): -eplis $N^{3-4c}W^{ac}$ *Ambros. R.22 sup.* $h^{ac}l_5$ *64*: (h)(i/y)belis R r^{ac}: hibepis *89*: epepis *8*: hyplepis *311*: hypeisplis (*ut uid.*) v_2: hyberis *34^{2c}*: *desunt P l.*

This report is itself very far from complete: it records only about fifty out of nearly 400 extant manuscripts, and it takes no account of the most common features of medieval orthography: presence or absence of h, i for y, and the differing treatment of the ae diphthong (i.e., as ae, as e-caudata, or as e). As a result, the forms *hypaepis, ypaepis, ipaepis, hipaepis, hypępis, ypępis, hipępis, ipępis, hypepis, ypepis, hipepis, and ipepis* are treated as identical. A comprehensive report would be many times the size of this sample. For the moment I will not ask whether a full account of the manuscript evidence would serve any useful purpose; I wish only to show that such an account, if extended to cover a poem of some 12,000 lines, is hardly feasible given the limitations of traditional scholarly publishing and editorial lifetimes.[11] (In the final chapter, I will consider whether conceiving of the apparatus as an electronic database provides a new approach to this question.)

In practice, therefore, all critical apparatuses in editions of classical texts are selective; the relevant questions are what degree of selectivity is appropriate and how to determine the criteria of selection, and on those points there is wide disagreement. There are two main competing ideologies of the apparatus, according to which editors can be categorized as minimalists or maximalists.

The minimalist approach is practised by most British editors or editors with British training; its results can be seen in the volumes of the OCT series, characterized by the 'breuis adnotatio critica' that has long been a standard description of the OCT apparatus. Its aim is encapsulated in a phrase used by E. J. Kenney in the preface to his 1961 edition of Ovid's amatory poems, the 'truly critical apparatus' or the 'apparatus uere criticus'. Kenney invoked this concept to explain his decision to remove (or 'relegate', in his exilic image) to an Appendix those manuscript variants which, although they do not contribute to the establishment of the text, are nonetheless useful in showing the character of the scribe or are for some other reason worthy of mention.[12] (Those words made a strong impression on me as a graduate student: in the margin of my copy I find 'good!' written in a youthful hand next to the paragraph in question.) In the revised edition of 1994, Kenney adopted an even more rigorous approach: one of his alterations was to eliminate the Appendix (literally 'send into exile', alluding to his earlier metaphor); some

---

[11] On the impractical nature of an 'apparatus plenus', see also Kovacs (1991), 35, who provides a full account of the conjectures made on just three lines of Euripides' *Medea*.

[12] 'Ut apparatum uere criticum reddam, lectiones eas quae, quamquam ad loci ubi occurrunt textum constituendum nihil adferunt, tamen librarii indolem utiliter declarent aut alioqui mentione dignae sint, in Appendicem relegaui': Kenney (1961), xi.

of the variants it contained were incorporated into the apparatus proper, but the majority were evidently thought no longer worthy of mention.[13] In addition to his several critical editions, Kenney's numerous reviews of editions in *Classical Review* have made him an articulate spokesman for this approach. Other exponents of this style would include R. A. B. Mynors, L. D. Reynolds, and M. Winterbottom.

At the heart of the minimalist approach is the idea that the apparatus as well as the text should be the product of the editor's judgement, and that it should contain only what is essential to the establishment of the text. The reasons for such a restriction are in part methodological, the belief that a carefully pruned apparatus allows readers to grasp significant differences without the distraction of minor or immaterial variants. Along with that view of the content of the apparatus goes an interest in how the material is presented, the aim being the greatest possible clarity and legibility. Another underlying assumption is aesthetic, the belief that a well-constructed *apparatus criticus* can be, if not a thing of beauty, then certainly an elegant piece of craftsmanship.

The maximalist approach tends to multiply the number of manuscripts reported and to be more inclusive in reporting variants of all kinds, such as grammatically or metrically impossible readings or the forms of proper names. The style is exemplified in an extreme form by F. W. Lenz, editor of several Ovidian and pseudo-Ovidian texts for the Paravia series in the mid twentieth century; here is a typical page of his edition of the *Nux*.[14]

> fit quoque de creta, qualem caeleste figuram   81
> sidus et in Graecis littera quarta gerit.
> haec ubi distincta est gradibus, quae constitit intus
> quot tetigit uirgas, tot capit ipsa nuces.
> uas quoque saepe cauom spatio distante locatur,   85
> in quod missa leui nux cadat una manu.
> felix secreto quae nata est arbor in aruo
> et soli domino ferre tributa potest.   88

81 de creta (decreta) **ABB$_1$C$_1$DEFGG$_{1,2}$H$_1$L$_{1,2}$MM$_3$PSUV$_{1,2,3,4}$β**: de certa (decerta) **A$_1$HOP$_{1,3}$οπ**: decretam **V**: de terra **R** *et i. m. m. recent.* **V$_1$**: de terra **C**, de greça *i. m.* **C^1**: delta (*glossa ad u. 82 pertinens*) **F$_2$**   qualem **ω** (*del. et tum quale est*

---

[13] 'Appendice exulare iussa lectiones quasdam ibidem commemoratas in ipsum apparatum recepi': Kenney (1994), xiv.

[14] Lenz (1956).

G): quale **D** (?) **V**: quale e **D** (? *dubit. Vo.*) **P**: ego quali est *i. m. m. recent., coniecit igit.* **V₁** figuram **B₁CEFF₂G₁.₂L₂M**(?) (**LP₂**) **P₃V**: figuram (m *del.*) **A₁**: figura **ABC₁DGHH₁L₁M₃OPP₁RSUV₁.₂.₃.₄β**: *nominat. non minus bonum defend. Vo. ut hyperbaton, qua de figura disput. SBerAk. Münch. 1918, 4, 3 sqq.*   82 quarta] quanta **V**
gerit] gerit **C**, uenit *i. m.* **C₁**: uenit **R₁**   83 H(a)ec] Nec **D**   distincta] di distincta
i
F: destincta **P**: destincta **H₁** o   qu(a)e **ω**: qua **L₁**: qui **E** o: q/ (3?) **M₃**   constitit
intus] constitu **V₃**   intus] intro **V**   84 Quot] Quod **BDG₂**: Tot **S**: Quę **P₂**   uirgas
Senftleb apud Burm. (*i. lineas parallelas trianguli*): uirga **ω** (**LP₂**): uirgo *nisi errau.*
Pol. **M**   *post* capit *uid. del.* l' **V₁**   ipsa **A₁DFGL₁.₂M**(?)**P₁SVV₃**: ipsae (a *corr. in*
e) **F₂**: ipse **ABB₁CC₁EG₁.₂LM₃NPP₂RV₁**: inde **HH₁OP₃UV₄β** *et i. m. m. recent.* **V₁**: ille
V₂   85 Vas] Vos **P**   cauum **ω**   Vas quoque saepe cauum spatio] Vasque cauum
saepe spatio **R**: Vas q°₃ sepe uacuum spacio (° *ssc. m. recent.*) **V₁**: Vasque cauum plenum
spatio **A**   dissate loquatur **R**   86 quod **DF** (*de hoc errau, Bae.*) **HL₄OV** *et m. recent.*
V₁: quo **AA₁BB₁CC₁EF₂GG₁.₂H₁L₂M**(?)(**LP₂**)**M₃PP₂RSUV₁.₂.₄**: qua **V₃**   cadat
A₁DEFGHH₁L₁M₃OP₃SUVV₃β: cędat **M₃**: cadit   **ABB₁CC₁F₂G₁.₂L₂M**(?)(**LP₂**)**NPP
₁RV₁.₂.₃** una **AA₁B₁CEFF₂GG₁.₂HH₁LL₁.₂M₃OPP₁.₂.₃RSUV₁.₂.₃.₄β**: uua (?) **B**: ima
D: ipsa **V**   87 in **G₂**   aruo **BB₁CC₁EFF₂G₂M**(?)(**LP₂**): est in arbor **NRVV₁²**: agro
AA₁DGG₁HH₁L₁/₂M₃OPP₁.₃SUV₂.₃.₄β: auro **V₁**   88 Et] ac **G₁**: Que **P**   fere **H₁**

Despite its size, Lenz's apparatus is far from exhaustive: a search for manuscripts by Martin Pulbrook in preparation for his own edition turned up twenty-eight witnesses unknown to Lenz. Here is Pulbrook's apparatus for the same lines, based on fifteen manuscripts 'chosen in order to illustrate … most important readings with the smallest number of primary manuscripts'.[15]

81 de creta] decretam *V*: de certa *HMU*   qualem] quales *V*   figura] figuram
EFLM¹RUVW   82 Graecis] gentis *G*   quarta] quanta *V*   83 distincta] did-
istincta *F*   qui *BE*: quae *X*: qua *a*   extra *Pulbrook*: intus *X*: intro *V*   84
quot … tot] tot … quot *S*   uirga] uirgas *incaute temptauit Sentleb* [sic] *receperuntque
editores*   capit] rapit *M*: gerit *a*   ille *a*: inde *HR*: ipse *AEU²W*: ipsa *X*   85 uas
quoque saepe cauum] uasque cauum plenum *A*   86 quod *DFHUV*: quo *X*   cadat]
cadit *ABLPUW*: cadet *a*   usque *Pulbrook*: una *X*: ima *D*: ipsa *V*   87 aruo
EFUV: agro *X* 88   et] ac *W*

In addition to reducing the number of manuscripts cited, Pulbrook's apparatus achieves greater compression by replacing long lists of individual *sigla* with collective *sigla*, X to represent the reading of all fifteen base manuscripts except those otherwise noted, and a to denote the reading of one or

---

[15] Pulbrook (1985), 28; he candidly remarks that 'the choice of these particular manuscripts is in some sense a matter of hazard'.

more manuscripts outside the core group (details are provided in a separate section following the text).

Expansive apparatuses of the kind produced by Lenz are a favourite target of minimalist scholars' scorn. Reviewing Lenz's edition of the *Ibis*, Kenney wrote that 'the apparatus criticus sprawls over two-thirds and more of most pages, recording with idiot zeal and impartiality the aberrations of ... witnesses of widely varying age and credibility.'[16] Almost fifty years later, Kenney had lost none of his edge or his aversion to maximalist apparatuses. Reviewing the first volume of Enrico Flores's edition of Lucretius, Kenney wrote that the apparatus 'is also encumbered with what Housman called the lees of the renascence, variants – sometimes unmetrical ... – of no critical significance which belong, if anywhere, to repertories of scribal delinquency (what George Goold called babble from the padded cell)'.[17]

It is tempting to connect the divergence of style between minimalists and maximalists to other divisions among textual critics. There is a general tendency for editors who have devoted themselves to studying the manuscripts of an author to take a conservative attitude to establishing the text, and also to display the fruits of their labour in the form of an expansive apparatus.

In this matter, I cannot pretend to be neutral. From my days as a graduate student, I have been influenced by critics of the minimalist school, and as my apparatus to the *Metamorphoses* shows, this is my editorial style. But I will try to identify as fairly as I can the drawbacks in both approaches, using as a first example the current Teubner and Oxford editions of Ovid's amatory poems.

A typical segment of Antonio Ramírez de Verger's Teubner text and apparatus (*Am.* 2.7.9–26):

> siue bonus color est, in te quoque frigidus esse,
> seu malus, alterius dicor amore mori.   10
> atque ego peccati uellem mihi conscius essem:
> aequo animo poenam, qui meruere, ferunt.
> nunc temere insimulas credendoque omnia frustra
> ipsa uetas iram pondus habere tuam.
> aspice ut auritus miserandae sortis asellus   15
> adsiduo domitus uerbere lentus eat.
> ecce novum crimen: sollers ornare Cypassis
> obicitur dominae contemerasse torum!
> di melius, quam me, si sit peccasse libido,

---

[16] Kenney (1958), 133.   [17] Kenney (2004), 369.

sordida contemptae sortis amica iuuet!   20
quis Veneris famulae conubia liber inire
tergaque complecti uerbere secta uelit?
adde quod ornandis illa est operata capillis
et tibi per doctas grata ministra manus:
scilicet ancillam, quae tam tibi fida, rogarem!   25
quid, nisi ut indicio iuncta repulsa foret?

Ramírez de Verger:

9 quoque] modo *Heinsius*   esse *S, y, recc., Heinsius* : esset *PY*   **11**
essem *PYS, recc. aliquot, cf. met. 13,805* : esse *T, recc.*   17 nouum
crimen sollers ornare *PYS, recc. aliquot* : tuum sollers caput exornare *V2,
recc. aliquot*   **19** quam me, si] quam, si mihi *Heinsius in notis* si *Itali,
Naugerius* : sic *codd.*   **20** sortis *y, recc. aliquot, Heinsius* : sordis *PYS,
recc. aliquot*   iuuet *T, recc., Heinsius* : iubet *PYS*: uiuet *L2*   **21**
Veneris *agnouit Heinsius*   **23** ornandis *T, recc., Heinsius* : ornatis *PYS,
recc. aliquot* illa est operata *PYS, recc. aliquot, prob. Heinsius, Martyn, cf.
2,13,17; epist. 9,35; art. 3,635, fast. 6,249* : illa est operosa *T, recc., h, Kenney,
cf. 2,10,5; 16,33* : ipsa est operanda *F*   **24** per doctas ... manus *T, recc.,
h, Heinsius, edd. plerique, cf. 2,4,28; art. 3,134* : perdocta est ... manus
PYS: perdoctaest ... manus *Müller* : perdocta est ... manu *Heinsius in notis,
prob. Riese* : perdoctae ... manus *Hilberg 1875* : *alii alia* grata *PYS, recc.*: apta
N, recc. aliquot, Bentley coll. 2,8,4   **25** quae tam *T, recc., Naugerius,
Heinsius, Ehwald, prob. Goold 1965; de hac iunctura, cf. e.g. Pl. Poen.
234:* quierat *P* : qua erat *Y (ut uid.)*: quae erat *S, recc. aliquot*: quod erat *y, coni.
Kenney 1958 et 1966* : quae sit *E2, Riese*: quia erat *corr. Palmer 1893, dub.
Luck post* rogarem *admirationis signum posuit Goold, qui hunc uersum ironice
explanauit*

Here is Kenney's corresponding apparatus:

Kenney:

11 essem *PYS* : esse ω   17 nouum crimen sollers ornare *PYS* : tuum s. caput
exornare ς 19 si *Itali, Naugerius* : sic *codd.*   peccasse *PYS* : peccare ω   20
sortis *yω* : sordis *PYS* 23 ornandis *ω* : ornatis *PYS*   operosa *ω* : operata
PYSCN : operanda *F*   24 per doctas *ω* : perdocta est *PYS*   perdocta ... manu
Heinsius   25 quod erat *y sicut coni. Kenney* : quierat *P* : quae erat *Sς* : quae sit
*BE*ₐ : quae tam *ω* : *de Y incert.* : quia erat *Palmer*

Ramírez de Verger is clearly a maximalist, whose apparatus is on average three times as extensive as Kenney's. The main reasons are these: readings of one older manuscript are cited even when ungrammatical or unmetrical; the agreement of later manuscripts with readings in earlier witnesses is regularly noted; variants in the form of proper names are generously listed; lists of parallels are included to justify Ramírez de Verger's choice of reading; modern scholars are named, not just as responsible for conjectures, but as supporting one or another competing reading.

The main objection to Ramírez de Verger's apparatus is that it is wasteful of space and unhelpful in directing a reader's attention. One example is his use of '*recc. aliquot*' of readings found in one or more of the older manuscripts that also appear in an unspecified number of *recentiores*; the term figures in that sense several times per page (nine times in the earlier sample). In addition to being typographically wasteful (Kenney's *siglum* ς conveys the same information with a single character), the practice is questionable on methodological grounds. In a large and contaminated tradition, nearly every reading found in an early witness that is not obviously impossible will appear in some number of later manuscripts. In such cases, the addition of '*recc. aliquot*' or an equivalent expression tells us nothing useful; the designation would be better reserved for readings that have bypassed the *antiquiores* and for which the *recentiores* are the earliest witnesses.

Particular problems do arise in deciding what kind of apparatus to construct in open traditions, where few if any manuscripts can be eliminated as *descripti* in the strict sense, but even so there is no benefit in multiplying witnesses, because in such traditions authority resides in the intrinsic merits of readings, not in the manuscripts that contain them. So the selective reporting that is required as a matter of practicality can also be defended on methodological grounds. One strategy for coping with a large open tradition is to report the minimum number of witnesses needed to provide manuscript attestation for all transmitted readings that are judged potentially authentic or worth recording for other reasons.[18]

A practice of Ramírez de Verger and of other maximalist editors that particularly incenses minimalists (myself included) is that of citing the names of previous editors who have adopted a given reading or conjecture; an example appears on line 25 of the sample mentioned earlier, where Naugerius, Heinsius, Ehwald, and Goold are named in support of the reading adopted.

---

[18] West (1973), 43–4 advocates a similar procedure.

This type of 'variorum' citation has been called 'totally useless'.[19] The policy may indeed be useless from the reader's perspective, but for the editor it can serve an important psychological function, that of providing protection by invoking the authority of like-minded critics, or in other words finding safety in numbers. An example from an earlier age is instructive. Rudolf Ehwald's apparatus entry on *Metamorphoses* 6.294 reads 'eiecerunt uersum Heins. Merkel, Haupt, Riese, Magnus'. Ehwald does not normally cite the decisions of earlier editors; his reason for doing so here is obviously to explain why he has taken the unusual step of bracketing a line found in all manuscripts. In that light his reference to Haupt, Riese, and Magnus is particularly useful, since it shows that not only the sceptics Heinsius and Merkel, but also his more conservative predecessors, had come to the same conclusion. For non-conservative editors, the incentives may be more varied: paying tribute to esteemed predecessors (as in the 'cultic' references to Heinsius and Bentley I mentioned previously (see p. 21)), the desire to impress readers with the editor's diligence, or simple *horror uacui*, an aversion to which makers of apparatuses are as prone as commentators.

There may be good reasons to cite a critic who has contributed significantly to the solution of a problem (e.g., by offering a cogent defence of a manuscript reading or conjecture, or by adducing a relevant parallel), but that is different from listing editors who have simply opted for one or another proposed solution.

It is all too easy to produce a *reductio ad absurdum* of this practice. In *Metamorphoses* 9.638–9 Ovid writes, of the love-maddened Byblis, *iam palam est demens inconcessamque fatetur | spem Veneris* ('now her madness is manifest and she confesses her forbidden hope of love'). That is how the passage appears in all the oldest manuscripts, but some *recentiores* and the Latin text presupposed by the Byzantine Greek translation of Maximus Planudes offer the variant *inconcessaeque ... Veneris* ('her hope of forbidden love'), which I and several previous editors have preferred.

The note in my apparatus reads as follows:

inconcessaeque *Plan ς (cf. 10.153)*: -amque Ω

Franz Bömer's commentary has the following note:

inconcessam codd. Magnus. Ehwald. Lafaye. Thes. VII 1,998,17. *-ae* Heinsius. Breitenbach. Anderson.

Drawing only on editions from 1900 onwards, one could produce the following note:

> inconcessaeque *Plan ς (cf. 10.153) Slater, Breitenbach, Anderson (in commentario, 1972), Miller–Goold, Hill, Kenney:* -amque Ω *Edwards, Magnus, Ehwald, Haupt–Ehwald, Miller, Lafaye, Ruiz de Elvira, Anderson (ed. 1977), Marzolla, Galasso.*[20]

But why limit the report to editions of the past century? If the purpose of the practice is to record the editorial history of a given problem, how can one not go back to the *editio princeps* of 1471?

Criticism of the minimalist approach has not been lacking, although its tone has generally been less strident. The language used often implies lack of nourishment (e.g., the 'skinny apparatus' of La Penna) or lack of generosity (e.g., the 'stingy apparatus' of Magnaldi).[21] The latter description rests on the assumption – almost always justified – that the editor knows considerably more about the manuscript evidence than is revealed in the apparatus.

The main weakness of the minimalist approach is that, in striving for concision and elegance, it may omit information of which the reader should be made aware. That danger is arguably greater than that posed by the opposite approach, since the reader of a maximalist apparatus can, with some effort, winnow out what is trivial, whereas the reader of a minimalist apparatus has no means of supplying information not presented by the editor. Martin West pithily remarked that 'editors are not always people who can be trusted, and critical apparatuses are provided so that readers are not dependent upon them'.[22] But as Juvenal asked in a different context, *Quis custodiet ipsos custodes*? Critical apparatuses are the work of the same editors against whose errors of judgement they are meant to protect readers. They can perform that function only if editors provide the information needed for them to do so. For example, I consider it an editor's duty to inform readers when a transmitted reading has been seriously questioned, even if the editor has concluded that the text is sound; otherwise the reader has no basis on which to assess the editor's decision. I also think that an editor is obligated to report cases in which a substantial part of the manuscript tradition presents a variant not adopted in the text, even if that variant has no chance of being right. That requirement might seem self-evident given the nature of a critical apparatus,

---

[20] My example is hypothetical, but an actual instance is to hand in Andreas Michalopoulos's edition of *Heroides* 16 and 17 (2006).

[21] La Penna (1982), 517; Magnaldi (2007), 627.

[22] West (1973), 9.

but not all editors have followed it, for example, Shackleton Bailey in his Horace.

The risks of minimalist reporting can be illustrated from a couplet in Ovid's *Remedia amoris* (565–6), described by a commentator as one of the most vexed passages in the poem:[23]

> hic male dotata pauper cum coniuge uiuit:
> uxorem fato credat obesse suo

> this poor man lives with a wife of meager dowry;
> let him think that his wife stands in the way of his destiny

The couplet is part of a series of *exempla* illustrating the precept given the poet by a vision of Cupid, *ad mala quisque animum referat sua, ponet amorem* ('just let each man turn his attention to his own ills, and he will forget his love' 559). Kenney and Ramírez de Verger print the same text, but their apparatus entries are radically different.

Ramírez de Verger:

> 566 *hunc uersum nondum sanatum dubitanter recipio*   fato *P2 fTSg, recc., Ma, Heinsius*: facto *RY(sed -c- eras.)E, To, recc. aliquot, Es3, Scaliger (ap. D. Heinsium), Ramírez de Verger-Socas 1998*: facito *Madvig 1873*   credat] credit *Af*   obesse *Tf, recc. aliquot, Ma, Heinsius* : adesse *RYEP2, To, recc. aliquot, Scaliger (ap. D. Heinsium), prob. Riese, Vollmer, Borneque, lege Lucke, Ramírez de Verger-Socas 1998; de uocis adesse sensu, cf. u. 663; Hor. serm. 1,9,38 et Kiessling-Heinze ad loc.; uide Luck 2002*: abesse *Es3*   suo] suam *Madvig 1873*.

Ramírez de Verger's apparatus is loaded with information, some of it superfluous;[24] but it shows that the verse has been the object of much scholarly attention. Kenney cites two manuscript variants without comment, from which a reader might reasonably, but wrongly, infer that the couplet is unproblematic:

> 566 fato *yKω* · facto *RYEC*   obesse *ς* : adesse *RYEKω*

In his first edition, Kenney had marked the couplet as controversial with the phrase 'haerent interpretes' ('commentators are stuck'). His silence in the second edition might reflect his policy of suppressing exegetical observations when in his view a passage has been satisfactorily explained in a

---

[23] Pinotti (1988), *ad loc.*

[24] For example, the separate citation of manuscripts in Spanish collections when they agree with other *recentiores*, as in the combinations '*recc.*, Ma[tritensis]', '*recc. aliquot*, Ma', and 'To[letanus], *recc. aliquot*'.

commentary.[25] But is it prudent for an editor to assume that readers will be consulting commentaries along with the edition? Should not a critical edition aim at being self-standing, at least as regards the constitution of the text?

My own conscience is not entirely clear on this score; I will mention two places in the *Metamorphoses* where I now think I should have reported a proposal that I did not accept.

Pentheus is set upon by the bacchants (3.715–18):

ruit omnis in unum   715

turba furens; cunctae coeunt fremituque sequuntur
iam trepidum, iam uerba minus uiolenta loquentem,
iam se damnantem, iam se peccasse fatentem.

the whole maddened throng rushes

against one man; they all converge and shouting pursue him,
now afraid, now speaking less violent words,
now condemning himself, now admitting he was wrong.

716 fremituque *Schepper*: trepidumque Ω (cunct(a)eque χ [*Heinsius*])

I found the *trepidumque … trepidum* of the manuscripts intolerable, and accordingly accepted Schepper's conjecture *fremituque* in 716, which I still believe is the most convincing solution; but I ought to have mentioned that Riese had proposed deleting 717, even though I would be inclined to keep the line: 717–18 describe an ordered sequence of reactions, and the repetition of *iam* with 'pathetic accusatives' has a plausibly Ovidian feel.

Pandion entrusts his daughter Philomela to his son-in-law Tereus (6.496–9):

hanc ego, care gener, quoniam pia causa coegit
et uoluere ambae (uoluisti tu quoque, Tereu),
do tibi perque fidem cognataque pectora supplex,
per superos oro, patrio ut tuearis amore …

This girl, dear son-in-law, because a pious reason compels me
and both daughters wished it (you wished it too, Tereus),
I give to you and by your loyalty and the ties that unite us
I beg you by the gods to guard her with a father's love.

497 et *B*: ut Ω

[25] Kenney (1994), xiv.

In the text as found in most manuscripts, 497 forms a rather limp expansion of 496 ('as both daughters wished', etc.). I chose to read *et* for *ut* at the start of the line with one older manuscript in order to connect the phrases more closely, but I did not mention Heinsius' suspicion that 497 might be an interpolation, a proposal that on reflection I think deserves to be seriously considered. If the line is interpolated, it was added by a reader who either thought that the *pia causa* of 496 called for a more explicit statement or who wished to underline the tragic irony of the scene and Pandion's ignorance of Tereus' true motives.

It may not be accidental that in these two passages the piece of information I did not mention was a proposal to bracket a line. Quite possibly, knowing that my propensity to suspect interpolation was likely to strike some as excessive, I chose not to mention such suspicions when I did not find them compelling. But elsewhere as well I would now record variants or conjectures that I previously omitted, either by oversight or because I did not find them sufficiently persuasive.

Questions can also be raised about the fundamental assumption of minimalist editors, that the apparatus should report only manuscript readings that have a bearing on the constitution of the text or that are essential for representing the testimony of the tradition. Manuscript evidence that falls outside this heading is likely to be characterized as 'rubbish' or a similarly pejorative term, such as Kenney's references to 'aberrations' or 'scribal delinquency' (see p. 132). But in fact an apparatus can serve useful functions beyond providing that basic level of information.

We may recall the discussion of manuscript variations of the name of Arachne's home town, Hypaepa. For the purpose of establishing what Ovid wrote, that information is useless. He presumably knew the correct form of the town's name, and it is irrelevant whether that form was accurately or inaccurately transmitted in his manuscripts; if the correct form had been entirely lost in the manuscript tradition, even the most conservative editor would not hesitate to restore it by conjecture. But from other points of view, some version of the data is useful. For understanding the shape of the *Metamorphoses* tradition it is instructive to see that a reading that has been corrupted in all the oldest manuscripts is correctly preserved in several twelfth-century manuscripts; we can be sure that the correct form was not produced by scribal conjecture, since even the most learned of twelfth-century scribes, faced with *hipelis* or *hypeis*, would not have been able to arrive at *hipepis*. Also, marginal or interlinear glosses on the word attest to a wide range of skill and enterprise: one fifteenth-century reader thought that *hypaepa* was not a place name at all, but an obscure synonym for *domus* or *uilla*, while another accurately noted a fleeting reference to the town in Strabo, 'libro xiii citra finem' (= 13.4.7). That example suggests that in order fully to exploit the potential interest of manuscript material, scholars need to look not only at the readings in the text but also at the glosses and comments appended to them.

Another consequence of a highly selective apparatus style is that 'maverick' manuscripts, whose readings are unlikely to be authorial, are prone to be discarded as unreliable witnesses, when they might offer valuable evidence of the taste and ability of medieval readers. As Derek Pearsall writes, 'manuscripts dismissed as worthless by editors of critical texts are often the very ones where scribal editors have participated most fully in the activity of a poem, often at a high level of intellectual and even creative engagement'.[26]

In the light of the foregoing discussion, La Penna's view of a variety of legitimate forms of critical apparatus looks even more appealing. In particular there may be a case for compiling as full an apparatus as possible for every text, to serve as a point of reference; ideally this would need to be done only once for a given author, then updated periodically to take account of new conjectures and additional manuscript collations. (In the next chapter, I will consider the role of electronic means of recording data in producing such an apparatus.)

*****

The previous pages have focused on the content and function of the critical apparatus, but one can also ask whether the current model of a critical edition is the most effective form of textual presentation. I believe that the format of Latin preface and text with Latin apparatus creates difficulties of several kinds for both editors and users of editions.

The convention of the Latin preface creates a distance between editors and readers; it suggests that the activity of the editor needs to be described in a special language that only initiates can fully comprehend. Today, many editors publish a full account of their analysis of the manuscript tradition and their editorial rationale as preliminary or simultaneous studies in their native language; that laudatory practice makes a Latin preface even more obviously ornamental, an occasion for classicists to display their skill in Latin prose composition

---

[26] Pearsall (1985), 103, on the quality of the editorial work in some manuscripts of the *Canterbury Tales* and *Piers Plowman*.

(with the risk of occasional embarrassment as a consequence). In the OCT series, there are clear indications that the convention is crumbling, having been abandoned by several editors of both Greek and Latin texts: first of all, Hugh Lloyd-Jones and Nigel Wilson in their edition of Sophocles (1990), followed by Roger Green in his Ausonius (1999), and more recently by Michael Reeve (Vegetius, 2004), Christopher Carey (Lysias, 2007), Nigel Wilson (Aristophanes, 2007), and Stephen Heyworth (Propertius, 2007a). It seems likely that within a generation the Latin OCT preface will be a thing of the past. But all the editors mentioned have chosen to draft the apparatus in Latin, finding the traditional Latin terminology still useful for its brevity and clarity.

The very qualities that have commended the Latin apparatus as a medium of scholarly communication entail difficulties. Even a carefully drafted apparatus presents challenges of decoding to the non-initiate; indeed, the well-crafted apparatus in particular, because of its higher degree of condensation, can be difficult to interpret by readers who are not themselves editors or textual critics. If one couples that fact with the diminished exposure classicists-in-training today receive to the mechanics of editing, it may be the case that relatively few professional classicists feel at home in reading an *apparatus criticus*.[27] Furthermore, critical editions are consulted more often than they are read, and it may be difficult for someone who opens an edition in order to check a specific passage to work out the conventions of the apparatus at a glance.

The traditional format of a critical apparatus conveys a false appearance of objectivity and certitude. Ideally the apparatus should be an invitation to the reader to engage in a dialogue with the editor, but one can only have a dialogue with a person, and the format of the apparatus tends to minimize or even elide the editor's personality.[28] Without descending into chattiness, editors could exploit the potential of the Latin critical vocabulary to a greater extent than they usually do, to give their notes a more personal voice.[29] (Heinsius' textual

---

[27] Zetzel (1993), 113 offers a more optimistic view: 'for the most part, the well-established conventions of the synoptic critical apparatus … allow any experienced reader to elicit the possible choices and the history of the text in medieval and modern times from the foot of the page of any competent edition'. Perhaps we differ only in our estimate of the number of experienced readers and competent editions.

[28] Paul Maas's statement that 'our present *apparatus critici* have too little life in them' (1958), 24 is undoubtedly true, though somewhat surprising to find in a book much of which has all the personality of a computer's instructional manual.

[29] Richard Rutherford draws my attention to several pungently expressed notes in Denys Page's OCT text of Aeschylus, e.g., on *Agam.* 871 'uersum miserrimum eiecit

notes offer an excellent example of critical writing that conveys a strong sense of a scholarly personality; see pp. 43–7 (Chapter 2).

More specifically, the black-and-white character of most apparatuses makes it difficult for the reader to gauge the editor's relationship to the edited text. It is a rare editor who feels confident that he or she has always chosen the correct variant or emendation, but if the only choices available are to place a reading in the text or to relegate it to the apparatus, it is hard for an editor to register varying degrees of confidence in the text as printed. In his OCT edition of Euripides' *Iphigenia in Aulis*, James Diggle ingeniously devised a set of marginal signs to mark degrees of suspicion attaching to a line or lines; once familiar with the notation, a reader could tell instantly whether Diggle regarded verses as *fortasse Euripidei*, *fortasse non Euripidei*, *uix Euripidei*, or *non Euripidei*.[30] The procedure was prompted by the specific problems of that play, but it could serve a wider purpose in helping editors express degrees of suspicion concerning possible interpolations. The editor can, it is true, append an expression such as 'fort. recte' to a reading not adopted, as I did in many places in the *Metamorphoses*, but that is at best a partial solution, and it also creates the false impression that readings not so designated have in the eyes of the editor no possibility of being correct. This might be another area where apparatus Latin could be used to convey a wider range of editorial attitudes. I have in mind such expressions as *utinam recte* ('if only correctly!') to describe a reading or conjecture to which the editor is attracted, but soberly refrains from adopting;[31] similarly, *aegre reicio* ('I reject with difficulty', used by Gian Biagio Conte in his apparatus to *Aeneid* 9.485).

In addition, the evidence or the reasoning on which the editor has based his or her choice of readings and conjectures can rarely be presented in conjunction with the choice itself. There are ways of alleviating that separation of text and rationale: one is the practice of publishing textual commentaries as companion volumes; another is the form taken by some recent Teubner apparatuses, which cite not only variants and conjectures, but also parallels, statements of the editor's understanding of the text, and bibliography. Neither solution is ideal, the former because it requires consultation of a

---

Schuetz' or on *Cho.* 386–7, where a reading generally accepted by editors is described as 'monstrum horrendum informe'. Colourful language in an apparatus is not to all tastes: Önnerfors (2006), 703 stigmatizes the apparatus of Michael Reeve's OCT Vegetius as 'oft rhapsodisch', a judgement as unfair as it is peculiar.

[30] Diggle (1994), vi, 358.

[31] Called 'strange' by Richmond (2006), 132.

separate volume and the latter because it makes the apparatus hard to negotiate, since information about variants and conjectures must be disentangled from other material. To some extent, the Teubner model has a forerunner in Housman's editions of Manilius, Juvenal, and Lucan. In each of them, the reporting of variants and conjectures is interwoven with a textual commentary, sometimes including extensive citation of supporting parallels. Such a format was only feasible, however, because Housman reduced the reports of manuscript evidence to a minimum (or, as many would think, even further).

A related drawback of the Oxford- or Teubner-style critical edition is the separation of text and apparatus from interpretative matter. Reviewing Roger Mynors's OCT edition of the *Panegyrici Latini*, W. S. Maguinness made the startling assertion that 'any Oxford Text of the *Panegyrici Latini* is of limited utility compared with an honest and competent Budé product';[32] his reasoning was that the format of the latter allows for explanatory notes to be included alongside the text itself. But recent Budé editions also demonstrate the problem of combining a substantial commentary with a text and translation: the space available for notes at the foot of the page is rapidly filled, and most of the commentary has to be placed at the back of the volume. The alternative, which is to reduce the amount of text per page to accommodate the commentary, also creates difficulties, as can be seen in Arthur Stanley Pease's edition of *Aeneid* 4, where a single line of text often sits stranded atop a mass of commentary.[33]

Finally, there are some texts where conditions magnify the drawbacks of the standard critical edition to the point where another form of publication may be preferable. For example, the admittedly unusual case of Vibius Sequester, the late antique author of the treatise *De fluminibus fontibus lacubus*, whose principal claim to fame is having preserved the only line of Cornelius Gallus' poetry known before the publication of the Qasr Ibrim papyrus. Vibius' text is transmitted in a single independent manuscript (V = Vat. lat. 4929, s. ix, owned by Heiric of Auxerre); it draws extensively on now lost ancient sources, and where it appears corrupt, it is often hard to tell whether the error arose in Vibius' source, in his misunderstanding of that source, or in the course of transmission. E. J. Kenney has suggested that in this case a traditional edition is less useful than a do-it-yourself kit consisting of a diplomatic transcription of V, an apparatus containing all conjectures with any plausibility, and a report of the extant sources used by Vibius.[34]

---

[32] Maguinness (1966), 65.   [33] Pease (1935).

[34] Kenney (1969), 183–5. Liberman's edition of Statius' *Siluae* (2010) is intended to furnish readers with the means of constructing their own text: it offers a lightly corrected

Several of the features of critical editions I have been discussing are linked to traditional methods of publication; it is therefore natural to ask whether developments in technology, which are changing so many aspects of classical studies, have the potential to transform our editorial practices as well. I will attempt an answer to that question in the final chapter, along with some thoughts about the future of classical editing.

text of the only extant manuscript and, in place of a traditional apparatus, an extensive 'commentaire critique' that calls attention to difficulties in the transmitted text and records possible solutions.

CHAPTER

8

The future: problems and prospects

E. R. Dodds: 'Our editions of Greek and Latin authors are good enough to live with'; D. R. Shackleton Bailey: 'Maybe, maybe not; it all depends on one's standard of living'.[1]

In this chapter, I will attempt a brief look forward into the future of editing classical texts. The questions I want to consider are these: What remains to be done in the area of textual criticism and editing? To what extent will traditional editing procedures be affected by new and emerging technology?

I

A natural starting point would be to ask which authors are and are not currently represented in satisfactory editions. 'Satisfactory' is a replacement for 'definitive', a concept that for reasons previously discussed I do not believe is applicable in this area. But that innocent-seeming question immediately raises another: what constitutes a satisfactory edition? The exchange between Dodds and Shackleton Bailey (even if only *ben trovato*) shows that eminent scholars can differ on that point. A minimal definition of a satisfactory edition might be one that accurately reports the essential manuscript evidence and reflects the current state of thinking about a text well enough to provide a basis for further study. Acceptable standards of living vary not only from person to person, but across time as well. Even an excellent edition will not remain satisfactory forever; for most authors, a good edition will have

---

[1] Probably apocryphal, based on Shackleton Bailey's remark that 'when E. R. Dodds pronounced that our editions are good enough to live with, he cannot have been thinking of G. Lehnert's Teubner edition (1905) of the longer declamations falsely attributed to Quintilian' (1976a, 73).

a useful lifespan of one or two generations, with fifty years an especially long life. (The obvious exceptions are editions of less-read texts, e.g., the *Agrimensores*, for which Lachmann's edition of 1848 was for more than 150 years the only critical edition of most of the corpus.)

There are certainly texts for which a new critical edition is not urgently needed. I think primarily of well-studied texts preserved in very few manuscripts or single manuscripts, such as Tacitus' *Annals* 1–6 or the Roman history of Velleius Paterculus, or texts with manuscript traditions that lend themselves to stemmatic analysis, such as the biographies of Cornelius Nepos. Even here what is in question is not a ban, but a moratorium.[2]

Much more numerous are texts for which a new edition would be welcome; it may be useful to divide them into rough categories:

(a) texts where further study of the manuscript tradition is needed. That is true for most classical texts that survive in numerous copies, since editors have rarely investigated the later stages of the tradition. (See pp. 55–6.)

(b) texts that exist in editions of very different kinds (often very conservative and very sceptical), where the main desideratum is a fresh assessment of the evidence. One such case is Juvenal, where the choice is currently between Clausen's OCT (very judicious, perhaps somewhat too cautious) and the editions of Knoche and Willis (both excessively sceptical). Another is Horace: Klingner's Teubner does the best job of presenting the manuscript evidence (although it could be improved on in that respect), but it is deficient in recording doubts of the transmitted text; Shackleton Bailey's Teubner offers a more sceptical alternative that is consistently thought-provoking but less consistently persuasive. The old OCT by Wickham (revised by Garrod) has always been unsatisfactory.[3]

Ovid's *Metamorphoses* presents a different situation: the latest editions are either conservative (Anderson) or moderately sceptical (my edition), so there is scope for a more aggressively sceptical approach, which is presumably what Antonio Ramírez de Verger and the *équipe* he has assembled will aim to provide.[4]

A subset of this category might include any text edited by Shackleton Bailey, for which his conjectures will need to be assessed by a future editor.

---

[2] Tarrant (1995a), 123, Reeve (2000), 204.

[3] Wickham (1901), iii prided himself on having printed only ten conjectures in the entire corpus. On the need for a new edition, see also Tränkle (1993).

[4] See Ramírez de Verger (2006) for criticism of my text, which he characterizes as conservative.

(c) texts in need of an improved apparatus. Until recently one such text was Virgil, where there was room for an apparatus more generous than that of Mynors's OCT but less expansive than that of Geymonat's Paravia edition. That is one of the contributions of the recent Teubner editions of the *Aeneid* by Gian Biagio Conte and of the *Eclogues* and *Georgics* by Conte and Silvia Ottaviano.

(d) texts for which advances in knowledge of the author make a new edition necessary. The metre of Plautus is better understood now than it was when Leo and Lindsay produced their editions, and a number of the textual decisions they made on metrical grounds now appear dubious or mistaken. New editions may be desirable when commentaries have improved our understanding of difficult passages or have sharpened our appreciation of an author. Examples would include several commentaries on individual Senecan tragedies that have appeared since Otto Zwierlein's OCT, and the recent spate of commentaries on single books of Martial.

(e) texts where the consensus of critical thinking has been questioned. An example is Catullus, on which John Trappes-Lomax has published a 'textual reappraisal' proposing more than 600 alterations of Mynors's 1958 OCT text in a corpus of about 2300 verses, the great majority of which are changes to the transmitted reading.[5] Among them are nearly fifty passages in which Trappes-Lomax suspects interpolation, a phenomenon that had been thought extremely rare in Catullus. It remains to be seen how many of his proposals will find general acceptance, but meeting his challenge to the modern *textus receptus* will require a thorough rethinking of the text.[6] Trappes-Lomax has at least succeeded in showing that Mynors's apparatus is often silent when there is reason to doubt the transmitted reading. Mynors's Catullus may therefore be an example of a meritorious edition that after more than fifty years has reached the end of its useful life.[7]

New editions can themselves destabilize existing views of a text, and sometimes the only adequate response to a provocative new edition is another edition.[8] Indeed any edition, to the degree that it stimulates thinking about the text, begins the process that will lead to its being succeeded by another edition.

---

[5] Trappes-Lomax (2007).

[6] For a balanced assessment, see Thomson (2009).

[7] On the need for a new critical edition of Catullus, see also Harrison (2000). Other critical work that a new edition will need to assess includes Nisbet (1978), Harrison and Heyworth (1998), Diggle (2006), and McKie (2009).

[8] So Ramires (2007), 400, reviewing Liberman's Valerius Flaccus.

(f) finally, there are texts that seem destined to remain the site of critical disagreement; in such cases new editions are periodically needed to take note of the latest contributions to the debate. Propertius is an obvious example (see Chapter 6). Another is the set of *Epistulae heroidum* attributed to Ovid; here the problems include a more than usually unreliable manuscript tradition, the possibility of frequent interpolation, and several cases of disputed authorship. The conservative edition of Heinrich Dörrie (1971) encountered criticism on several grounds,[9] and in the interim there has not been a new edition of the corpus. (If J. B. Hall is preparing a new edition for Teubner, we may look forward to a boldly sceptical treatment.) Here as well a new edition would be able to draw on a large body of recent commentary, although most of it has not been much concerned with textual problems.

A somewhat similar case is Lucretius. Enrico Flores's edition has been criticized for excessive conservatism, but the matter is complicated when dealing with a poem probably left unfinished or unrevised by the author; another controversial issue is the place of Poggio's manuscript, which Flores, contrary to the recent consensus, regards as an independent witness.[10] It is remarkable that Lucretius, the first classical text whose transmission was analysed in stemmatic terms, still lacks a critical edition based on the only independent witnesses; for that reason among others, David Butterfield's OCT edition is eagerly awaited.

So a great deal of useful editorial work remains to be done, and the traditional avenues of publication for critical editions are still open.[11] But will there be classicists willing to devote themselves to editorial work? A comment I made twenty years ago about 'a shrinking corps of trained editors'[12] is if anything more true now, at least in the English-speaking world, partly as a result of the institutional pressures I mentioned earlier.[13] (The situation seems very different in parts of Europe, notably Italy and Spain.) A few years ago, the American Philological Association (APA) launched an appeal for scholars willing to carry on the edition of Servius' commentary initiated by E. K. Rand and several of his students, the ill-starred 'Harvard Servius'. To my knowledge, only one proposal was received, from two scholars, one of whom has

---

[9] See, e.g., Goold (1974), Reeve (1974), and Hunt (1975).

[10] For critiques, see Liberman (2003), Kenney (2004), Deufert (2005), Reeve (2005), Butterfield (2011). Flores has not been silent in the face of criticism; see p. 37.

[11] There is also a place for periodic surveys of the editorial situation, such as Tarrant (1995a), 130–41 and Reeve (2000).

[12] Tarrant (1995a), 123.   [13] See, pp. 27–8.

since died; the APA decided to support the project, to be continued by the surviving editor. The incident provoked discussion about the need to incorporate
textual criticism and editing in the training of future classicists, but I am not
aware of substantive changes having been made in that area.

The scarcity of trained editors may help to account for the increasing
number of editions containing an introduction and commentary along with
a text taken unchanged or with minimal changes from an existing critical
edition. (Examples include most of the editions in the Cambridge Greek and
Latin Classics series.[14]) There are good reasons for the popularity this type of
edition enjoys, but it also entails less fortunate consequences: one is to separate the function of commentator from that of editor, and another is to suggest that the important editorial work on these texts has already been done.

II

I do not believe that technological advances will fundamentally alter the
way that classical texts are edited, but there have already been significant
changes in how editions are constructed and how the information they contain is disseminated.

Some of those developments are distinctly worrisome. For example, what
happens to textual criticism's focus on establishing the most reliable possible text in an environment in which texts circulate in electronic form and are
downloaded from out-of-date or uncritical editions? In some respects, the
use of electronic databases marks a return to conditions in the early days of
printing, when editions of classical texts were usually reproductions of late
manuscripts of no special merit.

To plunge briefly into the textual jungle currently on the Internet, I cite
two examples I encountered while downloading texts from The Latin
Academy/Ad Fontes.

Cicero, *Topica* I

Qua inscriptione commotus continuo a me librorum eorum sententiam
requisisti; quam cum tibi <u>euissem</u>, disciplinam inveniendorum argumen-
torum, ut sine ullo errore ad ea ratione et via perveniremus, ab Aristotele
inventam illis libris contineri … mecum ut tibi illa traderem egisti.

Excited by this inscription you immediately asked me about the books'
thesis; when <u>euissem</u> it to you, that they contained a system invented by

---

[14] See p. 28.

Aristotle for discovering arguments so that we can arrive at them correctly and in an orderly and rational fashion, you entreated me to impart it to you.[15]

The word *euissem*, a nonexistent form, is a mistake for *exposuissem* ('when I had explained it to you').

Florus, *Epit.* 2.21 (the subject is Mark Antony)

Quippe cum Parthos exorsus arma in otio ageret, captus amore Cleopatrae quasi bene gestis rebus in regio se sinu reficiebat ... Aureum in manu baculum, ad latus acinaces, purpurea vestis ingentibus obstricta gemmis: diadema deerat, ut regina ex et ipse frueretur.

Indeed when Parthos exorsus arma he was leading a life of leisure, seized with love for Cleopatra he sought relief in her royal bosom as if he had brought matters to a successful end ... In his hand was a golden sceptre, a scimitar at his side, his garment of purple fastened with enormous gems: a diadem was lacking, ut regina ex et ipse frueretur.

Here, two errors create serious problems in understanding. *Parthos exorsus arma* is a garbled version of *post Parthos exosus arma*. The omission of *post* and the alteration of *exosus* to *exorsus* almost reverses the sense: instead of 'detesting arms after defeating the Parthians', the text as recorded gives 'having initiated arms <against> the Parthians'. In the final clause, *ex* should be *rex*; the loss of the initial letter wreaks havoc with the entire phrase ('only a diadem was missing that he might himself be a king taking joy in his queen').

The same database presents the text of Catullus with *tituli* to individual poems similar to those found in the manuscripts, including inaccurate headings such as *Ad Arrium* for poem 84 (in which Arrius is never addressed) and even sheer nonsense, as in poem 36 (*Annales Volusi, cacata carta*), entitled *Ad lusi cacatam*.

A reader of corrupt texts such as those might well imagine how Poggio or Poliziano felt when coming upon a manuscript of a previously unknown author. Today a scholar can easily correct such errors by consulting a critical edition; the fact remains that some of the electronic texts now available do not meet minimal standards of reliability. Even more damaging than the

---

[15] The final sentence may contain a small textual problem: *illa* (neuter plural) should refer to *argumenta*, but the run of the sentence strongly suggests that what Cicero is asked to impart is the system for finding arguments (the *disciplina*); either *illa* refers loosely to what has been mentioned previously, or it is a slip for *illam*.

errors these texts contain are the misconceptions about texts that they foster; for example, the absence of a critical apparatus could suggest to an innocent user that there is a single text of Virgil or Cicero or Juvenal, and that those texts exist independently of any editor. All the more reason, therefore, to welcome the Digital Latin Library currently being developed under the auspices of the Society for Classical Studies (formerly the APA), which aims to provide online access to well-constructed critical editions with fully searchable apparatuses.

This is also a time in which changing technologies offer opportunities to re-examine traditional procedures.

Benefits are already visible in the study of manuscripts and the teaching of palaeography, through digitization and online access. Here technology makes it possible to advance far beyond the results attained in the latter decades of the nineteenth century, when many important Greek and Latin manuscripts were published in meticulous photographic reproductions. Entire collections of manuscripts are now available or are in the process of being made available electronically, and some particularly important manuscripts – including the Codex Venetus A of Homer – can be studied in greater detail in digitized form than by any other means, including autopsy.[16] Until recently the technology involved in digitizing manuscripts was costly and time-consuming, and the institutions that undertook such projects required outside support to carry them out.[17] But the pace seems to be quickening, and some major collections such as the Biblioteca Laurenziana in Florence and the Bayerische Staatsbibliothek in Munich have made substantial progress in digitizing their Latin manuscripts. In October 2011, the Vatican Library announced the largest digitizing project so far attempted, which when (or if) completed will make all 80,000 of its manuscripts accessible online in high-resolution photographs. The estimated time is ten years, and funding is not yet in hand for the entire enterprise, although the University of Heidelberg is supporting a first phase

---

[16] A reproduction in print form may still have advantages vis-à-vis a digitized version; see Elliott (2011), discussing the facsimile of Codex Sinaiticus in relation to the website version. The availability of manuscripts in digitized format could also have the undesirable consequence of making access to the original documents harder to obtain.

[17] The digitizing of the manuscripts of the Stiftsbibliothek in St. Gall was underwritten by a grant from the Mellon Foundation, which also funded the digitizing of the manuscripts of Parker Library in Corpus Christi College, Cambridge. A collaborative project of the Vatican Library and Oxford's Bodleian Library to digitize about 1.5 million pages of Greek manuscripts, Hebrew manuscripts, and incunabula is being supported by a donation from a private donor.

involving several hundred manuscripts in the Palatini Graeci and Latini collections (books from the Bibliotheca Palatina in Heidelberg obtained by Pope Gregory XV in 1623).

Digitized images of manuscripts can be far superior to the microfilm copies that editors have long relied on as a substitute for first-hand access. Widespread availability of digitized images might save future editors from the kind of error I made when collating a Paris manuscript of Seneca's tragedies from a microfilm: the manuscript had been extensively corrected, but because I failed to distinguish between original and altered readings I did not assign it to its proper place in the tradition.[18]

Next comes collation. Projects are underway to compile collations of texts in electronic form, but at the moment the data is being entered manually, so the role of the computer is limited to storing and reproducing the material. I doubt whether computer programs will soon be developed that can accurately read medieval script or that can distinguish between the hand of a scribe and that of a contemporary corrector. (If such programs were to be created, they might be too sensitive to minor differences in letter shapes to allow for the natural variations in a scribe's writing.) Even if those hurdles are eventually overcome, computer-generated collations would need to be carefully checked for accuracy and consistency.

Numerous attempts to perform stemmatic analysis of manuscript traditions by computer have been conducted outside the classical sphere, in medieval studies in particular; the results so far suggest that computer-based analyses of manuscript relations are not yet able by themselves to attain the level of precision that traditional stemmatic method can (under favourable circumstances) achieve.

Most computer-assisted approaches to stemmatics employ sorting techniques developed in the biological sciences to study the relationships of species or populations; analysis of this kind is called 'cladistic', from the Greek κλάδος or 'branch'.[19] In a cladistic analysis, shared variants are tabulated to determine which manuscripts are more closely related to one another than to other manuscripts or groups of manuscripts; the results can then be depicted in a tree graph, the analogue to a stemma.

Cladistic analysis by itself is a relatively blunt instrument, in part because of its inability to distinguish between original and non-original readings; a

---

[18] See Tarrant (1976), 392–3, corrected by Zwierlein (1977), 568–70, also MacGregor (1978).

[19] Robinson and O'Hara (1996) is a clear exposition of the process. Reeve (1998) subjects the analogy between biological species and textual variants to a probing investigation.

leading proponent describes it as 'fundamentally a method of blind count-ing'.[20] One of its limitations is that the tree graphs it produces are unrooted, that is, there is no indication of where in the graph the archetype is located. A recent study concludes that 'there is no way in text genealogy to identify the root, i.e., the position of the archetype … in a stemma, by mere numerical cal-culations. At least one substantial variant which is exclusively transmitted by a single group of manuscripts and which can be confidently judged as being original has to be identified on the basis of philological considerations'.[21] Accordingly, the most thorough discussions known to me supplement a first stage of mechanical tabulation with editorially chosen *Leitfehler* (indicative errors) to produce a usable stemma.[22] Those studies suggest that when dealing with lengthy texts or texts preserved in numerous copies, mechanical sorting of agreements could suggest tentative affiliations (in Peter Robinson's image, 'a broad "road-map"') to be tested or refined by further analysis.[23]

More tangible progress can be anticipated in preparing material for pub-lication, for example, by using programs such as Classical Text Editor to generate an apparatus criticus.[24] Here, too, the program's function will be to produce a first draft, which the editor will need to revise in order to elimi-nate trivial information and to secure consistency. In addition, for reasons discussed in the previous chapter, I think it would be a grievous loss if the apparatus were to be reduced to a mechanical record of variants and conjec-tures, and the editor's personal voice no longer heard.

At present perhaps the most important contribution of electronic data recording to classical editing is the ability to transcend the limits of tra-ditional book format and to generate a truly comprehensive apparatus. As we have seen (pp. 127–9), the selective character of apparatuses in classical editing is partly the result of an ideological bias that favours the omission of most non-authorial readings, but even more powerful have been practical

---

[20] Robinson (1997), 71.

[21] Maas (Philipp, not Paul!) (2010), 75.

[22] See, e.g., Robinson (1997) and Roelli and Bachmann (2010). In addition, contamin-ation is as serious a problem for computer-assisted analysis as for traditional stemmatic procedures.

[23] Robinson (1997), 80. The further analysis required is well described by Roelli and Bachmann (2010), 330, perhaps with a touch of wry humour: 'several methods based on *leitfehler* [*sic*] together with a good deal of intuition are used in ways that do not lend themselves to algorithmic description'.

[24] The program was devised by the editors of the *Corpus scriptorum ecclesiasticorum Latinorum*, published by the Österreichische Akademie der Wissenschaften in Vienna, and is available through the Academy's website.

factors: as M. C. Gertz rhetorically asked of Otto Rossbach in relation to the latter's proposed edition of Seneca's letters: 'where will he draw the line on citing the *codices deteriores*? ... How will he deal with the nearly countless mass of variants? Will he include them one and all in his apparatus? ... If so, I fear that, even if he is able to carry out the task, it will be hard for him to find readers for his book, and even harder to find a publisher'.[25]

Until recently, Gertz's words had as much force as they did in 1889. But manuscript data can now be encoded electronically so that a user who wishes to see a full rather than a selective account can click on a word or words and see all the relevant variants and conjectures. Depending on how they are constructed, electronic databases can also allow users to create subsets of information or to reconfigure data according to their interests; for example, to construct an entire text as it appears in any given manuscript. For that kind of manipulation of data to be possible, however, some of the means by which editors now condense information – for example, referring to groups of manuscripts by collective sigla or drafting apparatus entries in negative form – may need to be foregone.[26]

One use of online databases that is well within the bounds of what is currently feasible is to compile repositories of conjectures on a given author, such as that by Dániel Kiss for Catullus[27] and the repertory of conjectures to Horace produced at the University of Oslo by a team headed by Monika Asztalos.[28] An online database has a distinct advantage vis-à-vis such print repertories as Smyth's Propertius or Billerbeck and Somazzi's Seneca's tragedies in that it can be periodically updated to take account of new or previously overlooked conjectures.[29]

The ability to update material applies as well to other areas of online publication, whether of entire editions or of some portion thereof. Updating also entails challenges: in addition to the further labour demanded of the editor or a surrogate,[30] there is the problem of citing a work that is in constant flux. (A partial solution to the latter difficulty is to include the date on which the database was consulted.[31])

---

[25] Gertz (1889), 405, cited by Reynolds (1965a), 80.

[26] See the Appendix for explanation of the terms 'positive' and 'negative'.

[27] See Kiss (2013).   [28] tekstlab.uio.no/horace.

[29] See Smyth (1970), Billerbeck and Somazzi (2009).

[30] A point raised by Elaine Fantham in Gibson and Kraus (2002), 419, with reference to online commentaries.

[31] As recommended by *The Chicago Manual of Style Online*, section 15.51 (accessed 12 July 2013).

Granted that complete reporting is now possible (for the moment I will not ask how or by whom the data would be entered), who might wish to use it, and for what purposes? This might be an area where changes in technology will motivate changes in scholarly interest. Editors of classical texts have traditionally concentrated on variants that have some possibility of being authentic or that are indispensable for the construction of a stemma. They have shown little interest in the readings of later medieval and fifteenth-century manuscripts; indeed, editors often compliment themselves on not cluttering up their apparatus with what they regard as worthless material. That outlook is not likely to change at any time soon, and so one advantage of the electronic apparatus is that it can happily coexist alongside the conventional *apparatus criticus*. But the availability of fuller manuscript information for a given text could also stimulate interest in aspects of that text's transmission that lie outside the editorial task of recovering the original to the extent possible. Michael Reeve has shown that tracing the affiliations of fifteenth-century manuscripts of classical texts can contribute to the study of humanistic culture.[32] The rewards of studying thirteenth- and fourteenth-century manuscripts are not as obvious, since only rarely can those manuscripts be linked to specific individuals or writing centres, but the variants in those manuscripts can tell us much about how texts were read at that time.

Until now, the evidence that has been used to study medieval ways of reading classical texts has been paratextual: collections of excerpts (*florilegia*), introductions to authors or works (*accessus*), and sets of glosses or full commentaries.[33] Material in those formats is readily identified because it remains distinct from the classical text, even when an *accessus* or commentary shares space within the same manuscript. More complete reporting of variants would make it possible to see how the texts themselves were reshaped by their medieval readers, and thus open a new chapter in the reception history of the classics.

One specific area not yet investigated (at least to my knowledge) is the character of the variants found in medieval manuscripts and what they reveal about the skill and taste of scribes/readers. I am thinking, for example, of the quite sophisticated variants in some twelfth- and thirteenth-century manuscripts of the *Metamorphoses*, many of which display knowledge of a wide range of Latin poetry and constitute attempts to improve the text (e.g., by replacing a common word with a more elegant equivalent) rather than to

---

[32] For example, see the studies collected in Reeve (2011), 221–81.

[33] For representative work in this area see Burton (1983) and Allen (1971), also the ongoing catalogue of medieval commentaries in Kristeller *et al.* (1960–).

remove difficult or obscure terms – another form of collaborative intervention, at the level of individual words rather than interpolated material.[34]

Exploiting the potential of electronic recording and dissemination of data may call for more collaborative effort on the part of classicists; for example, to create databases of collations to which scholars in many countries could contribute. There are also good reasons for textual critics and editors to adopt a more collaborative intellectual attitude. Textual criticism's hopes for a healthy future depend in part on becoming more closely integrated with the disciplines to which it is connected by its nature and aims: on one hand with a set of historical disciplines – palaeography, history of the book, *Überlieferungsgeschichte* understood as a subdivision of the study of reception – and with literary criticism and analysis on the other.

Whatever changes the future may bring in the methods of editing classical texts, at the heart of the process will always be the scholar who applies his or her fallible judgement to the improvement of a text that can never be completely recovered. The age of heroes has passed and is not likely to return, but there remains something touchingly heroic about the enterprise: doomed, yet noble in its striving.[35]

---

[34] Tarrant (1989) is a foray into that territory, but my intention there was to argue that the variants in question were not authorial rather than to ask what they revealed about the reading habits of those responsible for them.

[35] Kenney (1974), 151 ends on a similar note, quoting Ovid's mock-solemn line *ardua molimur, sed nulla nisi ardua uirtus* ('what we attempt is difficult, but without difficulty there is no excellence' *Ars* 2.537).

Reading a critical apparatus

The following pages are meant for readers of critical editions who wish to make use of the information in an apparatus and who would welcome guidance in interpreting the form in which that information is presented. As in other areas of textual criticism, there are no strict rules about the form and content of an apparatus; there is also considerable diversity among editors and series of editions. I have promoted what I consider to be best practices and have tried to offer some rationale for my preferences.

General

Apparatuses can take many forms, serving a variety of purposes and audiences. In all cases, though, the principles on which an apparatus is based should be clearly explained and consistently applied. The preface to an edition will therefore usually contain a section setting out the types of evidence that the apparatus does and does not attempt to record and explaining any special conventions or vocabulary that the editor has employed. An apparatus should strive above all to be clear and easily legible; economy is often a means to that end, but when brevity requires a user to work harder, it defeats its purpose.

Latin versus English

The Latin preface may soon be a thing of the past, but even the editors who have opted to write their prefaces in English have retained Latin for the apparatus.[1] Since Latin is the language of all existing apparatuses and is likely to remain the primary language of those of the future, I have assumed it for the purpose of this introduction.

Manuscripts

Manuscripts are generally referred to by *sigla*, the most common form of which is a letter of the alphabet. That convention became standard in the course of the nineteenth century, replacing a fuller style in which manuscripts were designated by the Latin form of their location or owner, for example, *Vaticanus primus* or *codex Vossii*. Many single-letter *sigla* allude to those Latin designations (M is often used for *Mediceus* or *Monacensis*, P for *Palatinus* or *Parisinus*, and so on), but, depending on the number of manuscripts involved, it may not be possible to make all the *sigla* function in that way. When several manuscripts from the same source are cited, the editor may differentiate them by numerals: ten manuscripts from the Bibliothèque nationale de France in Paris might be designated as P1 to P10. Some editors use upper-case *sigla* for primary witnesses and lower-case *sigla* for secondary witnesses.

In addition to *sigla* that refer to individual manuscripts, many editions employ manuscript *sigla* of other kinds. One type is the collective *siglum* that represents the agreement of two or more manuscripts: for example, when manuscripts ABCDEF agree on a reading, an editor might choose to save space by designating the *siglum* X as the equivalent of ABCDEF. Many editors use collective *sigla* even when one or more members of the group that they represent do not agree with the reading of the majority; in such cases, the dissenters will be cited individually. Collective *sigla* are also used to refer to an indeterminate number of witnesses of a certain date or type. The most common example is a collective *siglum* for *codices recentiores*, either all or some number of them; ς is often used for that purpose. In my *Metamorphoses* edition, I used the *siglum* φ to represent the reading of at least three twelfth-century manuscripts, χ to represent the reading of at least one thirteenth-century manuscript, and ψ to represent the reading of at least one fourteenth-century manuscript; I thought it would be more helpful for a reader to know that a reading was attested at a given period than to have the details of which manuscripts contained the reading.

---

[1] See, e.g., Reeve (2004), xlii: 'where words are needed from me, I write them in Latin because the shorthand that has evolved in editorial Latin over the centuries allows a great deal of space to be saved'. See also pp. 140–1 (Chapter 7).

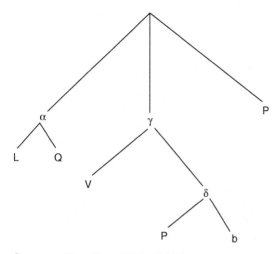

Stemma 5 From Reynolds (1965b), ix

Sigla can also stand for manuscripts whose existence is hypothesized on the basis of a stemmatic analysis. In Reynolds's stemma of Seneca's *Epistulae morales* 53–88, LQVPbp refer to existing manuscripts and αγδ to postulated common sources of those manuscripts.[2] (See Stemma 5.)

The *siglum* γ in his apparatus could refer either to the agreement of VPb or to the reading of the lost manuscript from which they are thought to descend. In the latter case, γ could represent the agreement of V with either P or b, since in stemmatic reasoning that will normally give the reading of δ and thus of γ as well. An editor therefore needs to spell out the meaning of such a *siglum*, for example, by a phrase like 'γ = *consensus codicum VPb*' or 'γ = *lectio codicis deperditi a quo VPb descendunt*'.

Many editions employ Greek-letter as well as Roman-letter *sigla*. Ideally, there should be a distinction between the entities denoted by the two alphabets, as in the Seneca stemma mentioned earlier, but sometimes matters are not so tidy, especially if an editor feels compelled to maintain the *sigla* used in previous editions. The most commonly used Greek-letter *sigla* are Ω (or ω) designating the agreement of all manuscripts and ς (stigma, a stylized ligature of sigma and tau) to represent *codices recentiores*.

It is standard practice to list all *sigla* used in an edition immediately before the opening of the text. When the manuscripts used to establish the

---

[2] See Reynolds (1965b), ix.

text change frequently (as with the late antique Virgil manuscripts), it is helpful to list the available witnesses at the head of each page of apparatus.

Manuscript readings

The simplest form of variant reading is represented by the appropriate manuscript *siglum* with no further qualification: if the majority reading is *errorem* and manuscript Q reads *terrorem*, the apparatus needs only to register 'terrorem *Q*'. Most medieval manuscripts, though, contain some degree of correction, whether by the original scribe or by later hands; many also contain variant readings (sometimes introduced by an abbreviated form of *uel* or *aliter*) and glosses (which may be signalled by '*i*' for *id est* or '*s*' for *scilicet*). In my view, an apparatus should record corrections and variants, especially when they appear to be made by hands close in time to that of the scribe, and should keep the two categories distinct; glosses have a lesser claim to inclusion, although a gloss that could also be a variant should be so treated. It is not always possible to make out the status of a reading entered above the line or in the margin; in such cases the apparatus should simply note it as superscript or marginal.

To represent readings other than those of the original scribe, editors employ a range of superscript numbers (for hands later than that of the scribe) and letters (for the various types of addition mentioned earlier: c for correction, g for gloss, m for marginal addition, s for superscript addition, v for variant reading).[3] If, for example, the scribe of Q wrote *terrorem* and a later hand drew a line through the *t* to mark it as deleted, the apparatus might read 'terrorem *Q*, *correxit Q²* '. If the text of Q reads *terrorem* and *errorem* appears in the margin in a later hand and preceded by *al.* (= *aliter*), the apparatus might add 'Q²ᵛ' to the *sigla* of the manuscripts that read *errorem*. (It would be cumbersome to add a further superscript specifying that the variant *errorem* is found in the margin; for this example I chose to ignore that piece of information, but if it were thought important it might be conveyed by, e.g., 'Q²ᵛ (mg.)'.)

Sorting out the hands in a manuscript is often difficult (in particular if the editor is working from a microfilm or digital reproduction rather than inspecting the actual codex), and recording them in an apparatus can also pose challenges. Some editors use superscript 2 to denote all hands other than that of the scribe, and that practice may be acceptable if all the hands in

---

[3] Some editors employ a more elaborate set of superscript letters to distinguish the reading of a manuscript before correction (ac = *ante correctionem*) from the corrected reading (pc = *post correctionem*).

question are fairly close in time. Some manuscripts call for a more nuanced approach. The Naples manuscript of the *Metamorphoses* (N in editors' apparatuses) has undergone correction over the course of several centuries: one can distinguish an early corrector using the same Beneventan script as the scribe, a particularly diligent corrector in the early Gothic period (thirteenth century), several nondescript thirteenth- and fourteenth-century hands, and finally a fifteenth-century scholar writing in an elegant humanist script. Editors may legitimately differ in deciding how much of that later activity to record, but to use 'N²' for both the earliest and the latest phase of correction would be to misrepresent the situation.

Conjectures

Verbal conjectures are recorded in the same way as manuscript variants, with the critic's name in place of a manuscript *siglum* or *sigla*: if Bentley proposed *rectis* for the transmitted *siccis* (as he did in Horace *Odes* 1.3.18), an apparatus might read 'siccis *Ω*: rectis *Bentley*'.[4] (It is not necessary to say *'coni. Bentley'* since the form of the entry makes it clear that *rectis* is a conjecture.) Conjectures should be attributed to the critic who first made them; if two or more critics hit upon the same conjecture independently, or if a conjecture has subsequently been found in one or more manuscripts, it is appropriate to register those facts. Some editors append to the author of a conjecture the names of later editors who have adopted or approved of it; I regard that practice as an abomination.[5]

Other forms of conjecture or editorial intervention are mentioned in independent sentences: for example, *'lacunam statuit Ribbeck* or *uu.* 465–6 *del. Brunck* or *uu.* 3–4 *post u.* 8 *transtulit Housman'*.[6]

---

[4] I prefer 'Bentley' to the Latinized 'Bentleius', but the matter is not clear cut; names of Renaissance and seventeenth-century critics are regularly cited in Latin form (e.g., Gronovius rather than Gronov), but Bentley's time marks something of a watershed. For fuller discussion, see Bywater (1914). When the syntax of an entry calls for the name of a scholar to appear in a case other than the nominative, Latin forms are required even for contemporary critics (e.g., *scripsi suadente Reevio*, although in that case *scripsi ut suasit Reeve* offers a more graceful alternative).

[5] See also pp. 134–6, for additional fulmination. Less offensive to me – probably because I have done it myself – is recording the views of an authoritative predecessor such as Bentley or Heinsius, although that policy too can be questioned; see p. 21.

[6] In Propertius suggested transpositions are so numerous that some editors dispense with a verb in recording them: so Barber (1960) on 3.6.3–4 reads simply '3-4 *post* 8 *Housman*'.

Editorial comments

Editors vary widely in the amount of comment they include in the apparatus, and in this area no general rule can be laid down. Citation of parallels can be an economical way for the editor to explain the reason for a choice of reading. In his apparatus entry for Seneca *Epist.* 12.7 *hoc alius aliter excepit*, Leighton Reynolds cites a variant *accepit* in *recentiores* and the conjecture *cepit* by Hense, and then adds *sed cf. p. 271.22*, where in *Epist.* 82.2 the *recentiores* once again read *accipe* for the *excipe* of older manuscripts; a similar comment (*sed cf. p. 27.25*) refers back to the earlier passage. Another useful category of comment relates to the soundness of the text that the editor has chosen to print; when the editor seriously doubts the transmitted text but has not felt confident enough of any conjecture to adopt it, an aside such as *an sanum dubito/nescio* ('I am doubtful/not sure whether <the text is> sound') appended to the transmitted reading both adds a touch of humanity to the apparatus and honestly reflects the editor's hesitation. Lengthy discussions of textual problems, however, will make the apparatus difficult to consult for the essential information about manuscript readings and conjectures. An apparatus is not a substitute for a full textual commentary.

Format: Positive versus negative

The most significant issue in the format of an apparatus is the choice between a positive and a negative style of recording variants and conjectures. In the positive style, both the witnesses that contain the reading adopted in the text and those that depart from it are cited, whereas in the negative form only those witnesses that deviate from the printed reading are listed. If a text is being established on the basis of manuscripts ABCDEF and in a given place ABC read *tandem* and DEF have the variant *tamen*, a positive entry would read 'tandem *ABC*: tamen *DEF*' and a negative entry would read either 'tandem] tamen *DEF*' or just 'tamen *DEF*'. (A lemma is often omitted when it is easy for the reader to relate the variant to the appropriate word or words in the text.) The negative form is particularly useful when a single manuscript or a small number of manuscripts differ from the reading of the majority: if in our example only F read *tamen*, it would not only be wasteful of space to write 'tandem *ABCDE*: tamen *F*', but that presentation would confer undue prominence on an isolated blunder.

For a negative style to function properly, the reader must know exactly which witnesses are being reported, in order to infer correctly *ex silentio* which ones have the reading printed in the text. Negative form is not the best way to depict complex manuscript evidence, since it puts too great a burden on the user. An apparatus can be positive throughout (albeit at great expense of space), but almost no apparatus can feasibly be cast in negative form throughout. Many apparatuses use a mixture of positive and negative entries; I see no objection to that procedure, provided that the principles governing the choice of format are clearly set out and consistently applied.

Miscellaneous aspects of format

If an entry begins with a lemma, the lemma reproduces the reading printed in the text.

Manuscripts that can be grouped into families are best cited together.

Within a given entry conjectures usually follow manuscript variants.

Variants are often cited in abbreviated form: if the reading *tacitum* has a variant *tacitam*, an apparatus might present them as 'tacitum] -am *M*'.

It is common practice to distinguish typographically between manuscript readings and conjectures and other matter (*sigla* and editorial comments). OCT editions, for example, use Roman type for the former category and italics for the latter, which is the style I have employed in this Appendix.

Other types of apparatus

Apparatus fontium. In its strictest form this is the equivalent of a set of footnotes, supplying references for texts quoted (= *fontes*) in the text being edited. Good examples can be found in Leighton Reynolds's OCT edition of Cicero's *De finibus* and Michael Winterbottom's OCT of Quintilian. A more expansive concept of *fontes* would include texts drawn on or alluded to; such an apparatus does not appear in most editions of classical texts, probably because it is impossible to attain complete coverage. The most useful specimens of the latter form are in the volumes of the *Monumenta Germaniae Historica* series *Auctores Antiquissimi*, which detail the indebtedness of late antique writers to earlier Latin literature.[7]

Apparatus testimoniorum. A listing of places where the text being edited is quoted by later authors (such quotations are known as *testimonia*); for an example see Friedrich Klingner's Teubner edition of Horace. An apparatus of this kind can be problematic if the text in question was widely cited: if one thinks of how often the opening words of the *Aeneid* (*arma uirumque cano*) were quoted in later texts, it is evident that such an apparatus for all of Virgil

---

[7] For example, Friedrich Leo's Venantius Fortunatus (1881), Rudolf Peiper's Avitus (1883), Karl Schenkl's Ausonius (1883), Theodor Birt's Claudian (1892).

would be dauntingly large. Difficulty also arises if the concept of *testimonium* is widened to include allusions to the text, as W. S. Anderson attempted to do for the *Metamorphoses*: as with the broader concept of *fonte*s, there is no way to achieve completeness.

Testimonia assume particular importance when they contain readings of interest for the establishment of the text, especially readings that are not represented in the direct manuscript tradition; those readings are properly cited in the main apparatus.

The *Apparatus fontium* and *Apparatus testimoniorum*, if present, are printed above the main apparatus.

Some editions include other forms of supplement to the apparatus, such as appendixes listing the variant forms of proper names or cataloguing morphological variants. Such supplements are a means of reserving the apparatus proper for more substantive material, while gathering together variants of certain kinds for the convenience of those readers with a particular interest in them. Supplements can also be used to record conjectures that the editor does not find attractive enough to cite in the apparatus proper, as in Nicolaus Wecklein's edition of Euripides, which includes for each play an *Appendix coniecturas minus probabiles continens*; that practice, though, seems to have fallen out of use in recent times.

Commonly used abbreviations and expressions

add. = *addidit*, usually referring to additions by a scribe or correcting hand; *add.* often appears in conjunction with *om.*, for example, 'nomen *om. M, add. M²*'

alii alia = *alii alia coniecerunt*; used when the editor has listed one or more conjectures made in a problematic passage and is noting that other proposals have been made

cett. = *ceteri*; refers to all manuscripts (or all of some designated subset) apart from those otherwise named, for example, 'numine *MP*: nom- *cett.*'

codd. = *codices*, often in the sense of 'all manuscripts', for example, 'nummo *Bentley*: minimo *codd.*'

coni. (sometimes *ci.*) = *coniecit* (less often *coniecerunt*)

corr. = *correxit*; usually applies to scribal correction, but some editors designate successful conjectures as corrections, for example, 'flere potest Ω, *corr. Baehrens*'[8]

---

[8] So Barber (1960) on Propertius 3.7.46. The note is cast in negative form: Baehrens's conjecture *fleret opes* is in the text.

def. = *deficit* ('is missing, is lacking'), most often applied to a manuscript (e.g., *'post hunc u. def. M''*)

del. = *deleuit*; could refer to a scribal action (e.g., crossing out a letter or letters), but more often denotes bracketing by a critic (see also *secl.*)

dett. = *deteriores*, a pejorative name for *recentiores*

dist. = *distinxit*, referring to punctuation or word division

dub. = *dubitanter*, usually applied to conjectures hesitantly proposed by
their authors or to choices made with hesitation by the editor

edd. = *editores*, often with the sense 'all editors'

eiecit, a strong way of describing athetesis

ex corr. = *ex correctione*, a synonym for *post correctionem*

fere 'nearly, almost', for example, *'u. 494 om. recc. fere omnes'*

fort. recte = *fortasse recte*, generally applied to a reading or conjecture
that the editor finds attractive but has not adopted

haud scio an recte ('I am inclined to think correctly'), a stronger version
of the previous expression

iam is used to indicate that a predecessor had already reached the same or
a similar conclusion (e.g., Heyworth on Propertius 3.6.3–4: '3–4
post 12 Heyworth (*iam post* 8 Housman').)

inc. or *incert.* = *incertum*

interpunxit etc.; *interpungere* is the generic term for punctuating: *leuiter
interpungere* refers to light punctuation (i.e., a comma), *grauiter
interpungere* to heavy punctuation (a colon or period)

inu. ord. = *inuerso ordine*, referring to disruption in the order of words in
a phrase or of lines of verse

l. = *linea* (and other cases)

lac. = *lacuna*; 'to posit a lacuna' is *lacunam statuere*[9]

n. l. = *non liquet* ('it is not clear')

non leg. = *non legitur* or *leguntur* ('it/they cannot be read'), referring to
illegible letters or words

om. = *omisit* or *omiserunt*, usually applied to scribal omission

praeeunte combined with the name of a scholar in an ablative absolute is
used when a conjecture or interpretation has been anticipated,
for example, 'Milanion *Heinsus praeeunte Politiano'* ('Heinsius
preceded by Poliziano'); the formula implies that Heinsius was
unaware of Poliziano's work

prob. = *probauit* ('gave approval to')

---

[9] More elliptical expressions are also found, e.g., Heyworth (2007a) on Propertius
4.5.29: *'ante* 29 *fort. lac.'*

ras. = *rasura* ('erasure')

redire can be used to describe a manuscript resuming ('returning') after a break in the text

retinere can refer to retaining a manuscript reading (usually one that has been doubted or emended by other editors)

s. l. = *supra lineam*

scripsi introduces a conjecture by the editor[10]

secl. = *seclusit*, referring to a critic's bracketing of material as interpolated; see also *del.*

signum interrogandi or *interrogationis*, a question mark

temptatum (*temptare*, etc.) refers to 'attempts on' (i.e., attempts to alter) a transmitted reading (e.g., Reynolds on Sen. *Epist.* 70.21 'deberet *frustra temptatum*')

teste combined with the name of a scholar in an ablative absolute denotes an editor's source for a piece of information, for example, *'teste Magno'* ('on Magnus's authority')

trans. = *transposuit* and *transt.* = *transtulit* refer to transposing of words or lines, whether by scribes or by critics

u., uu. = *uersus* (singular and plural)

u. = *uide*

ut uid. = *ut uidetur* ('as it seems'), used to qualify a statement about which the editor is less than sure; usually applied to manuscript readings

The following non-verbal symbols are commonly employed:

[] for letters or words deleted
< > for letters or words added
† † for words regarded as corrupt
/// indicates an erasure

Latin names for manuscript locations with English equivalents

I have omitted Latin designations that seemed self-evident, such as Londiniensis, Parisinus, or Vaticanus. Collections within libraries (*fondi*)

---

[10] Pontius Pilatus' *quod scripsi, scripsi* (John 19.22) could qualify him as the patron of textual critics.

are only included when I have seen manuscripts listed in editions by *fondo* without an accompanying indication of place: for example, Ambrosianus, Harleianus, Laurentianus. For a much fuller list of Latin forms of place names, see Hall (1913), 286–357.

The Latin forms are given in the masculine singular to agree with *codex*, the most common Latin rendering of 'manuscript'. The corresponding neuter forms would be used to refer to a fragment or fragments (*fragmentum*, *fragmenta*), the feminine plural for the few occasions when 'leaves' or 'pages' (*schedae*) are cited, as with the *Schedae Gottorpienses* and *Vindobonenses* of Lucretius.

Ambrosianus	Milan (Biblioteca Ambrosiana)
Amplonianus	Erfurt (Universitäts- und Forschungsbibliothek)
Argentoratensis	Strasbourg
Ariminensis	Rimini
Arretinus	Arezzo
Arundelianus	London (British Library)
Ashburnhamensis	Florence (Biblioteca Medicea-Laurenziana)
Atrabaticus	Arras
Audomaropolitanus	St. Omer
Augustodunensis	Autun
Aurelianus	Orléans
Bellovacensis	Beauvais
Bodleianus	Oxford (Bodleian Library)
Bodmerianus	Geneva (Bibliotheca Bodmeriana)
Bononiensis	Bologna
Brixiensis	Brescia
Budensis	Budapest
Cameracensis	Cambrai
Carnotensis	Chartres
Casinensis	Monte Cassino
Classensis	Ravenna (Biblioteca Classense)
Clm	Codex latinus Monacensis (Munich)
Coloniensis	Cologne
Daventriensis	Deventer
Dertusensis	Tortosa
Divionensis	Dijon
Dorvillianus	Oxford (Bodleian Library)
Eboracensis	York
Escorialensis	*See* Scorialensis
Estensis	Modena (Biblioteca Estense)
Exoniensis	Exeter
Floriacensis	Fleury

Gemblacensis	Gembloux
Genavensis	Geneva
Genuensis	Genoa
Graecensis	Graz
Guelferbytanus	Wolfenbüttel
Harleianus	London (British Library)
Hauniensis (*also* Hafniensis)	Copenhagen
Hispalensis	Seville
Holmiensis	Stockholm
Laurentianus	Florence (Biblioteca Medicea-Laurenziana)
Leodicensis	Liège
Lovaniensis	Louvain
Lucensis	Lucca
Lugdunensis	Lyon (*less often* Leiden)
Marcianus	Florence (Biblioteca Medicea-Laurenziana) *or* Venice (Biblioteca Marciana)
Matritensis	Madrid
Mediolanensis	Milan
Mellicensis	Melk
Monacensis	Munich
Montepessulanus	Montpellier
Mutinensis	Modena
Neo-eboracensis	New York
Palatinus	Heidelberg (Universitätsbibliothek) *or* Vatican (Biblioteca Apostolica Vaticana)
Patavinus	Padua
Perusinus	Perugia
Petriburgensis/ Petropolitanus	St. Petersburg
Pistoriensis	Pistoia
Puteaneus	Paris (Bibliothèque nationale de France)
Quirinianus	Brescia (Biblioteca Queriniana)
Riccardianus	Florence (Biblioteca Riccardiana)
Sangallensis	Sankt Gallen
Scorialensis	El Escorial
Senensis	Siena
Taurinensis	Turin
Tegernseensis	Munich (Bayerische Staatsbibliothek)
Thuaneus	Paris (Bibliothèque nationale de France)
Toletanus	Toledo
Traguriensis	Trau
Trevirensis	Trier
Tridentinus	Trento
Turicensis	Zurich

Turonensis	Tours
Vadianus	Sankt Gallen (Kantonsbibliothek)
Vallicellianus	Rome (Biblioteca Vallicelliana)
Vicentinus	Vicenza
Vindobonensis	Vienna
Vossianus	Leiden (Universiteitsbibliotheek)
Vratislavensis	Wroclaw

EXPLICIT EXPLICEAT LVDERE SCRIPTOR EAT

Bibliography

The following abbreviations are used in referring to journals:

AAHG	*Anzeiger für die Altertumswissenschaft*
AC	*L'Antiquité classique*
AJPh	*American Journal of Philology*
AR	*Atene e Roma*
BICS	*Bulletin of the Institute of Classical Studies*
BPhW	*Berliner philologische Wochenschrift*
BSL	*Bollettino di studi latini*
CPh	*Classical Philology*
CQ	*Classical Quarterly*
CR	*The Classical Review*
CSCA	*California Studies in Classical Antiquity*
EC	*Exemplaria classica*
G&R	*Greece and Rome*
HSCPh	*Harvard Studies in Classical Philology*
ICS	*Illinois Classical Studies*
JPh	*Journal of Philology*
JRS	*Journal of Roman Studies*
JTS	*Journal of Theological Studies*
LCM	*Liverpool Classical Monthly*
LI	*Literary Imagination*
MD	*Materiali e discussioni per l'analisi dei testi classici*
MH	*Museum Helveticum*
PACA	*Proceedings of the African Classical Association*
PBA	*Proceedings of the British Academy*
PCA	*Proceedings of the Classical Association*
PCPhS	*Proceedings of the Cambridge Philological Society*
QUCC	*Quaderni urbinati di cultura classica*
REL	*Revue des études latines*
RFIC	*Rivista di filologia e di istruzione classica*
RHC	*Research in Humanities Computing*

RhM	*Rheinisches Museum*
RHT	*Revue d'histoire des textes*
RPh	*Revue de philologie, de littérature et d'histoire anciennes*
SC	*Scrittura e civiltà*
SIFC	*Studi italiani di filologia classica*
TAPhA	*Transactions and Proceedings of the American Philological Association*
TLS	*Times Literary Supplement*
VP	*Victorian Poetry*
WZKS	*Wiener Zeitschrift für die Kunde Südasiens*

Alberti, G. B. (1968) '"Recensione chiusa" e "recensione aperta"', *SIFC* N.S. 40: 44–60.

Allen, J. B. (1971) *The Friar as Critic. Literary Attitudes in the Later Middle Ages.* Nashville, TN.

Alton, E. H., D. E. W. Wormell, and E. Courtney (1978) (eds.) *P. Ovidi Nasonis Fastorum libri sex.* Leipzig.

Anderson, W. S. (1975) 'A new pseudo-Ovidian passage', *CSCA* 8: 7–16.

(1977) (ed.) *Ovidius: Metamorphoses.* Second edn 1981. Stuttgart.

Arns, P. E. (1953) *La Technique du livre d'après Saint Jérôme.* Paris.

Ash, R. (2007) (ed.) *Tacitus: Histories II.* Cambridge.

Astbury, R. (2000) Review of Willis (1997), *Gnomon* 72: 309–13.

Austin, R. G. (1955) *P. Vergili Maronis Aeneidos liber quartus.* Oxford.

Ayerbe-Chaux, R. (1992) 'Critical editions and literary history: the case of Don Juan Manuel', in N. Spadaccini and J. Talens (eds.), *The Politics of Editing* (Minneapolis, MN *(Hispanic Issues* 8)): 22–38.

Badalì, R. (1992) (ed.) *Lucani opera.* Rome.

Barber, E. A. (1960 (ed.) *Sexti Properti carmina.* Second edn. Oxford.

Barchiesi, A. (2005) (ed.) *Ovidio: Metamorfosi I-II.* Rome and Milan.

Bauzá, H. F. (1990) (ed.) *Tibulo: Elegias.* Madrid.

Beard, M. and J. Henderson (1995) *Classics: A Very Short Introduction.* Oxford.

Belger, C. (1879) *Moritz Haupt als akademischer Lehrer.* Berlin.

Bergk, T. (1857) (ed.) *Aristophanis comoediae.* Second edn. Leipzig.

Billerbeck, M. and M. Somazzi (2009) *Repertorium der Konjekturen in den Seneca-Tragödien.* Leiden and Boston, MA *(Mnemosyne* Supplement 316).

Birt, T. (1892) (ed.) *Claudii Claudiani carmina.* Berlin.

Bömer, F. (1969–86) *Ovid: Metamorphosen.* Heidelberg.

Borzsák, I. (1984) (ed.) *Q. Horati Flacci opera.* Leipzig.

Brink, C. O. (1986) *English Classical Scholarship: Historical Reflections on Bentley, Porson and Housman.* Oxford.

Brittain, C. (2006) (trans.) *Cicero: On Academic Scepticism.* Indianapolis, IN.

Burnett, A. (1998) 'Poetical emendations and improvisations by A. E. Housman', *VP* 36: 289–98.

(2012) (ed.) *Philip Larkin: The Complete Poems.* New York.

Burton, R. (1983) *Classical Poets in the 'Florilegium Gallicum'.* Frankfurt.

Butler, H. E. and E. A. Barber (1933) (eds.) *The Elegies of Propertius.* Oxford.

Butrica, J. L. (1997) 'Editing Propertius', *CQ* 47: 176–208.

Butterfield, D. J. and C. A. Stray (2009) (eds.) *A. E. Housman: Classical Scholar.* London.

Butterfield, D. J. (2011) Review of Flores (2009), *Gnomon* 83: 597–608.

Bywater, I. (1914) 'The latinizations of the modern surname', *JPh* 33: 76–94.

Camps, W. A. (1966) (ed.) *Propertius: Elegies Book III*. Cambridge.

  (1967) (ed.) *Propertius: Elegies Book II*. Cambridge.

Canfora, L. (2002) *Il copista come autore*. Palermo.

Carey, C. (2007) (ed.) *Lysiae orationes cum fragmentis*. Oxford.

Cazzaniga, I. (1959) (ed.) *Carmina ludicra Romanorum (Pervigilium Veneris – Priapea)*. Turin.

Clausen, W. V. (1959) (ed.) *A. Persi Flacci et D. Iuni Iuvenalis saturae*. Oxford.

Consolino, F. E. (1988) Review of Hall (1985), *Athenaeum* 66: 257–62.

Conte, G. B. (2009) (ed.) *P. Vergilius Maro: Aeneis*. Berlin and New York.

  (2013) *Ope ingenii: Experiences of Textual Criticism*. Berlin and Boston, MA.

Courtney, E. (1968) 'Some remarks on the Ilias Latina', *CR* 18: 22–3.

  (1970) (ed.) *C. Valeri Flacci Argonauticon libri octo*. Leipzig.

  (1999) Review of J. Amat (ed.), Consolatio ad Liviam (Paris 1997), *CR* 49: 397–9.

Cucchiarelli, A. (2012) 'Nonae Decembres. Un'interpolazione in Hor. carm. 3, 18, 9–16', *MD* 68: 203–21.

Damon, C. (2003) (ed.) *Tacitus: Histories I*. Cambridge.

  (2008) 'Tritus in eo lector: Grotius's emendations to the text of Tacitus', *Grotiana* 29: 133–49.

Davis, G. (2010) (ed.) *A Companion to Horace*. Malden, MA.

Dawe, R. D. (1965) *Repertory of Conjectures on Aeschylus*. Leiden.

Della Corte, F. (1989) (ed.) *Tibullo: Le elegie*. Second edn. Milan.

Deremetz, A. (2006) Review of Viarre (2005), *REL* 84: 285–7.

Desy, P. (2003) Review of Willis (1997), *AC* 72: 407–8.

Deufert, M. (2005) Review of Flores (2002), *Gnomon* 77: 213–24.

Dewar, M. (1991) Review of R. Sueur (ed.), Stace, Thébaide Livres I-IV (Paris 1990), *CR* 41: 332–4.

Diggle, J. (1994) (ed.) *Euripidis fabulae III*. Oxford.

  (2006) 'On the text of Catullus', *MD* 57: 85–104.

Dörrie, H. (1971) (ed.) *P. Ovidii Nasonis Epistulae heroidum*. Berlin and New York.

Donaldson, E. T. (1970) 'The psychology of editors of Middle English texts', in *Speaking of Chaucer* (London): 102–18.

Eggert, P. (2009) *Securing the Past: Conservation in Art, Architecture and Literature*. Cambridge.

Ehwald, R. (1915) (ed.) *P. Ovidius Naso 2: Metamorphoses*. Leipzig.

Elliott, J. K. (2011) Review of Codex Sinaiticus: A Facsimile Edition (London 2011), *TLS* May 27: 26.

Fedeli, P. (1984) (ed.) *Sexti Properti Elegiarum Libri IV*. Stuttgart.

  (1986) 'Sul modo di costituire il testo di Properzio', *RFIC* 114: 238–50.

  (1998) 'Congetturare sì, ma con cautela', in A. Ferrari (ed.), *Filologia classica e filologia romanza: esperienze ecdotiche a confronto*. Spoleto: 267–80.

  (2006) 'The history of Propertian scholarship', in H.-C. Günther (ed.), *Brill's Companion to Propertius*. Leiden and Boston, MA: 3–21.

  (2007) Review of Tarrant (2004), *Gnomon* 79: 605–12.

  (2013) Review of Riesenweber (2007), *Gnomon* 85: 512–17.

(2014) Review of H. P. Syndikus, *Die Elegien des Properz. Eine Interpretation* (Darmstadt 2011), *Latomus* 73: 281.

Fedeli, P. and V. Paladini (1976) (eds.) *Panegyrici Latini*. Rome.

Finglass, P. J. (2006) 'The interpolated curse', *Hermes* 134: 257–68.

Flores, E. (2002–09) (ed.) *Titus Lucretius Carus, De rerum natura*. Naples.

   (2006) 'Risposta a K. Mueller, M. Deufert, M. D. Reeve', *Vichiana* ser 4.8: 117–33. Republished in Flores (2012b): 87–105.

   (2012a) 'Butterfield, la sua critica e la riscrittura di Lucrezio', *Vichiana* ser. 4.14: 253–65. Republished in Flores (2012b): 111–26.

   (2012b) *Il testo anglo-tedesco di Manilio e Lucrezio*. Naples.

Fohlen, J. (1979) 'Recherches sur le manuscrit palimpseste Vatican, Pal. Lat. 24', *SC* 3: 195–222.

Fowler, D. (1991) Review of Zwierlein (1990), *G&R* 38: 235–7.

   (2000) *Roman Constructions*. Oxford.

Fraenkel, E. (1951) Review of Munari (1951), *Athenaeum* N. S. 29: 349–52.

   (1952) 'The Culex', *JRS* 42: 1–9. Republished in Fraenkel (1964): 2. 181–97.

   (1960) (ed.) Friedrich Leo, *Ausgewählte kleine Schriften*. Rome.

   (1964) *Kleine Beiträge zur klassischen Philologie*. Rome.

Gertz, M. C. (1889) Review of O. Rossbach, *De Senecae philosophi librorum recensione et emendatione* (Breslau 1888), *BPhW* 1889: 405.

Geymonat M. (1973) (ed.) *P. Vergili Maronis opera*. Turin. Second edn 2008. Rome.

Giardina, G. C. (2005) (ed.) *Properzio: Elegie*. Second edn 2010. Rome.

   (2006) 'Verg. "Aen." 2.255: una "crux" esegetica o una "crux" testuale?', *QUCC* 83: 93–5.

   (2007) 'Munera Cereris in Catullo 68,10?', *Philologus* 151: 182–3.

Gibson, R. K. (in press) 'Fifty shades of orange: Cambridge Classical Texts and Commentaries', to appear in Kraus and Stray.

Gibson, R. K. and C. S. Kraus (2002) (eds.) *The Classical Commentary: Histories, Practices, Theory*. Leiden and Boston, MA.

Gnilka, C. (2000) *Prudentiana I: Critica*. Munich and Leipzig.

Goold, G. P. (1966) 'Noctes Propertianae', *HSCPh* 71: 59–106.

   (1969) 'Catullus 3.16', *Phoenix* 23: 186–203.

   (1974) Review of Dörrie (1971), *Gnomon* 46: 475–84.

   (1988) 'On editing Propertius', in N. M. Horsfall (ed.), *Vir bonus discendi peritus: Studies in Celebration of Otto Skutsch's Fightieth Birthday* (London (*BICS* Supplement 51)): 27–38.

   (1989) 'Problems in editing Propertius', in J. N. Grant (ed.), *Editing Greek and Latin Texts* (New York): 97–119.

   (1990) (ed.) *Propertius: Elegies*. Cambridge, MA.

Gorni, G. (2003) 'Material philology, conjectural philology, philology without adjectives', in T. Barolini and H. W. Storey (eds.), *Dante for the New Millennium* (New York): 44–55.

Gotoff, H. C. (1971) *The Transmission of the Text of Lucan in the Ninth Century*. Cambridge, MA.

Gowers, E. (2012) (ed.) *Horace: Satires I*. Cambridge.

Grafton, A. T. (1983) *Joseph Scaliger: A Study in the History of Classical Scholarship I: Textual Criticism and Exegesis*. Oxford.

Gratwick, A.S. (1993a) (ed.) *Plautus: Menaechmi*. Cambridge.

(1993b) Review of Zwierlein (1990), *CR* 43: 36–40.

Green, R. P. H. (1987) Review of Hall (1985), *CR* 37: 183–4.

(1999) (ed.) *Decimi Magni Ausonii opera*. Oxford.

Greetham, D. (2013) 'A history of textual scholarship', in N. Fraistat and J. Flanders (eds.), *The Cambridge Companion to Textual Scholarship* (Cambridge): 16–41.

Grier, J. (1988) 'Lachmann, Bédier and the bipartite stemma: towards a responsible application of the common-error method', *RHT* 18: 263–77.

Günther, H.-C. (1997) *Quaestiones Propertianae*. Leiden and New York.

(2008) Review of Heyworth (2007a), *MH* 65: 236–9.

Hall, F. W. (1913) *A Companion to Classical Texts*. Oxford.

Hall, J. B. (1969) (ed.) *Claudian: De raptu Proserpinae*. Cambridge.

(1980) Review of Anderson (1977), *PACA* 15: 62–70.

(1985) (ed.) *Claudii Claudiani carmina*. Stuttgart.

(1995) (ed.) *P. Ovidi Nasonis Tristia*. Stuttgart.

(2007) Review of Viarre (2005), *CR* 57: 95–7.

(2008) (ed.) *P. Papinius Statius: Thebaid and Achilleid*. Newcastle Upon Tyne.

Hanslik, R. (1979) (ed.) *Sex. Propertii Elegiarum libri IV*. Leipzig.

Hardie, P. R. (1994) (ed.) *Virgil: Aeneid IX*. Cambridge.

Harrison, S. J. (2000) 'The need for a new text of Catullus', in C. Reitz (ed.), *Vom Text zum Buch* (St. Katharinen): 63–79.

(2007) (ed.) *Cambridge Companion to Horace*. Cambridge.

Harrison, S. J. and S. J. Heyworth (1998) 'Notes on the text and interpretation of Catullus', *PCPhS* 44: 85–109.

Havet, L. (1911) *Manuel de critique verbale appliquée aux textes latins*. Paris.

Hawkshaw, P. and T. L. Jackson (2001) 'Anton Bruckner', in S. Sadie (ed.), *The New Grove Dictionary of Music and Musicians* (London): 4. 458–87.

Hertz, M. (1851) *Karl Lachmann. Eine Biographie*. Berlin.

Heyworth, S. J. (1985) Review of Fedeli (1984), *CR* 35: 281–4.

(2007a) (ed.) *Sexti Properti Elegi*. Oxford.

(2007b) *Cynthia: A Companion to the Text of Propertius*. Oxford.

Hinds, S. E. (1993) 'Medea in Ovid: scenes from the life of an intertextual heroine', *MD* 30: 9–47.

Holford-Strevens, L. (2008) 'Martial's dandy book', *CQ* 58: 386–8.

Horsfall, N. (2006–7) 'Fraud as scholarship: the Helen Episode and the Appendix Vergiliana', *ICS* 31–2: 1–27.

Housman, A. E. (1882) 'Horatiana', *JPh* 10: 187–96. Republished in Housman (1972): 1–8.

(1893) 'The manuscripts of Propertius', *JPh* 21: 101–60. Republished in Housman (1972): 232–76.

(1894) Review of K. P. Schultz (ed.) *Catulli Veronensis liber* (Leipzig 1893), *CR* 8: 251–7. Republished in Housman (1972) 305–13.

(1902) 'Remarks on the Culex', *CR* 16: 339–46. Republished in Housman (1972): 563–76.

(1903) (ed.) *M. Manilii astrnomicon liber primus*. London.

(1905a) (ed.) *D. Iunii Iuuenalis saturae*. Second edn 1931. London.

(1905b) Review of R. Ellis (ed.), *Catulli carmina* (Oxford 1904), *CR* 19: 121–3. Republished in Housman (1972): 623–7.

(1917) 'The Thyestes of Varius', *CQ* 11: 42–8. Republished in Housman (1972): 941–9.

(1922) 'The application of thought to textual criticism', *PCA* 18: 67–84. Republished in Housman (1972): 1058–69.

(1926) (ed.) *M. Annaei Lucani belli ciuilis libri decem.* Oxford.

(1930) (ed.) *M. Manilii astronomicon liber quintus.* London.

(1931) (ed.) *D. Iunii Iuuenalis Saturae.* Cambridge.

(1972) *The Classical Papers of A. E. Housman*, J. Diggle and F. R. D. Goodyear (eds). Cambridge.

Hubbard, M. (1975) *Propertius.* London.

Hunt, J. M. (1975) Review of Dörrie (1971), *CPh* 70: 215–24.

(1998) Review of Badalì (1992), *Gnomon* 70: 497–504.

Jocelyn, H. D. (1991) Review of R. Marache (ed.), *Aulu-Gelle: Les nuits attiques, livres xi–xv* (Paris 1989), *CR* 41: 80–2.

(1993) Review of Zwierlein (1990), *Gnomon* 65: 122–37.

(1996) Review of Zwierlein (1991), *Gnomon* 68: 402–20.

Johnson, S. (1968) 'Preface to Shakespeare', in A. Sherbo (ed.), *Johnson on Shakespeare* (New Haven, CT, and London (*The Yale Edition of the Works of Samuel Johnson* 7)): 59–113.

Keller, O. (1879) *Epilegomena zu Horaz.* Leipzig.

Kenney, E. J. (1958) Review of Lenz (1956a and 1956b), *CR* 8: 133–5.

(1961) (ed.) *P. Ouidi Nasonis Amores, Medicamina faciei femineae, Ars amatoria, Remedia amoris.* Second edn 1994. Oxford.

(1965) Review of R. Verdière (ed.), *Grattii Cynegeticon* (Wetteren 1964), *CR* 15: 55–8.

(1969) Review of R. Gelsomino (ed.), *Vibius Sequester* (Leipzig 1967), *CR* 19: 183–5.

(1972) Review of Börner (1969–86), vol. I, *CR* 22: 38–42.

(1974) *The Classical Text.* Berkeley and Los Angeles, CA.

(2002) 'Ovid's language and style', in B. W. Boyd (ed.), *Brill's Companion to Ovid* (Leiden): 27–89.

(2004) Review of Flores (2002), *CR* 54: 366–70.

(2012) (ed.) *Ovidio: Metamofosi VII-IX.* Rome and Milan.

Kiss, D. (2013) *Catullus online* (www.catullusonline.org).

Kissel, W. (1999) Review of Willis (1997), *AAHG* 52: 185–91.

Klingner, F. (1957) (ed.) *Q. Horati Flacci opera.* Third edn. Leipzig.

Knoche, U. (1950) (ed.) *D. Iunius Iuvenalis: Saturae.* Munich.

Knox, B. M. W. (1966) *The Heroic Temper: Studies in Sophoclean Tragedy.* Berkeley and Los Angeles, CA.

Knox, P. E. (1995) (ed.) *Ovid: Heroides.* Cambridge.

Kortekaas, G. A. A. (1984) (ed.) *Historia Apollonii Regis Tyri.* Groningen.

(2004) (ed.) *The Story of Apollonius, King of Tyre.* Leiden and Boston, MA.

Kovacs, D. (1991) 'Euripides, Medea 1–17', *CQ* 41: 30–35.

Kraus, C. S. and C. Stray (in press) (eds.) *Classical Commentaries: Explorations in a Scholarly Genre.* Oxford.

Kraus, T. J. (2015) Review of O. Zwierlein (ed.), *Die Urfassungen der Martyria Polycarpi et Pionii und das Corpus Polycarpianum* (Berlin 2014), *BMCR* 2015.5.14.

Kristeller, P. O. *et al.* (1960–) *Catalogus translationum et commentariorum: Medieval and Renaissance Translations and Commentaries.* 9 vols. to date. Washington, DC.

Lachmann, K. (1848) (ed.) *Gromatici veteres*. Berlin.

  (1850) (ed.) *T. Lucreti Cari de rerum natura libri sex*. Berlin.

Lafaye, G. (1928–30) (ed.) *Ovide: Les métamorphoses*. Paris.

La Penna, A. (1982) Review of Hanslik (1979), *Gnomon* 54: 515–23.

Lassandro, D. (1992) (ed.) *XII Panegyrici Latini*. Turin.

Lebek, W. D. (1978) 'Love in the cloister: a pseudo-Ovidian metamorphosis', *CSCA* 11: 109–25.

Lenz, F. W. (1956a) (ed.) *P. Ovidii Nasonis Ibis*. Turin.

  (1956b) (ed.) *P. Ovidii Nasonis Halieutica–Fragmenta–Nux; Incerti Consolatio ad Liviam*. Second edn. Turin.

Leo, F. (1881) (ed.)*Venanti Honori Clementiani Fortunati presbyteri italici opera poetica*. Berlin.

Liberman, G. (2003) Review of Flores (2002), *RPh* 87: 355–7.

  (2010) (ed.) *Stace: Silves*. [Paris].

Lloyd-Jones, H. and N. G. Wilson (1990) (eds.) *Sophoclis fabulae*. Oxford.

Longo, O. (1981) 'Critica del testo', in E. Flores (ed.), *La critica testuale greco-latina, oggi: Metodi e problemi* (Rome): 65–80.

Lowe, E. A. (1964) 'Codices rescripti: a list of the oldest Latin palimpsests with stray observations on their origin', *Mélanges Eugène Tisserant* 5 (Vatican City 1964): 67–112. Republished in *Palaeographical Papers*, ed. L. Bieler (Oxford 1972): 2.480–519.

Luck, G. (1988) (ed.) *Albius Tibullus: Carmina*. Second edn 1998. Stuttgart.

  (2005a) 'Naugerius' notes on Ovid's Metamorphoses', *EC* 9: 155–224.

  (2005b) Review of Tarrant (2004), *EC* 9: 249–71.

  (2010) 'Lucubrationes Propertianae', *EC* 14: 43–87.

Maas, P. (1958) *Textual Criticism*. Oxford.

Maas, P. A. (2010) 'Computer aided stemmatics—the case of fifty-two text versions of Carakasaṃhita Vimanasthana 8.67–157', *WZKS* 52–3: 63–119.

MacGregor, A. P. (1978) 'Parisinus 8031: cod. opt. for the A-MSS of Seneca's tragedies', *Philologus* 122: 88–110.

  (1980) 'Mussato's commentary on Seneca's Tragedies: new fragments', *ICS* 5: 149–62.

  (1985) 'The manuscripts of Seneca's Tragedies: a handlist', in H. Temporini and W. Haase (eds.), *Aufstieg und Niedergang der Römischen Welt* 32.2 (Berlin and New York): 1134–1241.

Magnaldi, G. (2007) Review of Reynolds (1998), *BSL* 37: 622–38.

  (2008) (ed.) *Le Filippiche di Cicerone: edizione critica*. Alessandria.

Maguinness, W. S. (1966) Review of Mynors (1964), *CR* 16: 65–6.

Mankin, D. (1995) (ed.) *Horace: Epodes*. Cambridge.

Manuwald, G. and J. Ramsey (2009) (eds.) *Cicero: Philippics*. Cambridge, MA.

Marshall, C. W. (2006) *The Stagecraft and Performance of Roman Comedy*. Cambridge.

Marshall, P. K. (1977) *The Manuscript Tradition of Cornelius Nepos*. London.

  (1999) Review of J.-Y. Boriaud (ed.), *Hygin: Fables* (Paris 1997), *CR* 49: 410–12.

McCue, J. (2012) 'Dilemmas and decisions in editing Eliot', *LI* 14: 2–24.

McGann, J. J. (1983) *A Critique of Modern Textual Criticism*. Chicago, IL.

McKeown, J. C. (1987) (ed.) *Ovid: Amores I: Text and Prolegomena*. Liverpool.

McKie, D. S. (1977) 'The manuscripts of Catullus: recension in a closed tradition.' Diss. Cambridge.

(2009) *Essays in the Interpretation of Roman Poetry*. Cambridge.

Mercati, G. (1934) (ed.) *M. Tulli Ciceronis De re publica libri e codice rescripto vaticano latino 5757 phototypice expressi*. Vatican City.

Merkel, R. (1875) (ed.) *P. Ovidius Naso ex iterata R. Merkelii recensione II: Metamorphoses*. Leipzig.

Meusel, H. (1906) (ed.) *C. Iulii Caesaris commentarii de bello civili*. Leipzig.

Michalopoulos, A. (2006) (ed.) *Ovid Heroides 16 and 17*. Cambridge.

Momigliano, A. (1974) Review of Housman (1972), *Athenaeum* 52: 368–71. Republished in *Sesto contributo alla storia degli studi classici e del mondo antico* (Rome 1980): 745–8.

Mülke, M. (2008) *Der Autor und sein Text. Die Verfälschung des Originals im Urteil antiker Autoren*. Berlin and New York.

(2010) 'Adulteratio und Aemulatio—Verfälscher als Co-Autoren?', *RhM* 153: 61–91.

Munari, F. (1951) (ed.) *P. Ovidi Nasonis Amores*. Fourth edn 1964. Florence.

(1957) *Catalogue of the Mss. of Ovid's Metamorphoses*. London (*BICS* Supplement 4).

(1965) *Il codice Hamilton 471 di Ovidio*. Rome.

Munk Olsen, B. (1982–9) *L'Étude des auteurs classiques latins aux xie et xiie siècles*. Paris.

(2007) 'Chronique des manuscrits classiques latins (ixe–xiie siècles), VI', *RHT* N.S. 2: 49–106.

Myers, K. S. (2009) (ed.) *Ovid: Metamorphoses XIV*. Cambridge.

Mynors, R. A. B. (1958) (ed.) *C. Valerii Catulli carmina*. Oxford.

(1964) (ed.) *XII Panegyrici Latini*. Oxford.

(1969) (ed.) *P. Vergili Maronis opera*. Oxford.

Naiditch, P. G. (1996) '"The slashing style which all know and few applaud": the invective of A.E. Housman', in H. D. Jocelyn (ed.), *Aspects of Nineteenth-century British Classical Scholarship* (Liverpool (*Liverpool Classical Papers* 5)): 137–49.

Nisbet, R. G. M. (1960) 'Cicero, Philippics ii 103', *CR* 10: 103–4.

(1978) 'Notes on the text of Catullus', *PCPhS* 24: 91–115.

(1991) 'How textual conjectures are made', *MD* 26: 65–91.

(1995) *Collected Papers on Latin Literature*, S. J. Harrison (ed.), Oxford.

Nisbet, R. G. M. and N. Rudd (2004) *A Commentary on Horace, Odes, Book III*. Oxford.

Ogilvie, R. M. (1971) 'Monastic corruption', *G&R* 18: 32–4.

Önnerfors, A. (1993) Review of L. Stelten (ed.), *Vegetius: Epitoma rei militaris* (New York 1990), *Gnomon* 65: 494–8.

(2006) Review of Reeve (2004), *Gnomon* 78: 699–703.

Ottaviano, S. (2013) 'Una culla scomoda: proposta di espunsione di Ecl. 4,23', *RhM* 156: 401–5.

Ottaviano, S. and G. B. Conte (2013) (eds.) *P. Vergili Maronis Bucolica et Georgica*. Berlin and New York.

Page, D. (1972) (ed.) *Aeschyli septem quae supersunt tragoediae*. Oxford.

Pasquali, G. (1932) 'Edizione critica', *Enciclopedia italiana* 13: 477–80.

(1952) *Storia della tradizione e critica del testo*. Second edn. Florence.

Pearsall, D. A. (1985) 'Editing medieval texts: some developments and some problems', in J. McGann (ed.), *Textual Criticism and Literary Interpretation* (Chicago, IL): 92–106.

(2010) Review of Schmidt (2008), *Speculum* 85:701–3.

Pease, A.S. (1935) *Publi Vergili Maronis Aeneidos liber quartus*. Cambridge, MA.

Peiper, R. (1883) (ed.) *Alcimi Ecdicii Aviti Viennensis episcopi opera quae supersunt*. Berlin.

Peirano, I. (2012) *The Rhetoric of the Roman Fake: Latin Pseudepigrapha in Context.* Cambridge.

Peskett, A. G. (1914) (ed.) *Caesar: The Civil Wars.* Cambridge, MA.

Pinotti, P. (1988) (ed.) *Publio Ovidio Nasone: Remedia amoris.* Bologna.

Pulbrook, M. (1985) (ed.) *Publii Ovidi Nasonis Nux elegia.* Maynooth.

Ramires, G. (2007) Review of G. Liberman (ed.), *Valerius Flaccus: Argonautiques* (Paris 1997–2002), *Maia* 69: 398–401.

Ramírez de Verger, A. (2003) (ed.) *Ovidius: carmina amatoria.* Munich and Leipzig.

(2006) Review of Tarrant (2004), *Latomus* 65: 790–1.

Reed, J. D. (2013) (ed.) *Ovidio: Metamorfosi X–XII.* Rome and Milan.

Reeve, M. D. (1970) 'Seven notes', *CR* 20: 135–6.

(1974) Review of Dörrie (1971), *CR* 24: 57–64.

(1986) 'Stemmatic method: "qualcosa che non funziona"?', in P. Ganz (ed.), *The Role of the Book in Medieval Culture* (Turnhout): 57–69. Republished with additions in Reeve (2011): 28–44.

(1998) 'Shared innovations, dichotomies, and evolution', in A. Ferrari (ed.), *Filologia classica e filologia romanza: esperienze ecdotiche a confronto* (Spoleto): 445–505. Republished with additions in Reeve (2011): 55–103.

(2000) 'Cuius in usum? Recent and future editing', *JRS* 90: 196–206. Republished with additions in Reeve (2011): 339–59.

(2004) (ed.) *Vegetius: Epitoma rei militaris.* Oxford.

(2005) 'The Italian tradition of Lucretius revisited', *Aevum* 79: 115–64.

(2008) 'Josef Delz', *Gnomon* 80: 379–83.

(2009) 'Dust and fudge: manuscripts in Housman's generation', in Butterfield and Stray: 139–52. Republished in Reeve (2011): 323–38.

(2011) *Manuscripts and Methods: Essays on Editing and Transmission.* Rome.

Reinhardt, T. (2003) (ed.) *Cicero: Topica.* Oxford.

Reynolds, L. D. (1965a) *The Medieval Tradition of Seneca's Letters.* Oxford.

(1965b) (ed.) *L. Annaei Senecae Epistulae morales.* Oxford.

(1983) (ed.) *Texts and Transmission: A Survey of the Latin Classics.* Oxford.

(1998) (ed.) *M. Tulli Ciceronis De finibus bonorum et malorum libri quinque.* Oxford.

Reynolds, L. D. and N.G. Wilson (2013) *Scribes and Scholars: A Guide to the Transmission of Greek and Latin Literature.* Fourth edn. Oxford.

Ribbeck, O. (1858) *Emendationes Vergilianae.* Bern.

Richmond, J. A. (1962) (ed.) *The Halieutica Ascribed to Ovid.* London.

(1990) (ed.) *P. Ovidi Nasonis Ex Ponto libri quattuor.* Leipzig.

(2006) Review of Tarrant (2004), *Hermathena* 180: 129–32.

Riesenweber, T. (2007). *Uneigentliches Sprechen und Bildermischung in den Elegien des Properz.* Berlin.

Rizzo, S. (1973) *Il lessico filologico degli umanisti.* Rome.

(1991) (ed.) *Marco Tullio Cicerone: Lettere ad Attico.* Milan.

Robinson, P. and R. O'Hara (1996) 'Cladistic analysis of an Old Norse manuscript tradition', *RHC* 4: 115–37.

Robinson, P. (1997) 'A stemmatic analysis of the fifteenth-century witnesses to the Wife of Bath's Prologue', in N. Blake and P. Robinson (eds.), *The Canterbury Project, Occasional Papers* 2: 69–132.

Roelli, P. and D. Bachmann (2010) 'Towards generating a stemma of complicated manuscript traditions: Petrus Alfonsi's Dialogus', *RHT* N. S. 5: 307–31.

Rosati, G. P. (1996) 'Sabinus, the Heroides and the poet-nightingale. Some observations on the authenticity of the Epistula Sapphus', *CQ* 46: 207–16.

    (2009) (ed.) *Ovidio: Metamorfosi V–VI*. Rome and Milan.

Rudd, N. (1989) (ed.) *Horace: Epistles Book II and Epistle to the Pisones ('Ars Poetica')*. Cambridge.

Salvadore, M. (2005) 'Una recensione inutile', *RFIC* 133: 478–83.

Savon, H. (1987) Review of Hall (1985), *AC* 56: 392–4.

Scaffai, M. (1997) (ed.) *Ilias Latina*. Bologna.

Schenkl, K. (1883) (ed.) *D. Magni Ausonii opuscula*. Berlin.

Schmidt, A. V. C. (2008) (ed.) *William Langland, Piers Plowman: A Parallel-text Edition of the A, B, C and Z Versions*. New York.

Schröder, B.-J. (1999) *Titel und Text*. Berlin and New York.

Shackleton Bailey, D. R. (1956) *Propertiana*. Cambridge.

    (1976a) Review of L. Hakanson, *Textkritische Studien zu den grösseren pseudoquintilianischen Deklamationen* (Lund 1974), *AJPh* 97: 73–9.

    (1976b) Review of Kenney (1974), *CPh* 71: 185–7. Republished in Shackleton Bailey (1997): 392–4.

    (1982) *Profile of Horace*. Cambridge, MA.

    (1985) (ed.) *Q. Horati Flacci opera*. Stuttgart.

    (1990) 'Emil Baehrens (1848–1888)', in H. Hofmann (ed.), *Latin Studies in Groningen, 1877–1977* (Groningen): 25–37.

    (1997) *Selected Classical Papers*. Ann Arbor, MI.

    (2001) Review of Reynolds (1998), *CR* 51: 48–9.

Smyth, W. R. (1970) *Thesaurus criticus ad Sexti Propertii textum*. Leiden.

Stoppard, T. (1997) *The Invention of Love*. London.

Stringer, G. A. (2000) (ed.) *The Variorum Edition of the Poetry of John Donne*, vol. II: *The Elegies*. Bloomington and Indianapolis, IN.

Syme, R. (1983) *Historia Augusta Papers*. Oxford.

Tarrant, R. J. (1976) (ed.) *Seneca: Agamemnon*. Cambridge.

    (1978) Review of P. Dufraigne (ed.), *Aurelius Victor: Livre des Césars* (Paris 1975), *Gnomon* 50: 355–62.

    (1981) 'The authenticity of the letter of Sappho to Phaon (Heroides XV)', *HSCPh* 85: 133–53.

    (1982) 'Editing Ovid's Metamorphoses: problems and possibilities', *CPh* 77: 342–60.

    (1983) 'Ovid', in Reynolds (1983), 257–84.

    (1987) 'Toward a typology of interpolation in Latin poetry', *TAPhA* 117: 281–98.

    (1989) 'The reader as author: collaborative interpolation in Latin poetry', in J. N. Grant (ed.), *Editing Greek and Latin Texts* (New York): 121–62.

    (1989) 'Silver threads among the gold: a problem in the text of Ovid's Metamorphoses', *ICS* 14: 103–17.

    (1995a) 'Classical Latin literature', in D. C. Greetham (ed.), *Scholarly Editing: A Guide to Research* (New York): 95–148.

    (1995b) 'The *Narrationes* of "Lactantius" and the transmission of Ovid's *Metamorphoses*', in O. Pecere and M. D. Reeve (eds.), *Formative Stages of Classical Traditions: Latin Texts from Antiquity to the Renaissance* (Spoleto): 83–115.

(1999) 'Nicolaas Heinsius and the rhetoric of textual criticism', in P. Hardie, A. Barchiesi, and S. Hinds (eds.), *Ovidian Transformations* (Cambridge (Cambridge Philological Society supplementary vol. 23)): 288–300.

(2000) 'The soldier in the garden and other intruders in Ovid's Metamorphoses', *HSCPh* 100: 425–38.

(2004) (ed.) *P. Ovidi Nasonis Metamorphoses*. Oxford.

(2006) 'Propertian textual criticism and editing', in H.-C. Günther (ed.), *Brill's Companion to Propertius*. Leiden and Boston: 45–65.

(2012) (ed.) *Virgil: Aeneid XII*. Cambridge.

(2015) Review of G. Giardina (ed.), *Properzio: Elegie* (Pisa and Rome 2010), *Gnomon* 87: 754–6.

Taylor, G. (2007) *Thomas Middleton and Early Modern Textual Culture: A Companion to the Collected Works*. Oxford.

Taylor, G. and S. Wells (1987) *William Shakespeare: A Textual Companion*. Oxford.

Testard, M. (1965) (ed.) *Cicéron: Les devoirs*. Second edn 1974. Paris.

Thomas, R. F. (1988) (ed.) *Virgil: Georgics*. Cambridge.

(2008) 'David Roy Shackleton Bailey 1917–2005', *PBA* 153: 3–21.

(2009) Review of Heyworth (2007b), *TLS* 26 March: 24.

(2011) 'Epigram and Propertian elegy's epigram riffs: radical poet/radical critics', in A. M. Keith (ed.), *Latin Elegy and Hellenistic Epigram* (Newcastle Upon Tyne): 67–85.

Thomas, R. F. and J. M. Ziolkowski (2014) (eds.) *The Virgil Encyclopedia*. Chichester.

Thomson, D. F. S. (1997) (ed.) *Catullus*. Toronto.

(2009) Review of Trappes-Lomax (2007), *Mnemosyne* 62: 679–85.

Timpanaro, S. (1953) 'Delle congetture', *AR* 3: 95–9. Republished in Timpanaro (1978): 673–81.

(1963) *La genesi del metodo del Lachmann*. Third edn 1985. Florence/Padua.

(1978) *Contributi di filologia e di storia della lingua latina*. Rome.

(1981) 'Un nuovo commento all'Hercules Furens di Seneca nel quadro della critica recente', *AR* 26: 113–41.

(1995) Review of Badalì (1992), *RFIC* 123: 218–21.

(2005) *The Genesis of Lachmann's Method*, trans. G. Most. Chicago.

Tränkle, H. (1993) 'Von Keller-Holder zu Shackleton Bailey. Prinzipien und Probleme der Horaz-Edition', in W. Ludwig (ed.), *Horace. L'oeuvre et les imitations, un siècle d'interprétation* (Vandoeuvres-Geneva (*Entretiens sur l'antiquité classique* 39)): 1–29.

Trappes-Lomax, J. M. (2007) *Catullus: A Textual Reappraisal*. Swansea.

Verdière, R. (1988) Review of Hall (1985), *Latomus* 47: 890–1.

Viarre, S. (2005) (ed.) *Properce: Elégies*. Paris.

Wallace, D. F. (2011) *The Pale King: An Unfinished Novel*, ed. M. Pietsch. New York.

Watt, W.S. (1968) Review of Testard (1965), *CR* 18: 58–61.

(1982) (ed.) *M. Tulli Ciceronis Epistulae ad familiares*. Oxford.

Wecklein, N. (1898–1902) (ed.) *Euripidis fabulae*. Leipzig.

West, M. L. (1973) *Textual Criticism and Editorial Technique*. Stuttgart.

Wickham, E. C. (1901) (ed.) *Q. Horati Flacci opera*. Oxford.

Willis, J. (1972) *Latin Textual Criticism*. Urbana, IL (*Illinois Studies in Language and Literature* 61).

(1997) (ed.) *D. Iunii Iuvenalis saturae sedecim*. Stuttgart.

Wilson, N. G. (2007) (ed.) *Aristophanis fabulae*. Oxford.

Winterbottom, M. (2008) Review of E. M. Morales (ed.), *Jérôme: Trois vies de moines. Paul, Malchus, Hilarion* (Paris 2007), *JTS* 59: 372–4.

Wiseman, T. P. (1969) *Catullan Questions*. Leicester.

   (1979) *Clio's Cosmetics: Three Studies in Greco-Roman Literature*. Leicester.

Zetzel, J. E. G. (1993) 'Religion, rhetoric, and editorial technique: reconstructing the classics', in G. Bornstein and R. G. Williams (eds.), *Palimpsest: Editorial Theory in the Humanities* (Ann Arbor, MI): 99–120.

   (2005) *Marginal Scholarship and Textual Deviance*. London (*BICS* Supplement 84).

   (2010) Review of Mülke (2008), *Gnomon* 82: 273–5.

Zwierlein, O. (1977) Review of Tarrant (1976), *Gnomon* 49: 565–74.

   (1986) (ed.) *L. Annaei Senecae tragoediae*. Oxford.

   (1990) *Zur Kritik und Exegese des Plautus I: Poenulus und Curculio*. Mainz (Akademie der Wissenschaften und der Literatur, Abhandlungen der Geistes- und Sozialwissenschaftlichen Klasse, Jahrgang 1990.4).

   (1991) *Zur Kritik und Esegese des Plautus II: Miles Gloriosus*. Mainz (Akademie der Wissenschaften und der Literatur, Abhandlungen der Geistes- und Sozialwissenschaftlichen Klasse, Jahrgang 1991.3).

   (1999) *Die Ovid- und Vergil-Revision in tiberischer Zeit I: Prolegomena*. Berlin and New York.

   (2000) *Antike Revisionen des Vergil und Ovid* (Vorträge der Nordrhein-Westfälischen Akademie der Wissenschaften, Geisteswissenschaften 368).

General index

Index of passages discussed

Index of scholars

Alton, E. H., 25
Anderson, William S., 25, 29, 38, 86, 105, 146, 164
Asztalos, Monika, 154

Bachmann, D., 153
Badalì, Renato, 25
Baehrens, Emil, 25, 71, 122, 164
Barber, E. A., 106, 109, 122, 161, 164
Barchiesi, Alessandro, 87
Beatus Rhenanus, 70
Beltrami, Achille, 61
Bentley, Richard, 19, 20, 21, 22, 32, 36, 43–8, 49, 66, 71, 77, 79, 81, 86, 135, 161
Bergk, Theodor, 125
Billerbeck, Margarethe, 154
Birt, Theodor, 163
Bömer, Franz, 29, 135
Bonazzi, Giuliano, 118
Boot, Joannes, 114
Borzsák, Istvan, 25, 68
Bothe, F. H., 92
Brodeau, Jean, 74
Buecheler, Franz, 19, 21, 23, 32, 74
Burman, Pieter, 64
Butler, H. E., 107
Butrica, James, 79, 92, 93, 107, 108, 109, 111
Butterfield, David, 22, 148

Camps, W. A., 111, 113
Canfora, Luciano, 88

Carey, Christopher, 141
Cazzaniga, Ignazio, 127
Chabotius, 45
Clausen, Wendell V., 90, 146
Constantius Fanensis, 46
Conte, Gian Biagio, 41, 42, 69, 73, 75, 90, 142, 147
Courtney, E., 25, 36, 98
Cucchiarelli, Andrea, 81

Dacier, A., 45
Dain, Alphonse, 10
Damon, Cynthia, 16
Dawe, R. D., 68
Delz, Josef, 66
Diggle, J., 142
Dodds, E. R., 145
Donaldson, E. Talbot, 58, 86
Dörrie, Heinrich, 148
Dousa senior, 66

Eggert, P., 124
Ehwald, Rudolf, 25, 29, 72, 86, 134, 135
Ellis, Robinson, 20

Faber, Tanaquil, 45
Fantham, Elaine, 154
Fedeli, Paolo, 25, 37, 70, 75, 87, 106, 107, 111, 122
Fish, Stanley, 25, 69
Flores, Enrico, 37, 132, 148
Fontein, Pierre, 116